To George F. Ku[illegible]

With appreciation for your

work for the people of Illinois.

Best wishes,

Bob Krueger ———— Kathleen Krueger

17 Dec. 2007

D0946652

MORE PRAISE FOR

From Bloodshed to Hope in Burundi

AND FOR

ROBERT AND KATHLEEN KRUEGER'S

WORK IN BURUNDI:

"Murder, massacre, and ethnic cleansing are no longer mere news items but terrifying realities in this tense personal account, written from the eye of the storm." —JOHN CAREY, PROFESSOR EMERITUS OF ENGLISH LITERATURE, OXFORD UNIVERSITY

"Kathleen Tobin Krueger's compelling story of an ambassador's family coping with an explosive revolution in Burundi should be 'must-reading' for diplomats. She leads the reader breathlessly from sentence to sentence as she details the dangers amid the desire to teach her small children how to cope in a world of turmoil. I was proud of her as a mother, an author, and a Texan." —LIZ CARPENTER

"Reading Kathleen Krueger's vivid and captivating story of embassy life in Africa shatters the stereotype of a traditional diplomat's wife. Leaving the bone china and chandeliers behind, Kathleen chose to visit refugee camps, face down armed soldiers to protect a household employee, and put her young children to bed to the sounds of machine-gun fire and grenades exploding outside. Americans reading her vividly told, captivating story will be proud to have had a person of such grace and strength representing our country overseas." —TIPPER GORE

"Ambassador Krueger's courage in defending democracy gave courage to the members of FRODEBU and inspired all other Burundi political democratic parties to believe that democracy could succeed and prevail in Burundi." —THE HONORABLE DR. JEAN MINANI, SPEAKER OF THE BURUNDI PARLIAMENT, JANUARY 2002–AUGUST 2005; PRESIDENT OF THE FRODEBU PARTY, JANUARY 1995–OCTOBER 2005; AND MEMBER OF PARLIAMENT 2005–2010

"Robert Krueger is certainly the most influential and the best ambassador ever to serve in Burundi since we received our independence in 1962. He fought for the preservation and consolidation of democracy with all his heart and his intelligence. He never took partisan sides, as many were tempted to do. On the contrary, he based every single statement and any action on his own careful inquiries made on the ground in every corner of Burundi. He saved many lives and gave hope to those who lost their cherished ones." —JEAN-MARIE NGENDAHAYO, MEMBER OF THE BURUNDI PARLIAMENT AND MINISTER OF COMMUNICATIONS, 1993; FOREIGN MINISTER OF BURUNDI, 1994–1995; AND MEMBER OF THE BURUNDI PARLIAMENT AND CHAIRMAN OF THE FOREIGN RELATIONS COMMITTEE, 2005

"While providing leadership characterized by his attachment to peace, his Excellency Ambassador Robert Krueger represented his country, the United States of America, during the most critical moments in the history of Burundi. An ambassador out of the ordinary, he would go to the countryside to see for himself the atrocities committed against a population that left many too afraid to speak out. He went wherever there were massive violations of human rights. He was not afraid to face down armed men and call out their transgressions; he met with the media to cry out loud and clear to the world what was happening in Burundi; yet he never failed to call the protagonists to dialogue rather than confrontation. His phone was always available twenty-four hours a day, ready to receive calls for help from the people. Even if he could not understand their language, his interpreter was always by his side. Ambassador Robert Krueger viewed massacre sites and visited the wounded at their hospital beds. His Excellency Ambassador Robert Krueger even risked his own life in an ambush planned by those who feared his outspokenness. This political man of vision had always said that the problems of Burundi would only find resolution through dialogue among Burundians. When he returned to Burundi in 2007, events had proven him to have been right all along, as he found Burundi to be now entering a phase of reconciliation and reconstruction. This man of peace and exceptional courage has contributed immensely to the defense of human rights for the population of Burundi—so much so that thirteen years after his official service to Burundi ended, the name of this ambassador reminds people of the love and hope that he gave to the people of Burundi." —THE HONORABLE NORBERT NDIHOKUBWAYO, MEMBER OF BURUNDI PARLIAMENT, 1993–1994 AND 2004–PRESENT

The one who dared to go and see what others couldn't or were afraid to see . . .

"When Burundi was destroying itself, God raised up a man eager to see for himself the plight the population was living. Courageous, persistent, unwavering and above all loving, Ambassador Robert Krueger, against all expectations, was probably the only diplomat who dared to venture outside the capital city of Bujumbura and reach down to the villages, where the war was raging, to get acquainted with the depth of the crisis. Being a man of compassion, it is obvious that Ambassador Krueger was determined to suffer with these people he so much loved, regardless of all the threats on his life that this represented. This led him to speak openly against the cruelties that were being inflicted on the population. Many a time, his mere presence and his eyewitness at the spot of the drama have inspired hope in the victims. More than anyone else, he is worthy to bear this witness. May this be to him an expression of too many unexpressed thanks of the Burundian population he has jeopardized his life to love and serve." —BISHOP JETHRON NSABIYAREMYE, PRESIDENT OF THE ASSOCIATION OF BURUNDI SEVENTH-DAY ADVENTIST CHURCHES

"Robert Krueger was the ambassador of the United States of America in Burundi from 1994 to 1996, the hardest time in the history of Burundi. I first of all want to express our heartfelt appreciation and gratitude to the United States of America as a country and to his parents who made the important decision of sending this strong man, Robert Krueger, to a war-torn country like Burundi in those years, for the service of the nation. He and his beloved wife were persecuted and were sometimes in danger because they were not afraid of speaking out against the ills the Burundians were going through. However, they did not give up. I am talking here about a man who could not sleep while he heard the cries of innocent people being killed every day and night. He is a fearless man and sensitive to injustice. Ambassador Robert Krueger fought energetically for justice, peace, reconciliation, human rights, and democracy for all Burundians. He hated bloodshed and he advocated for the unjustly treated Burundians. I knew him personally, and he is one of the rare foreign diplomats who knows the reality the country of Burundi went through. He is among the people to be consulted if one wants to know the history of Burundi well. I can simply say that his work in Burundi helped to save lives and preserved democracy. The peace Burundians are enjoying today is the result of the work of strong and courageous men like Robert Krueger."

—BISHOP SIMEON NZISHURA,
PRESIDENT AND LEGAL REPRESENTATIVE OF THE
UNION OF CHRISTIAN CHURCHES IN BURUNDI

FROM BLOODSHED TO HOPE IN BURUNDI

Focus on American History Series
Center for American History
University of Texas at Austin
Edited by Don Carleton

FROM BLOODSHED
TO HOPE
IN BURUNDI

*Our Embassy Years
during Genocide*

AMBASSADOR ROBERT AND KATHLEEN TOBIN KRUEGER

FOREWORD BY DESMOND TUTU
Archbishop Emeritus and Nobel Peace Prize Laureate

UNIVERSITY OF TEXAS PRESS
Austin

Publication of this book was made possible
by the John Henry Faulk Fund
of the Center for American History and by a
generous gift from the Jess and Betty Jo Hay Endowment.
Copyright © 2007 by the University of Texas Press
All rights reserved
Printed in the United States of America
First edition, 2007

Requests for permission to reproduce material from
this work should be sent to:
Permissions
University of Texas Press
P.O. Box 7819
Austin, TX 78713-7819
www.utexas.edu/utpress/about/bpermission.html

∞ The paper used in this book meets the minimum requirements of
ANSI/NISO Z39.48–1992 (R1997) (Permanence of Paper).

Library of Congress Cataloging-in-Publication Data
Krueger, Robert, 1935–
From bloodshed to hope in Burundi : our embassy years
during genocide / Robert Krueger and Kathleen Krueger ; foreword by
Desmond Tutu. — 1st ed.
    p.   cm. — (Focus on American history series)
Includes bibliographical references and index.
ISBN-13: 978-0-292-71486-1 (alk. paper)
ISBN-10: 0-292-71486-6
1. Burundi—History—1993–   2. Massacres—Burundi.
3. Burundi—Ethnic relations.   4. Krueger, Robert, 1935–
5. Krueger, Kathleen, 1958–   6. Ambassadors—Burundi—Biography.
7. Ambassadors—United States—Biography.   8. United States—Foreign
relations—Burundi.   9. Burundi—Foreign relations—United States.
I. Krueger, Kathleen, 1958–   II. Title.
DT450.863.K78A3 2007
967.57204—dc22
2006101398

For the people of Burundi

CONTENTS

FOREWORD

DESMOND TUTU, ARCHBISHOP EMERITUS

AND NOBEL PEACE PRIZE LAUREATE, 1984

*F*rom *Bloodshed to Hope in Burundi* is, partly, a story of faith: faith in the power of the people in a small, little-known nation in central Africa, Burundi, to be capable of reestablishing peace and democracy in their war-torn homeland, which for over a century has suffered from colonialism and its own tyrannous military government. The authors, Ambassador Bob Krueger and his wife, Kathleen, document their experience of living amid genocide in a country heroically seeking to throw off decades of domination by a small group of Burundians whose armed forces have employed murder, torture, intimidation, and segregation to keep the majority of the population under their control. The authors had faith that if the world knew the truth of conditions in Burundi, the truth could help set Burundi's people free. Using the advantage of outsiders who were freer to travel, discover, and speak the truth than were most of Burundi's own citizens, they also believed that only by revealing the truth of Burundi's suffering could reconciliation between its warring factions be achieved.

The story they tell is frank, unsparing, and directly documented by personal observation and experience. The narrative recounts scenes including the annihilation by the Burundi Army of 430 people in the village of Gasorwe, and the selling of tickets by a group of young thugs to allow buyers to watch and participate in the torture and killing of a group of eight laborers whose only crime was to have been born into a different ethnic group. But their account equally recounts the heroism of courageous citizens, ranging from civilians in government to educators at the university and peasants living in the countryside, who were willing to step forward at their own peril to reveal the horror being perpetrated against Burundi's people.

Recognizing, then, that only after the truth of genocide and tyranny is revealed can reconciliation be possible, the authors proceed to a call for forgiveness by all parties in this ethnically divided nation, and for attention and support from a world that has ignored the Burundi genocide as if killing tens of thousands of people in a little-known country somehow didn't matter. Yet Jesus reminded his followers, "Inasmuch as ye have done it unto one of the least of these my brethren, ye have done it unto me." Therefore we in the twenty-first century should surely be able to see that if democracy is denied, if tyranny and injustice anywhere in the world go unreported and unattended, then all of us suffer from our neglect and indifference toward our brothers and sisters with whom we share this planet.

The story of Burundi is therefore our story: not simply the story of Africans, or Americans, but of all of us. This particular story takes place in Africa, and this is an important book about Africa. But the practices of tyranny, of ethnic and cultural division and oppression, and of unattended suffering and apathetic inattention take place in various forms around the world. This account, written with pain and compassion, but with scrupulous specificity, makes that clear. After its searing report, it offers a hopeful vision of the budding green shoots of a democratic future for Burundi that even now seem to be emerging. The book is thus a reminder that, in the words of the spiritual sung by slaves in America over a century ago, "All God's children got wings."

If we are to fly to our full height, we must all fly together.

PREFACE

This is a love story. A story told by a couple who fell in love with a people and their country: a tiny, mountainous, remote nation in the heart of Africa, seemingly set apart from the world in distance and time. The story includes horror and hope, calumny and courage, pain but also personal triumph. It is told by two narrators. One, a recently defeated American officeholder whose workplace shifted from the shining mahogany of the U.S. Senate chamber to the killing fields of equatorial Africa, and whose activity changed from decorous debate to digging up graves. The second, his wife, who plucked our two small children from the security and familiarity of small-town Texas and found herself putting them to bed under African mosquito netting, listening to the clatter of machine guns and thud of grenades outside. Sent there expecting to find a nascent democracy, we found genocide and a fledgling, frightened government under threat:

> And we [were] here as on a darkling plain
> Swept with confused alarms of struggle and flight,
> Where ignorant armies clash[ed] by night.

— MATTHEW ARNOLD, "DOVER BEACH"

We arrived in this ancient country familiar with it through books, but as strangers to its people. The longer we stayed, the tighter grew the bonds of affection; and upon our departure, having been given a view into such a distant and different world, where the suffering of the people is immense, but where their sacrifice and service are also ennobling, we felt a responsibility to tell their story.

Burundi is one of the world's ten poorest countries. When one adds to its material poverty pitifully inadequate health care, daily murder, and intermittent massacres, one has an equation combining penury, disease, and terror. It is perhaps not surprising, then, that in July 2006, an analytic social psychologist at the University of Leicester, Mr. Adrian White, reported that after receiving responses from 80,000 people in 178 countries to assess their level of overall happiness, he found that the people of Burundi ranked 178th, and were the unhappiest in all the world.

Burundi is, for its citizens, one of the world's most difficult places to live. Facing its challenges is made more difficult because through experience Burundians have realized that no one in the outside world seems to care about their plight. Burundi has suffered through several large genocides, as in 1972, when 10–15 percent of the total male population was massacred in a couple of months. Those victims included, by design, probably three-quarters of those in the largest ethnic group who had received formal education beyond age fifteen. But the world said and did nothing.

More recently there has been what some have referred to as a "creeping genocide," in which individuals and groups of people are targeted because of their ethnicity and put to death. I calculated in 1995 that in Burundi at least 100 people a day were being so killed. Adjusted for the difference in population between Burundi and the United States, the numbers killed would equal 4,200 victims of premeditated murder every day in the United States. That many deaths would be equivalent to a new Oklahoma City bombing every hour of the day, 365 days a year; or ten World Trade Center attacks each week. Yet that level of violence continued, without notice or intervention from the world outside, well into the twenty-first century.

In the final years of the twentieth century, tens of thousands of people were imprisoned by the Burundi dictatorship in "regroupment camps"— actually concentration camps—where families were forced to live outdoors or in hovels put together from grass, reeds, sticks, scraps of board and twine, and mud. They were subject to rape, torture, theft, abuse, and sometimes murder. The people were not the victims whom Hitler chose for genocide: Jews, gypsies, and homosexuals. They were Hutus: an ethnic group in Burundi that has been subjugated and persecuted throughout most of the twentieth century. Yet the world has taken remarkably little notice of their plight.

Some attorneys and governmental officials deny that there was genocide, either creeping or swift, taking place in Burundi at all. We do not wish to quibble over words, but we challenge that notion.

Webster's *Third New International Dictionary* defines genocide as "the use of deliberate systematic measures (as killing, bodily or mental injury, unlivable conditions, prevention of births) calculated to bring about the exter-

Eighty-five percent of the population lives by subsistence farming, done largely by women. Photo by Judy Walgren, 1994. Courtesy of the Dallas Morning News ©.

Many peasant farming families live in small houses with conical thatched roofs.

The American embassy was an unostentatious two-story building.

Burundian children entertaining themselves with simple homemade toys, such as balls of twine. Photo by Judy Walgren, 1994. Courtesy of the Dallas Morning News ©.

Sarah, Kathleen, Bob, and Mariana at a village market near Bugarama, on the way to the Hansens, 1995.

Unknown to the world, a hundred lives were being saved by the United Nations, 1995.

Pastor Hansen's church, with pews carved in Denmark, 1995.

A villager removing straw and blankets with a long stick because the smell of decaying human flesh is so repugnant, Butaganzwa, 1995.

Bob contemplating Ngayabosha's body, Butaganzwa, 1995.

Bob recording survivors' tales, Butaganzwa, 1995.

*The UN camp of Magara, housing over 45,000 Rwandan Hutus under blue plastic
UN sheeting, 1995.*

Bob addressing hundreds of displaced Tutsi families near a school building, 1995.

Passing carefully through tens of thousands of refugees from Gasorwe headed toward Tanzania, March 31, 1995.

Bob with President Clinton at the entrance to the Oval Office, 1995.

Photo shown to President Clinton in the Oval Office, 1995.

mination of a racial, political or cultural group or to destroy the language, religion, or culture of a group."

"Killing"? In my first three weeks as ambassador, I visited with Amnesty International and Physicians for Human Rights a mass grave where at least 120 bodies had been thrown into a pit and covered, the legs and skulls picked clean by animals and the elements. The night before our group went to investigate, the military authorities responsible had tried to hide the horror by pouring diesel fuel on the grave to mask the stench of rotting bodies. The killing of these refugees by the Burundian and Rwandan armies was "deliberate" and "systematic," and I call it *genocide.*

I wonder what those who deny that genocide existed in Burundi would say to three of the many people whom I visited in a hospital in the village of Butaganzwa after a Burundi Army attack on the local population in January 1995. A twelve-year-old boy whose arm had been snapped like a tree branch by a Burundian soldier; a twelve-year-old girl, Hakizimana, who delicately lifted her clothing to show me the healing scars on her abdomen, where the soldiers had thrust bayonets; or Louis Ntawarushwashaka (whose name translates as "No one wants to be miserable"), a man in his seventies with slices all across his bald skull from army machetes. All were suffering "bodily or mental injury" from "deliberate systematic" attacks against victims personally unknown to the attackers.

"Unlivable conditions"? After 800,000 of the nation's six million people fled to other countries after the presidential assassination of 1993, and 400,000 more were internally displaced from their homes, Burundi was a country with 20 percent of its population uprooted. Houses were burned, furniture destroyed, and often only ashes remained. Even for those accustomed to poverty, these had become "unlivable conditions." Thus, many Burundians sought refuge in surrounding countries, even as fleeing Rwandans came to Burundi. Many of these, in both groups, proceeded to live on bare earth, under blue plastic United Nations sheeting, in hovels the size of pup tents with neither running water, heat, nor insulation, but with tuberculosis, malaria, and rampant dysentery.

"Prevention of births"? Had those who deny genocidal intent been with me in April 1995 in a hospital in Muyinga, we would together have witnessed an eighteen-month-old girl who had been bayoneted in the vagina by a Burundian soldier so that she might never be able to have children. Had those who deny genocide been at the Monument to National Unity in Bujumbura in September 1995, they too would have seen, as we pulled back the cloth covering his body, a five-year-old boy whose skull had been split open and whose penis had then been cut off by the soldiers, who compounded murder with mutilation and sought to send a message that no more Hutus should be born.

There is no doubt in my mind that all these acts were "calculated to bring about the extermination of a racial, political, or cultural group," in an attempt to destroy not only their bodies but also their dignity and their hope for a better future. One of my colleagues in the U.S. Congress once said in debate, "If it looks like a duck, quacks like a duck, and walks like a duck, it's a duck." I would say if there is a pattern of massive killing, bodily or mental injury, unlivable conditions, and prevention of births directed toward a group of people, not because of who they are as individuals, in personal vengeance, but because of the ethnic group into which they were born, this is *genocide.*

In the pages that follow, we have in several chapters documented with first-hand observation this "creeping" genocide, whether represented by large massacres or individual murders. This genocide was particularly formidable and terrifying because it was an effort of the combined powers of the national army, the police or gendarmerie, the judiciary, and many in the legislative and executive branches of the government. With the state propelling the genocide, the populace had nowhere to turn for safety. We have written not to shock, but rather to awaken the world to the horrendous cruelty and suffering of human beings in an isolated and forgotten land. But we wish to provide not simply a catalogue of horrors. As *King Lear* is arguably the cruelest and most painful of all of Shakespeare's great tragedies, so it also portrays qualities of redeeming love, personal sacrifice, bravery, and extraordinary compassion in fuller measure than any of his comparable works. As in drama, so in life, in Burundi. We have seen the examples of Bishop John Berchmans Nterere, who performed the Mass, even though he was fired upon by soldiers as he elevated the host in Muyinga, an attack that succeeded in slaughtering over one hundred communicants as they fled the church, and wounded many more. Or Prosper Mpawenayo, a professor of physics who risked his life to accompany me into the countryside in order to give a true and accurate account of armed massacres in Butaganzwa. Or Jytte and Knud Hansen, Danish missionaries who spent approximately thirty years living in Rwanda and Burundi in order to teach and minister, reading Greek and Hebrew texts at night by candlelight, since they had electricity only two hours a day. Or members of parliament from the Front for Democracy (Frodebu) political party, who courageously continued to serve even after twenty-one of their fifty-seven members had been assassinated, one by one.

The story of Burundi is charged with ethnic tension. Some, unfamiliar with Burundi's history and jumping too readily to conclusions, assume that the conflict between Tutsi and Hutu has gone on for centuries. Not true. The tension is palpable and the most defining feature of daily life and conversation today, but it has not always been so. There had been intermarriage and commercial and social exchange between Hutu and Tutsi for generations. What has happened in recent years, however, is that deeper motivations of fear, pride, avarice, and wrath—all the seven deadly sins and more—have found their expression by polarizing people into two groups, Hutu and Tutsi. And though the conflict between them certainly bubbles from deeper sources, once it is aboveground, it is almost always expressed as ethnic hatred.

When we went to Burundi, we sought to avoid categorizing people ethnically. But when almost everyone in the country defines himself or herself daily and often hourly as Hutu or Tutsi, it becomes impossible to understand a culture and what is happening in it unless one accepts the existence of the patterns of thought by which the people define their own cultures, thoughts, and actions. One might as well try to talk in terms of feet and pounds in a world where everyone else is using centimeters and kilograms. To communicate and to understand how local culture communicates, one must accept that even if citizens share the same language, a similar history, much intermarriage, and many biological connections, they still consider themselves to be either Hutu or Tutsi. And, unquestionably, the structure of government, commerce, and education, and above all the killing, looting, and attempts to instill fear and to subjugate, revolves around perceived ethnic differences between these two major groups. The majority of the population, having been tricked or coerced by their leaders into thinking in this ethnic framework, continue to do so. As observers, we should not limit our understanding to the perceptions of these groups; but to ignore their vision would be to bury our heads in the sand because we did not like what we saw.

There are many reasons that the world has paid little attention to the fate of Burundi: it is isolated and poor, and neither its culture, its economy, nor its politics has ever significantly affected the developed world; and it is perhaps easier to ignore people who are suffering terribly than to know their fate, because to know it might make us subject to caring about them. If we assume that Burundi's struggles are the result of historic rivalries and as inevitable as tropical rain, then we can no more change the violence than we can stop the rain from falling. We must, instead, recognize that we can be separate from people because of language, culture, distance, time, habits, race, and color—and yet know that these are ultimately superficial differences. If we close our eyes and hear a baby cry, we cannot tell whether it is Burundian or American; if we see skeletons in a field, we do not know whether they are African or European; but in either case we know that they are human beings. They could be our children or our forebears. Recognizing that, perhaps we can be reminded that those things that separate us are only tangential, while those things that unite us are fundamental and universal.

Our family had the opportunity to experience something of that basic truth by living for a time in this extraordinary country. We feel like people who were witness to a murder: the murder of a democracy, a nation, and its people. And we feel that, through some strange fate, we have an obligation to tell the story of that murder and to try to bring to some public justice the perpetrators of this genocide. It was a role we neither asked for nor expected, but from which, having been witnesses, we could not withdraw in silence. Ours was no epic voyage, but we were given a glimpse into an underworld where millions of people, some brave, some vicious and cowardly, are suffering immensely.

One thing not killed in Burundi was hope. The citizens continue to hope that the world will take notice and will help them as they work to restore decency and justice to their lives. To achieve that, the first step is for their story to be told.

—Robert Krueger

ACKNOWLEDGMENTS

Kathleen and I feel immense appreciation to the people of Burundi for sharing themselves and extending their friendship to us, and to President Bill Clinton, who assigned me as ambassador to Burundi and who continuously expressed personal support for my actions there, even when some people in the State Department questioned them. Together they have given us a life-enriching experience.

Following our departure from Burundi, Kathleen spent many midnight hours reviewing home videos of our time there, consulting her diary and re-visiting documents and conversations as she began writing an account of our family's experience in that treasured but troubled land. As she was completing her manuscript, I had occasion to visit Merton College, Oxford, where I had earned my doctorate many years ago. When I related some of my observations and experiences in Burundi to the Merton Professor of English Literature, Dr. John Carey, he said, "You've written about this, haven't you, Bob?" I replied that I hadn't, since my time was currently fully occupied as ambassador to Botswana. "Once you finish that assignment, let me know, and we will give you a position as visiting research fellow at Merton to write about Burundi. This is a story that must be told."

When I returned to Botswana a few days later, Kathleen very generously suggested, "Why don't we do a book together?" We agreed that offering two perspectives—that of a mother rearing children amid genocide and satisfying the many responsibilities of a diplomatic spouse, and that of an ambassador seeking to assist in preserving what could be saved of Burundi's fragile democratic institutions—would offer a more complete, and we hoped a more engaging, picture than could be provided by either of us alone.

When our family arrived in Oxford a year later, the assistance of many people in that venerable university and the special hospitality of the warden, fellows, and administrative staff of Merton College were exceptional and deeply appreciated. Not only did John Carey review and offer encouragement and helpful advice for our manuscript, but so did many of the old Mertonians with whom I had studied forty years ago. Three in particular gave their time and suggestions as our manuscript was being prepared: Oliver Miles, who served the UK in three ambassadorial posts; Tony Nuttall, fellow of New College; and Joe McDonald, a classicist now retired after many years of teaching. Mauro de Lorenzo of Linacre College brought to me his extensive knowledge of central Africa on many occasions and his impeccable French, as he accompanied me to Belgium to interview Mme Laurence Ndadaye, the widow of Burundi's assassinated president. Frances Wickes, who served as my incomparable personal secretary in Washington, Burundi, Botswana, and Oxford, offered help in many ways, for many years.

The generous assistance of these friends was but one more reminder of the depth of my lifelong debt to Oxford University, and to my college, now almost 750 years old, which graciously accepted a young man from a small town in Texas, many years ago, and offered me an opportunity to expand my horizons, nurturing my aspirations and never belittling my failings. Many of the roots, the cultivation, and the fruits of this book are grounded in Merton College, an institution to which I am deeply grateful.

Finally, although I owe thanks to countless Burundians who in many ways made this book possible, I shall here publicly mention only one, my good friend, the former foreign minister, and now member of Parliament, Jean-Marie Ngendahayo. We lived next door to one another, were side-by-side when assassins sought to kill us both, and have remained in touch through all the years since. He not only shared information and experience available nowhere else, but read our entire manuscript, correcting my errors with patience and goodwill. He is a true patriot and a great servant of democracy in Burundi. And Kathleen and I are proud to be considered his friends.

SOME NOTES ON THE TEXT

In Burundi we shared the experiences described in this book, and we likewise shared the responsibility for recounting them. Kathleen wrote Chapters 6, 7, 11, 12, 13, 14, and 15; Bob took care of the rest.

Parts of the story are told through dialogue. The words attributed to speakers come either from tape recordings, Kathleen's video camera, written notes and speeches, or recollections from participants in the conversations. While recollections will include slight inaccuracies, they nevertheless conform more closely to what was said than would attempts to paraphrase. While most names in the text are accurate as given, in a very few instances pseudonyms are used to protect the identities of certain persons still in Burundi, whose lives might be endangered if their identities were revealed.

FROM BLOODSHED TO HOPE IN BURUNDI

ONE

THE COUP

Burundi's Army Kills Its President

THE PRESIDENT'S CABINET ROOM

It was late afternoon on Wednesday, October 20, 1993, in Bujumbura, the capital of Burundi, and President Melchior Ndadaye was meeting with members of his newly formed cabinet. He had been installed in office only 102 days earlier, Burundi's first-ever democratically elected president, and most of his cabinet members had been elected to Parliament just ten days before his inauguration. There was, therefore, a sense of newness, eagerness throughout the room. People who had never before been allowed to vote for anyone or anything were now heading cabinet agencies and deciding policy for their nation of six million people. The atmosphere was heady.

At one end of a long, attractive, but unostentatious room, the president sat alone behind a large light-colored wooden desk, no advisers nearby to whisper to him. His policy was that everything said in cabinet meetings should be known to all. Before him, along an extended table of matching wood, sat the twenty-three members of his cabinet, each with a separate microphone. Although the president had been elected by a 2–1 majority, and his political party, Front pour la Démocratie au Burundi (Frodebu), had won 80 percent of the seats in Parliament, Ndadaye's cabinet was bipartisan and multiethnic. Like Ndadaye, fourteen cabinet members were Hutu, the ethnic group that composed most of Frodebu and 85 percent of the population. One Frodebu member was Ganwa, a descendent of Burundi's earlier royal families, and eight cabinet members were Tutsi, the minority ethnic group (14 percent of the total population) that had held all political power among Burundians for over half a century. They were mostly members of the Parti de l'Union et du Progrès National (Uprona), which, until then, had governed since independence in 1962. Its early leaders, the military dictators Michel Micombero and Jean-Baptiste Bagaza, had forced Ndadaye and numerous other Burundians to live many years in exile, and its last leader and military dictator, Pierre Buyoya, had imprisoned Ndadaye for expressing his democratic views.

Having just passed the 100-day mark, the new cabinet was comparing its accomplishments with its election promises. The president had called for a report from his minister of social action, human rights, and the protection of women, Marguerite Bukuru, who, at precisely 5:00 p.m., was just stating, "This event can shake the situation," when the table, chairs, light fixtures, and entire building were for several seconds shaken violently by earthquake tremors. When the motion stopped, the room was hushed. Then, Minister Bukuru broke the silence with her comment, "I was not meaning such a heavy shake," and laughter broke forth. But it was nervous, apprehensive laughter. Every person in that room, whatever his or her later education in science or geology, had grown up in households and communities where everyone—grandparents, parents, relatives, and neighbors—shared a basic, pervasive belief: earthquakes foreshadow events of major turmoil and violent upheaval in government. Further, whether or not those present believed earthquakes to be prophetic, they all knew as unavoidable historical fact that four years after the country gained independence from colonial rule in 1962, Tutsi political leaders had captured every Hutu elected to Parliament, imprisoned the entire group without an opportunity for defense or trial, and murdered them all in a single night. In more recent memory were the events of July 2–3, 1993, when, just a week before his inauguration, Ndadaye only narrowly averted death in an attempted coup by members of the all-Tutsi Burundi Army at his residence.

Nonetheless, once the murmur of conversation following the tremors stopped, with only a smile and without comment Ndadaye returned to the previous agenda: the review by his cabinet of his administration's achievements and shortfalls.

- The minister of finance, Salvator Toyi, reported that in its first three months the administration had brought in more tax revenues than had been gathered in the entire previous year. Before, most people, including especially the peasant farmers whose families composed 85 percent of the population, had avoided, when possible, paying taxes to a military dictatorship unresponsive to their concerns. Now, however, with confidence in the purposes and honesty of the new administration, they were willing to pay.

- Minister of Communications Jean-Marie Ngendahayo reported that several new newspapers had begun publication. Although he had suspended one for gross irresponsibility in its attacks on the president, the newly established Commission on Press Freedom had overturned his decision, and the newspaper was now back in print. Burundi's press had never before been so free.

• Construction of a major prison in northern Burundi had been stopped, and at Ndadaye's direction, plans were underway to convert it to a school.

• A general amnesty releasing all prisoners except those convicted of murder, cannibalism, arson, drug trafficking, and armed robbery was in effect, to the great relief of the population. Five thousand persons, including all political detainees, had been released.

• On presidential instruction, the Intelligence Service had destroyed the torture cells used to force confessions from prisoners.

The meeting then concluded with a discussion between the president and his former campaign manager, Léonard Nyangoma, minister of public works and repatriation of refugees. A leitmotif in campaign speeches had been that Burundi should be a country open to all, and Burundian citizens living in other countries, whatever their political party or ethnicity, had been encouraged to come home to rebuild a multiethnic nation. The most prominent returnee was Colonel Jean-Baptiste Bagaza, Burundi's military dictator from 1976 to 1987, who had been banished from the country when overthrown by Major Pierre Buyoya in 1987. Far more numerous, however, were the Hutus who had fled to neighboring Tanzania, Zaire, Rwanda, and other countries during various genocidal slaughters over the past thirty years, the worst being in 1972, when the Burundi Army executed 150,000–300,000 Hutu civilians. Many of these refugees, estimated to number 240,000, were now returning, some having been away almost three decades.

Their return, while popular, was not without problems. Burundi is one of many African countries in which property ownership sometimes rests on oral tradition— villagers knowing and remembering where families farm and live—rather than on written and recorded deeds. Knowing this, Ndadaye believed it would be impossible accurately to ascertain the legitimate property rights of all returning refugees. He concluded that, instead, government-owned land would have to be distributed as fairly as possible to those who could not prove their ownership of particular properties.

And with that, darkness having fallen some hours ago, President Ndadaye ended the meeting. Before he could get away, however, he was approached by Communications Minister Ngendahayo, spokesperson for the government, who said, "Mr. President, as I told your *chef de cabinet* earlier today, I need urgently to talk with you, privately."

"Come into my office now," the president responded.

The issue was the president's safety. The previous day, Ngendahayo's wife had been approached by an army officer who believed that something inimical to the president—he was not sure what—was going on at army headquarters. Apprehensive, but thinking the report too unspecific to be convincing, Ngendahayo approached the President differently, saying,

> Mr. President, I have two matters to raise with you. First, we are in late October, and elections in the communes are scheduled for December. Yet Uprona is attacking our policy of encouraging the return of refugees, which is overwhelmingly supported by the general population. Uprona cannot win at the polls if they take this position. Therefore, I fear they have a hidden agenda that smells of presidential assassination. Second, over a month ago I sent to you a report stating that presidential protection is inadequate and that we must carry further our discussions with Israel about training a presidential guard force. But I've had no reply to my message.

In response, the President instructed Ngendahayo to go immediately to fetch the defense minister, Colonel Charles Ntakije, who was in another office, talking on the telephone. There, Ngendahayo found Ambassador Melchior Ntamobwa, senior adviser to the cabinet, listening intently to the telephone conversation and sweating profusely. He turned and whispered, "The minister has been told that a coup against the president is being planned for tonight."

Once the telephone conversation ended, Ngendahayo and Ntakije rushed to the private office of the president and shut the door. Ngendahayo spoke first: "Mr. President, the defense minister now has hard, factual information, much more specific than my speculation, that a coup is right now being prepared." The president turned toward his defense minister, squinted slightly, and said, "Mr. Minister, what do you have to tell me?"

Ntakije replied, "I've just been informed by telephone that there is a coup d'état being prepared. Troops from the 11ème Bataillon-Blindé (Eleventh Armored Car Battalion) are to attack the Presidential Palace at 2:00 a.m.—in about five hours." The president replied carefully and directly: "Mr. Minister, how are you preparing to counter the attack?"

"First, I'll contact officers I trust, who should be meeting right now in the Officers' Mess Room, to get the accurate information. If this plot is true, I'll prepare an ambush at the exit of the military camp to stop the *blindés.*"[1]

Weighing the defense minister's response, Ndadaye inquired, "Is Siningi still in the Rumonge Prison?" Colonel Sylvestre Ningaba, nicknamed "Siningi," had been chef de cabinet to former military dictator Pierre Buyoya for seven years. He was currently under arrest for his role in the failed coup attempt of July 2–3 against Ndadaye.

Upon Ntakije's reply that Siningi was still imprisoned, Ngendahayo asked, "Mr. President, shouldn't we move him to a different location, since the putschists may seek his help?"

But the defense minister demurred, insisting that prison administrators did not like to move prisoners during the night, when they can be easily killed. He then added, "Concerning your own security, Mr. President, I will send an additional blindé to the Presidential Palace."

Deferring to the defense minister's recommendations, the president added only, "It's a good idea to send an additional blindé to the Palace; yesterday the motor wouldn't start on one of the blindés there now."

That a president as intelligent as all of Ndadaye's associates found him to be would accept so readily such scant preparations for his protection seems, in retrospect, remarkable to an outsider. Suspicion of a possible coup had been coursing through Bujumbura conversations all week and had reached the presidential couple in Mauritius, where they were attending a meeting of heads of state from francophone nations.

Upon their return from Mauritius on October 18, the president and his wife had been greeted at Bujumbura Airport by all the Frodebu cabinet members (as is customary in many African countries for a president returning from abroad), but not one Uprona cabinet member was present. That could have been viewed as a warning. However, in a capital perpetually nervous with rumor, it becomes exhausting to take seriously every reported threat. Moreover, Ndadaye may have had a kind of *che sarà, sarà,* fatalistic attitude that could come to a person who, having overcome numerous life-threatening challenges, was unwilling to run away from the position and responsibilities he had so recently assumed.

Without commenting further on the possible coup, Ndadaye returned briefly to the subject of getting the Israelis to Burundi to help train the presidential guard, and then dismissed the two of them at 9:15 p.m.

As he was driven home, the president knew that it would be his last night in the old, historic Presidential Palace downtown. To provide him better protection, plans had been made several weeks earlier to move his family the next day to a more secure residence, where former president Buyoya had once lived. What the president did not know was that the move would never be made, and that this would be his last night on earth.

THE PRESIDENTIAL PALACE

The Presidential Palace to which President Ndadaye returned stood in faded splendor in the heart of Burundi's capital city of 275,000 inhabitants. Designed and constructed as the official residence of the Belgian vice governor-general for Ruanda-Urundi (today known as Rwanda and Burundi) after Belgium had been granted trusteeship for the twin countries after the First World War, it was easily the most striking building in Bujumbura. The large, high-ceilinged structure, its stucco exterior painted white, immediately drew attention away from the smaller drabber buildings surrounding it. Its tall windows and columned façade had been designed in grand African colonial style, and its very form bespoke the message of colonial civilization and the ethos of expatriate elegance in the tropics. Jean-Paul Harroy, as colonial governor, had extended its grandeur by filling its extensive gardens, which led to the main entrance, with an arboretum of trees and plants from around the world. While the gardens were laid out in a geometric pattern, the extensive grounds were interspersed with a rich variety of palm trees, including the rare traveler's palm, the long leaves of its crown arched like a lady's fan or a peacock's tail. Fragrant oil exuding from the leaves of eucalyptus trees, originally imported from Australia but today found across Africa, hung heavy in the moist night air. Beneath grew roses, hibiscuses, birds-of-paradise, and poinsettias in a climate that never knew frost and seldom saw barrenness. The scene had been enjoyed not only by colonial governors but also by King Mwambutsa IV, King Ntare V, and the general public until 1966. Then, Colonel Micombero overthrew the government, fear entered the garden, white walls were raised, and the public was no longer allowed inside.

On this night, like every night, the city was quiet. Since Burundi has only one car for every one hundred people, vehicular traffic is small by day and almost nonexistent after dark. By midnight, the city has few lights, even downtown, and is essentially as silent as the rich panoply of multitudinous stars that sparkle in the African night sky from horizon to horizon.

This was the palace to which the president returned by 10:00 p.m. He mentioned the rumor of a coup to his wife, Laurence, but both he and Communications Minister Ngendahayo had accepted the assurances of the Defense Minister that the matter would be addressed. The Ndadayes spent more time puzzling over the unusual character of the evening newscast, which reported at length on strange happenings in northern Burundi, where some farmers, thought to have been bewitched, were burning their coffee crops instead of harvesting them. Why, they wondered, should that story rather than the work discussed at cabinet meetings be aired? But the conversation was not long, for the day had been full. Soon thereafter they were in bed and falling asleep, only to be awakened by a telephone call from Brussels. Alfred Ndoricimpa, the Methodist bishop in Burundi, was calling to ask about the truth of rumors circulating among the Burundian community in Brussels that a military coup was being planned against the president that night. Once again, the president seemed unconcerned.

Unknown to him then, but evident by morning, was that a widespread conspiracy within the armed forces, in which the majority of the upper-echelon officer corps were active coconspirators and to which the remainder of the armed forces was complicit either out of sympathy, indifference, or fear, was underway against him. Earlier that day, at 3:00 p.m., Major Isaïe Nibizi, who concurrently held positions as commander of the 2nd Commando Battalion, commander of Camp Muha, and the officer responsible for presidential security, had informed Ndadaye's chef de cabinet of suspicious army troop movements. Nibizi was credited with having helped prevent the earlier July 3 coup attempt against Ndadaye, and was therefore trusted by him. Although Nibizi later claimed that on October 20 he had surrounded Camp Muha with antitank mines in order to prevent blindés from leaving the camp, others stated that Nibizi had removed the mines later that night on orders from army chief of staff Colonel Jean Bikomagu. In any case, around midnight, blindés were rolling out of Camp Muha, headed toward the Presidential Palace and other key locations in the city, and no one stopped them.

Within the hour, the Presidential Palace was surrounded by blindés from the 11th Armored Car Battalion at Camp Muha, troops from the 1st Parachute Battalion, and other soldiers from the twelve military camps in the capital, including some from the 2nd Commando Battalion, commanded by Nibizi. As the night proceeded, hundreds of commandos, parachutists, and gendarmes surrounded the Presidential Palace. While more than a dozen blindés were underway to mount the attack, and while hundreds of troops surrounded the palace, there were but two blindés and thirty-eight soldiers inside the palace enclosure for defense.

Shortly before 1:00 a.m. the telephone rang, and Mme. Ndadaye answered. The minister of defense was calling. "Is the president there?" he immediately asked. Responding yes, Mme. Ndadaye then stayed on the line and heard Colonel Ntakije inform the President that blindés had left Camp Muha but that he did not know their destination—perhaps the Ngagara quartier, perhaps the Presidential Palace. In any case, his message was "*Il faut sortir*" (you must leave). But he did not suggest where or how to go.

While Mme. Ndadaye hurriedly dressed, the president tried to call Captain Mushwabure, the officer in charge of the palace guard. When he did not answer, the president himself went out into the gardens. Then, at 1:30 a.m. Mme. Ndadaye heard a single shot. Fearing the worst, she called her husband on his cell phone. He was fine; she was relieved. Moments later, a burst of gunfire. She called again. No answer. She was convinced her husband was dead.

According to Mme. Ndadaye, the fusillade against the palace began just after 1:30 a.m. At least one blindé (perhaps more) blasted a hole through the outer perimeter wall, and, taking position there, barraged the house with cannon fire. To protect her three small children from the shattered glass of the tall palace windows, Mme. Ndadaye took them into a windowless inner hallway, laid them beneath long tables, and waited. Even so, she and her son Tika were each grazed by shrapnel from one of the bursts of cannon fire that recurred at five-minute intervals throughout the night. Between 1:30 and 2:00 a.m., the defense minister again called, asking to speak to the president, and Mme. Ndadaye replied that he was outside in the gardens. During that same period, in spite of the recurrent artillery attacks, Mme. Ndadaye managed to reach by telephone Foreign Minister Sylvestre Ntibantunganya, Agriculture Minister Cyprien Ntaryamira, President Habyarimana of Rwanda, and various Frodebu leaders and provincial governors to inform them of the coup.

During this period, unknown to his family, the president had been taken by members of the Presidential Guard, dressed in a military camouflage uniform as a disguise, then placed inside one of the two blindés in the palace gardens. He was to remain there for the next six hours—essentially, a president prisoner to his own nation's army, trapped in a blindé in his front garden while his wife, children, and servants waited apprehensively inside. It was a surreal situation, to which our narrative will return.

Meanwhile, the cannonade may have been the signal for the packs of army jackals to begin their nocturnal hunt for Frodebu's political leaders. One of the most influential and therefore most endangered among them was Sylvestre Ntibantunganya, the foreign minister. A passionate supporter of Frodebu and a former editor of its newspaper, *L'Aube de la Démocratie,* he was considered one of the strongest intellects in his party. Small and wiry in physique, he was also assertive and loquacious in manner. His critics complained that he could talk for an hour and neither listen to anyone else nor give them an opportunity to interrupt. But with his lively though sometimes frenetic mind, he had the kind of intellectual curiosity, restlessness, and freedom from insularity that made him a rarity in Bujumbura.

After Mme. Ndadaye telephoned his home to tell Ntibantunganya of the attack on the palace, he immediately began calling Frodebu leaders in hopes that the government could be saved. At 2:10 a.m. he awakened Jean-Marie Ngendahayo, the communications minister, who only a few hours earlier had warned the president of a possible coup, and at 2:45 a.m. he made the first of three calls within an hour to Paul Patin, chargé d'affaires of the American embassy. Initially, he was optimistic, telling Patin, "*On semble maîtriser la situation*" (the situation seems to be under control), and saying he thought the president was safe for the moment. He urged the United States government vigorously to condemn this attempt to overthrow democracy—assurance Patin immediately granted him.

His second conversation was less sanguine. And his third call, at about 3:30, came in a panicked voice, as he pleaded for the United States immediately to denounce the attack, and revealed that he was preparing to flee and go into hiding.

His flight was shrewd and successful. Knowing better than to trust the government soldiers assigned to protect him, Ntibantunganya called in his gardener and, exchanging clothes with him, put on some of his gardener's poorest and most ragged clothing, including his cap. Barefoot and disguised, he walked out his front gate, undetected by his own guards, and made his way through the streets to the home of a friend, where he hid for the next two days.

While trudging along Bujumbura's dirt streets, he could hardly have guessed that eleven months later he would be inaugurated as president, with a public assurance of support from the army. Nor could he know that less than two years after that, the army would engage in yet another coup, this time against him, to bring back once more into office the very military dictator, Pierre Buyoya, whom Ndadaye had defeated at the polls and who, as has become increasingly clear, was behind the putsch then in progress.

Knowing that their home had almost certainly been targeted, Sylvestre Ntibantunganya and his wife, Eusébie Nshimirimana, had decided that she should take their children and a houseguest, Sylvana Katabashinga, to seek refuge elsewhere. Not knowing when they might return, they dressed hurriedly but properly, in clothes befitting their station in life, since doing so might make it easier to bluff their way through roadblocks or opposition. Then, after gathering Eusébie's daughters and infant son, they all fled to the home of her close friend Dominique Barumpozako, where Sylvana Ntaryamira, wife of the minister of agriculture, was also staying. It was a decision that, in the bizarre irrationality of that terrifying night, would soon cost both fleeing women their lives.

The fate of another Frodebu leader and his family was strangely tied to that of the Ntibantunganya family that night. Cyprien Ntaryamira had been given the ministry of agriculture, a key post in a country where 85 percent of the population tills the soil. Fearing that they both would be targeted, the Ntaryamiras decided to seek safety separately. His wife went to the same home as Mrs. Ntibantunganya, and Cyprien sought refuge with his next-door Tutsi neighbors.

When a truckload of troops arrived at the Ntaryamira house, only the servants were there. Angry at their quarry's having escaped, the soldiers went next door, where Cyprien was hiding. To protect him, the lady of the house, a tall elegant woman with the style of beauty Burundians particularly admire, turned on her outside lights and walked confidently into the front garden. There she calmly told the soldiers that she had seen Cyprien fleeing, and pointed in the direction of his supposed escape. The soldiers left in hot pursuit, and Cyprien, safe inside, survived to become the president who, four months later, would succeed Ndadaye.

The frustrated soldiers, however, somewhere learned that the Ntaryamiras might be staying with Dominique Barumpozako, and proceeded to her house. There they found the well-dressed Eusébie Nshimirimana (Mrs. Ntibantunganya, the foreign minister's wife) and her friend Sylvana Katabashinga, and Sylvana Ntaryamira (wife of the agriculture minister), who was dressed like a peasant.

Upon entering the front room, the soldiers saw an elegantly dressed woman holding a baby, her two young daughters beside her, and a woman whom they took to be a peasant or servant. Furious that their real target, the cabinet minister, had escaped, they attacked the well-dressed woman—piercing her head with a bayonet. As she struggled to maintain her balance, Mrs. Ntibantunganya handed her baby to Mrs. Ntaryamira, saying, "Take care of my baby," and fell to the floor. Then the soldiers shot her in the presence of her children. Perhaps uncertain whom they had slain, but knowing Mrs. Ntaryamira's first name to be "Sylvana," they asked the woman in peasant dress, "Where is Madame Sylvana?" Sylvana Ntaryamira replied that she did not know; she was in the house by accident. The soldiers then entered a back bedroom and discovered Sylvana Katabashinga, well dressed and hiding. They asked, "Are you Madame Sylvana?" When she replied yes, a soldier raised his machine pistol and shot her dead. Thus, in a night of mindless violence, the agriculture minister's wife, Sylvana, who was the intended victim but was dressed as a peasant and was holding a baby, escaped unharmed, whereas the better-dressed visitor named Sylvana was murdered.

Less fortunate than Cyprien Ntaryamira was another of Frodebu's strong and early leaders, Juvénal Ndayikeza, minister of home affairs and communal development, to whom Ndadaye had given the difficult assignment of heading the ministry responsible for the national police, or gendarmerie. As a Hutu heading an agency manned almost completely by Tutsis, his challenge was inevitably overwhelming. He had therefore sought to avoid confrontation, having recognized, like Ndadaye, that integrating Hutus into the gendarmerie and the army would require years. Facing a coup, he must have wondered whether the gendarmerie would prove faithful to the government and to his direction, or to the ethnic group to which they were tied by blood and to which they owed their position. At 2:45 a.m., in a telephone conversation with Communications Minister Ngendahayo, Ndayikeza reported that he had been phoning governors in the fifteen provinces to alert them to the events in Bujumbura, but that he did not know what could be done in the capital. "What place is safe? Who can be trusted?" he asked. Even as they spoke, he exclaimed, "Jean-Marie, it's all right. I see the headlights of a car coming. It must be someone coming to take us to a safe place." But evidently the car passed by, for fifteen minutes later he telephoned Paul Patin, chargé of the American embassy. Hurried and desperate, he said, "Paul, the soldiers are coming; I hear the trucks. I want to slip out through my backyard and go to the American embassy. Can I have safe haven there?" Patin replied, "I'll be waiting at the gate to let you in." "I'll be there in ten or fifteen minutes," Ndayikeza responded.

So Patin waited outside. When Ndayikeza had not arrived half an hour later, Patin telephoned his house. His call was answered by a gruff male voice, undoubtedly that of a soldier, who told Patin that he had the wrong number and hung up. Between those two conversations, Ndayikeza had been captured and murdered.

The stories of several other democratic leaders that terrifying night concluded like that of Ndayikeza—with death.

Gilles Bimazubute held the third-highest position in government, deputy speaker of the National Assembly. As a Tutsi committed to majority rule, he knew that he was viewed by Uprona and the army as a traitor to the larger Tutsi "family," and therefore could not have been surprised when the soldiers arrived at his house. Nevertheless, he insisted that they wait to take him away until he had put on a suit, coat, and tie: he was determined to die in the dress of a man serving his country in high office, not as a fleeing refugee.

When soldiers arrived to take away the director of intelligence, Richard Ndikumwami, he drew his pistol to defend himself and his family, but, outnumbered and outgunned, was quickly overpowered. Then, as his family watched helpless and aghast, the soldiers began beating and bayoneting Ndikumwami. In their final act of humiliation and torture, several soldiers together stuck bayonets into Ndikumwami's quivering body, lifted him, and dropped him in the back of their truck like a useless, dying fish tossed onto a pier.

The fate of Pontien Karibwami, speaker of the National Assembly and therefore vice president of the republic, was no better, though he was able to resist slightly longer. Pontien and his brother escaped the genocide of educated Hutus in 1972 because they were studying at a university in Belgium at the time. Later, after working as a mining engineer in Zaire, he returned to become Ndadaye's right-hand man. After his election as vice president in 1993, he moved into a spacious government residence on a hill overlooking Bujumbura. Once the home of President Bagaza, it came with extensive safety features: bulletproof glass, reinforced steel doors, warning systems, and various escape routes from the large surrounding grounds. All that, however, proved useless. When a truckload of soldiers arrived, his guards offered no resistance, although the building's protective features briefly delayed the soldiers' entry. Frustrated for more than an hour, they finally blasted away the security doors with a bazooka. The family survived the shelling, but was forced to watch as Pontien, beaten, bayoneted, and bleeding, was led stumbling away to his death.

IN A COUP, SURVIVAL IS UNPREDICTABLE

Amid this night of horrors, not every story ended in death. There was also escape, rescue, relief, help, hope, heroism, and survivors who looked to a better day.

Two who unexpectedly survived were deputy prime ministers, Bernard Ciza and Melchior Ntahobama. Like Vice President Karibwami and many others, Ciza and Ntahobama were betrayed rather than protected by their military guards. But instead of being beaten to death, they were taken to prison. There, in the early darkness of that morning, a junior military officer whom they did not know came quietly to them, instructing them not to talk. He silently led them out of the prison, past an unquestioning guard, hid them under a canopy in the back of an army truck, and asked where they wished to be taken. Ciza chose the French embassy; Ntahobama, the house of the deputy chief of mission of the Belgian embassy, M. Koen Vervaeke, where he was later joined by Communications Minister Ngendahayo's wife, Antoinette, and her two daughters. An unusually courageous and compassionate man, Vervaeke provided sanctuary to several threatened families over the next few days.

Another diplomat who gave refuge to several individuals and families over the next few months (sometimes harboring as many as fifteen people) was Paul Patin, chargé d'affaires of the American embassy on the night of the attack and director of the U.S. Information Services (USIS) in Bujumbura. A cerebral, wiry, intense man in his thirties, Paul not only spoke the best French among Americans in the embassy, but was also one of the few Americans to have, in addition to "contacts," genuine friends from across Burundian society, including students, journalists, and political figures. During the night of the putsch and afterward, many of them requested his help. Selections from his journal entries convey some of the confusion and desperation felt on that night.

At about 2:20 a.m., on the morning of 21 October 1993, I was awakened from a half-sleep by my wife Maja, who nudged me and told me to listen. The firing of weapons was clearly audible not too far from our house, in the direction . . . of the Presidential Palace. The Army was rebelling against the government. No more than 2 minutes after this grim reckoning, the telephone rang. Amy Hart Vrampas, of USIS, told me that they were seeing troops and *auto-blindés* moving up and down the street. Immediately following that conversation, our Embassy's Regional Security Officer, Chris Reilly, called. We agreed we must both get to the embassy ASAP. The plan was for Chris to drive to the embassy, then come to my house in the ambassadorial vehicle—with flags flying. In about 10 minutes, Chris and the vehicle were at the gate of my house. But so was a group of about 25 soldiers, from a variety of different units, judging by their different colored berets. They were in a state of high agitation and insisted that the night guard, Evariste, not open the gate to let the vehicle onto my property. I joined in the melee, and told Evariste, who was obviously frightened out of his wits, to let the vehicle in. I refused to let the soldiers in as well, although their attempt to force entry was half-hearted at best. They had other things to do.

I have occasionally wondered whether the incident with the soldiers at my gate did not provide just the margin of time needed for Communications Minister Jean-Marie Ngendahayo, a neighbor, to escape with his life. It subsequently became clear that soldiers were prowling the streets of Bujumbura that night looking for ministers and other Frodebu officials of importance to murder. Jean-Marie was one of the lucky ones to slip away as he did, and I cannot otherwise explain why the soldiers were so close to my house. Had they been serious about preventing me from leaving, it would have been an easy matter to do so. But they were obviously flustered and uncertain how to act.

With Chris Reilly at the wheel, and a Marine in the front seat, we made it to the embassy in a few minutes. . . . My first act was to call the State Department Operations Center. . . . [For the next few hours, Patin and Reilly manned the embassy telephone lines, taking calls from Burundi officials.] At about 4:00 a.m. the phones went dead. I later learned that the reason the phones stayed operational for so long was that the technician that the *putschistes* had rousted out of bed that morning was unable to cut the phone lines. . . . [By morning] I had decided with the wholehearted approval of Chris, the security officer, that it was pointless to sit in the embassy, when it was just possible that something useful could be done outside. So Chris Reilly and I went out to—to do what?—to look for the president, I suppose, or at least to try and find out something useful. Chris met a soldier of his acquaintance, who told us we should not be prowling around the streets, and that we should return to the embassy, which advice we ignored. . . . We learned there . . . that President Ndadaye had been forcibly moved from the Palace by soldiers and taken to a military camp.

From the Palace we proceeded towards the *État-Major* [military headquarters], U.S. flag flying. On one occasion we were stopped at a roadblock by soldiers who told us that we must not continue. We argued with them a bit, but in the end we moved on in spite of their protests. I felt that my vehicle, a big black *voiture américaine,* with its flags flying, afforded me some protection and would intimidate the lowly soldiers assigned to guard the street corners. It was a game of bluff. They could have shot at us or our tires, but they did not. We proceeded to the *État-Major* . . . and then to the Officers' Mess . . . where we found a large group of officers, as well as a few French military attachés. . . . We understood that something important was happening at one of the camps down the road, *Camp Muha.* . . . I decided that we should proceed to the camp. But a couple of French military officers dissuaded us. They assured us that the Burundians in charge at the Officers' Mess were serious when they said that they would not let us proceed, and that we could be in danger. So we didn't go.

I regret the decision not to proceed. . . . I'm almost certain that Ndadaye was there, and equally so that he was already dead. . . . It is possible, though not probable, that he was alive, and that had Chris Reilly and I forced our way through (which we probably could not have done, the soldiers would have simply held us back physically, not bothering to shoot us, just holding us) we might possibly have saved the day, Ndadaye's life, and all the tragedy which ensued. I don't believe that to be the case, but I wish we had tried just a bit harder to get through.

One of the fortunate few among leaders of Frodebu was Communications Minister Jean-Marie Ngendahayo. As a relative of Burundi's last king, he was Ganwa, considered by Tutsis to be part of their ethnic group. Hence, they considered his support of democracy to be apostasy: how could someone in the royal line believe that peasants were as worthy as he to participate in government? Ngendahayo was therefore undoubtedly on the list of those to die; but those planning the coup had failed to provide clear directions to the homes of Frodebu leaders. Thus, soldiers turned up by mistake at the home of Paul Patin, the American chargé, and were bewildered when a white, five-foot-eight-inch American met them at the gate instead of a six-foot-two-inch Tutsi.

Ngendahayo himself was but a few houses away. Awakened just after 2:00 a.m. by a phone call from Foreign Minister Ntibantunganya, Ngendahayo began his own telephoning. He first reached the cell phone of the defense minister, who said the situation was under control. When Ngendahayo called again half an hour later, the defense minister, somewhere in hiding, said the situation was worse, and then inquired, "Where are you?" Ngendahayo replied, "At home. As communications minister, I have to keep in touch with members of the government, and I have no cell phone." The defense minister replied, "You are a fool, Jean-Marie. They are looking for all Frodebu leaders. If they find you, they will surely kill you."

Ngendahayo decided he was right. So he made one more call, asking for refuge from his friend, Michel Ramboux, a Belgian *cooperant* (i.e., aid and development official) whose home was likely to be secure. Driving his own Toyota rather than his official Mercedes with identifiable government license plates, he gathered his family and sped to Ramboux's house.

Next door to Ramboux lived Ngendahayo's brother, Déo, a businessman who had been joined by the minister of refugee repatriation, Léonard Nyangoma (later to become the leader of the CNDD, the political movement that took arms against the Burundi Army). Not wanting to risk being seen on the street, shortly before daylight Ngendahayo climbed over the side wall separating the houses, and the three of them discussed what to do and telephoned friends—or those they hoped would be friends in a time of crisis.

At about 7:00 a.m., desperate for information, Ngendahayo took the risk of phoning Colonel Jean Bikomagu, army chief of staff. Surprisingly, Bikomagu said that the situation was "under control" and that the president was "in a safe place." As communications minister, Ngendahayo then requested a military escort to take him to the radio and TV broadcast building so that he might inform the nation. Col. Bikomagu, sounding hurried and nervous, said he would call back and send more protection when time allowed.

Elated that the President was safe, Ngendahayo leapt into the air for joy, exclaiming, "The president is alive. The president is alive." But when, half an hour later, Bikomagu had not called back, Ngendahayo phoned again. This time Bikomagu hastily replied that he was with President Ndadaye but that the president could not speak with Ngendahayo, because at that moment soldiers were outside, threatening them both. Then Bikomagu hung up.

Upon reflection, the group agreed that they could not trust Bikomagu. If the President was indeed both with him and well, why was Ngendahayo not allowed to speak with him? And if he was not, Ngendahayo's having given away their location meant that army trucks might be on the way, not to escort but to capture them. They must flee.

In Déo's car, they headed for the Hutu residential sector of Kamenge, but at the first traffic circle were stopped by a military contingent. The soldiers walked to the car, looked in, and, perceiving the long frames and angular Tutsi faces, were prepared to let them pass, when a military commander shouted, "Tell them to go home." So Déo wheeled about and headed for the industrial sector, driving to the office and warehouse of a Belgian business associate, Michel Carlier. After admitting them, the businessman bolted the outer gates. The four of them then moved large packing crates behind some heavy industrial machinery, creating a small hiding place where they might be unobserved if workers, or soldiers, arrived. From this position, the communications minister used his brother's cell phone to reach Ndadaye's chef de cabinet, Frédéric Ndayegamiye, who stated that the president had been assassinated and that as spokesman for the government, Ngendahayo had the responsibility of informing the world.

Ngendahayo knew that, having killed the President, the army would soon capture the radio station. While contemplating the import of the chef de cabinet's instructions and formulating his own message, Ngendahayo was telephoned by two engineers from the telecommunications station. Though unable to broadcast from the station itself, they still had working telephone landlines and were, at that moment, in touch with Radio Rwanda. The engineers took the listening end of the telephone on which they were speaking to Ngendahayo, placed it next to the speaker end of the handle on the set in which they were talking to Rwanda, and broadcast Ngendahayo's message that a coup had been attempted. Not wanting abruptly to reveal the full horror of the truth to the people of Burundi, and to the world, Ngendahayo said:

> I do not know for certain the fate of President Ndadaye at this time. What I do know is that, whether alive or dead, no one will stop the democratic process in Burundi. The people have decided to choose freedom. The wheel of history is going forward. I therefore call upon the free world's representatives to rescue the nation of Burundi and its democracy. And I particularly call upon the francophone countries to assist, because at the recent francophone summit attended by President Ndadaye, they highlighted the virtues of democracy. I hope that they will spearhead this process in Burundi. And I call upon all Burundians to fight for democracy wherever they are.

Miraculously, the message was broadcast in both Kirundi and French, and was repeated, and repeated, and repeated throughout the day.

But when Ngendahayo finished, his brother asked, "Do you realize that in making that statement you have just signed your own death warrant?"

In fact, all three realized that, if captured by the army, they would be summarily slain. So they slipped into Michel Carlier's adjoining office, and borrowing some plain lined paper, each wrote his final will and testament. For the remainder of the day and through the night, the three remained in hiding. But as Carlier's workers began to arrive on October 22, they realized that their hiding place could not remain secure. Déo therefore sent a worker to get from his business a minivan that had been converted into a kind of pickup truck by removing all but the front seat and installing a board platform behind it. Nyangoma slipped between the platform and the frame, a space hardly bigger than a coffin, and both brothers got into the front seat with the driver and prayed they would not be recognized.

It was by then 9:00 a.m., but the streets were almost empty. On the road they expected to take, they sighted a military checkpoint ahead, turned around, and took a different route. Their destination, the French embassy, would provide both international protection and the opportunity to join other government leaders. As they neared the embassy, they passed the Presidential Palace. Through its shattered wall they saw the building, now an empty shell, its life stolen away. The only activity was soldiers and civilians scurrying about, carrying off chairs, lamps, clothes, and even light fixtures. The leader was gone; the plunder was underway—a sickening symbol of the fragility of all laws once an assault on government is begun.

A few blocks farther, at the corner of Uprona Boulevard and Rue de la France, they reached the embassy. The large metal gates were opened; they drove in, and as the gates shut, they almost collapsed with exhaustion. They were safe—at least for the moment. They sat briefly in the minivan, too relieved to move. Then, after lifting the platform so that Nyangoma could climb out, the three of them walked upstairs to reunite with colleagues.

There, everyone was speaking of the president's fate. And his final hours proved to have been the strangest of all during that phantasmagoric night.

From 1:30 a.m. to 7:30 a.m. on October 21, President Ndadaye had remained inside a blindé in the front palace garden. He was undoubtedly a prisoner. Had he been free to leave, he would have either sent for his family or made an escape. Yet the telephone records indicate that throughout this period he received only two calls on his cell phone, each lasting less than a minute, and that he initiated none. His widow told me that during that period he spoke with no one by phone. Undoubtedly, his cell phone did not work properly inside the closed steel blindé. Unfortunately, any accounts from his army captors regarding this time could only be unreliable and self-serving. When responding to such official inquiries as were made, no one wished to take responsibility for fomenting or furthering the coup. The pretense has been that it was conceived, formulated, and directed by a lowly army lieutenant, Jean-Paul Kamana, who somehow had the authority to gather hundreds of troops from various locations and deliver a battalion of blindés without the collaboration of army and political superiors. That is preposterous. Only officials of a country accustomed to the lies of despots could suppose that free, rational people would accept such an implausible explanation.

Kamana himself, living in exile in Uganda since soon after the coup, has stated that he has witnesses to his having been at home when the attack began, where he remained until he and others were taken to the Presidential Palace near daybreak. My conversations with him convince me of the obvious: he was but a minor player chosen by higher-ups to be the scapegoat for a major catastrophe—a practice not unusual anywhere in political and military circles, but especially prevalent in military dictatorships.

Given, then, that part of the accounts received are not credible, it is nevertheless true that the events that can be documented often seem incredible as well.

At about 7:00 a.m., Mme. Ndadaye recounts, soldiers broke into the shattered palace and, to their surprise, found that Mme. Ndadaye and her children had lived through the cannonade. They insisted that she take her children and servants to the safety of one of the two blindés stationed inside the gardens for presidential protection. It took them almost thirty minutes to run, crawl, and creep the 100 yards toward it, and they were frequently told to lie flat to avoid gunfire. Once there, the group climbed onto the blindé's turret and dropped inside. But the blindé would not start.

At that juncture, the second blindé inside the palace grounds pulled alongside, and the family members and servants climbed across and into it—where, to their astonishment, they found the president. His cell phone had not worked inside the enclosed metal blindé; he had therefore been unable to receive his wife's calls, and she had thought him killed. Once reunited, the entire family and their servants then sought to climb over a wall facing the Meridien Hotel, but found escape impossible because the palace was surrounded by troops. With nowhere else to go, they returned to the second blindé. By then it was clear that they had to go to the military camp as Captain Mushwabure directed. So the president told his family, "Now we must go to Camp Muha." As they moved outside the palace walls, the attacking blindés held their fire and followed the president's blindé from the palace grounds. It was 7:30 a.m.

Throughout the period from 1:30 a.m., when firing began, until the departure of the president and his family at 7:30, there were only two reported casualties among all army members across the city: two infantrymen following a blindé that entered the palace grounds and then retreated were reportedly wounded by gunfire. But no one, from Minister of Defense Colonel Ntakije and Army Chief of Staff Colonel Bikomagu to the lowest recruit ever stepped forward at personal risk to protect the president or other government leaders, and no guard ever seriously sought to repel an attack. According to Mme. Ndadaye, not one of the thirty-eight palace guards ever fired a single shot in their defense. Those who say that the putsch was the work of only a small group led by a junior officer are therefore left with cowardice as the only explanation for the unwillingness of anyone in the army to defend the nation's elected leaders. No doubt the cowardice and fear were ample, but the sadder truth is that, in addition, the complicity of the army in the treasonous coup was complete.

The route taken to Camp Muha was extremely circuitous, and at one point passed the French embassy, which, if Captain Mushwabure had genuinely wished to save the president, would of course have offered international sanctuary. But the president and his family were, nonetheless, taken to Camp Muha, where they arrived at precisely 8:00 a.m. Surrounded by putschists from the 1st Battalion, the family remained in the blindé while the president went away with Colonel Bikomagu and several high-level officers.

President Ndadaye returned after slightly more than an hour and, along with Colonel Lazare Gakoryo, secretary of state for security, climbed into the blindé to try to put into final form an agreement that had been verbally reached in the larger meeting. Once Gakoryo exited the blindé, however, all the soldiers surrounding it—red and green berets alike—began shouting mockingly for the president to come out.

When he did so, Colonel Bikomagu quieted them for a moment, and speaking in a steady voice, the president said,

> Soldiers, I am a man of negotiation, a man of peace. Tell me your problems, and we will discuss them and find a solution. But for heaven's sake, don't shed blood. Think of your country, think of your families, think of the future of this country.

As the troops crowded more closely around the blindé, Bikomagu told them, "Let the family go; they are of no interest to you." Then, calling for a jeep, he instructed the driver to take Mme. Ndadaye and her children away—though he gave no instructions about where to go. Mme. Ndadaye believes that Bikomagu intended that she and her children be killed. Since he had given the driver and accompanying soldiers no specific instructions, however, they took direction from the president's wife. She first ordered them to go to the Belgian embassy. Finding that road blocked, she then ordered the driver to go the wrong way down a one-way street and take her immediately to the French embassy, where she and her children were given sanctuary at 9:45 a.m.

As she was being driven away, she looked back and saw Col. Bikomagu speaking to the troops. In words remarkably reminiscent of Pontius Pilate's, he told them as he pointed to Ndadaye, "He is the one you were looking for. Here he is. Do whatever you want with him." And with that, Bikomagu, the deputy minister of defense, and Nibizi, the officer directly responsible for presidential security, turned and walked away.

Ndadaye was then put in a jeep and driven to the nearby camp of the 1st Parachute Battalion. Bikomagu, Nibizi, and Gakoryo followed in a Land Rover, hungry jackals nearing a kill. At the parachutists' camp, the troops were spread out, some sitting, others lying lazily on the grass around the parade grounds and basketball court. Inside the battalion commandant's office sat François Ngeze, wearing a grey jogging suit and "looking like a fat worm," according to one observer. He was waiting for his moment of triumph, when he could be presented to the troops as their new president.

Meanwhile, in another office inside, ten lower-ranking officers were given the task of killing the president. According to the coroner's report, Ndadaye was held with a cord around his neck while being pierced by bayonets, seven of the fourteen stabbings penetrating the thorax, thereby causing his lungs to fill with blood.

The president's body was left lying in the office where he had collapsed, for troops to witness and to mock. The assassins had so little respect for their president, world opinion, or common decency—and so little understanding of what it meant to depose a head of state and slaughter the principal leaders of a freely elected government—that they dug a mass grave right in the military camp. Into it they tossed the bodies of Melchior Ndadaye, president of the republic; Pontien Karibwami, vice president and speaker of the National Assembly; Gilles Bimazubute, deputy speaker of the National Assembly; Juvénal Ndayikeza, minister of lands and communal development; and Richard Ndikumwami, director of intelligence.

Some hours later, upon realizing the world's outrage at the assassinations, army leaders ordered the bodies exhumed so that they might be collected by their families. The soldiers took the bodies, some bayoneted, some shot, all battered and filthy, and dropped each one into a simple wooden coffin. The followers and families were then allowed to fetch the coffins, take them to the morgue, and prepare for a state funeral.

TWO

BURUNDI'S TORTURED HISTORY, ITS CHAMPION OF DEMOCRACY, AND ITS LEGACY OF ASSASSINATION

The bayonets thrust into President Melchior Ndadaye's thorax, and the bullets that felled his vice president and cabinet members, critically injured the world's newest democracy, born only 102 days before. Six million people, more than the population of Denmark or Ireland, and equal to the population of Israel, were suddenly thrust back into a miasma of misrule and uncertainty after a brief season of hope while the outside world took only temporary measures to stanch the bleeding. Then the international community once again relegated Burundi to the status of a forgotten nation, powerless to affect the developed world economically, socially, or politically and peopled by silent masses buried in unmarked graves.

It seems always to have been so. As a nation-state, Burundi has affected only its immediate neighbors. Nonetheless, if human life everywhere has meaning, then the story of people surviving on limited rations and frail hopes in the center of Africa can carry universal relevance. What happens when one ethnic group tyrannically subjugates another is painted in bold tropical colors in Burundi, and thereby highlights the subtler forms of domination and discrimination still found worldwide. Just as the Belgian Congo was used as the setting for Joseph Conrad's *Heart of Darkness* to illustrate the horror that potentially lives in every person, so an account of the murder of democracy and the persistent genocide in Burundi can illuminate our understanding of less obvious threats to liberty and justice in our own society. To facilitate that understanding, it helps to know a little of Burundi's past, seldom mentioned in the history books that most of us have read.

BURUNDI: A BRIEF HISTORY

The basic geography of Burundi is easily understood. It is a small, beautiful, landlocked, and isolated country located just below the equator in central Africa, shaped like an arrowhead pointing south. Across the Kanyaru and Kagera rivers, which form its northern border, lies Rwanda. Beyond the Ruzizi River and Lake Tanganyika on the west is the Democratic Republic of the Congo (once called the Belgian Congo, then Zaire), and across its eastern and southern borders lies Tanzania. Burundi's land area is about the same as that of Maryland or Wales—only 10,747 square miles, or 27,834 square kilometers. On the northern shore of Lake Tanganyika sits the capital, Bujumbura (population: 275,000), at 2,600 feet; the mountains farther north rise to more than 9,000 feet, which prompted the country at one time to be called "the Switzerland of Africa." The southeast is marked by level and slightly rolling plains. Overall, however, the country is hilly or mountainous, covered with volcanic soil once rich, though now often eroded. The landscape is largely verdant, either with terraced farms or natural foliage, dotted throughout with small, individually cultivated plots of land and groups of houses or villages forming "communes," often perched on hillsides, or *collines*. Apart from the capital, there are no other cities; Gitega, Rumonge, and Ngozi, the largest towns, have populations of only 15,000–50,000 people.

Burundi's early history is uncertain and difficult to describe. A major reason that we know little about the countries of the vast African continent—which is larger than the United States, Russia, France, Germany, Italy, the United Kingdom, Japan, and Argentina combined—is that except for two countries, all of Africa south of the Sahara was essentially without written records until missionaries, traders, and colonial powers arrived to introduce writing to the continent. Such was the case in Burundi. Thus, its early history is largely lost, as inaccessible as the inner treasures of a misty, primeval forest viewed from a distant airplane. We can speculate on the life and activity that we suppose went on there, but from our distance we tend to see a uniform forested canopy, largely opaque to us.

The people of Burundi identify themselves as belonging to one of three ethnic groups: Hutu (85 percent), Tutsi (14 percent), or Twa, i.e., Pygmy, (1 percent). This breakdown of the population, provided by the Belgian colonial government, has been almost universally accepted for over three-quarters of a century, although the percentages and ethnic distinctions are themselves only approximations. Intermarriage has blurred ethnic descriptions that had only partial accuracy to begin with, but since no population counts have been done based on ethnicity in the past half century, these are the only, and therefore the best, numbers we have.

Most historians in the late nineteenth and early twentieth centuries held that the first people in Burundi were the Pygmies whose descendants are now identified as Twa, and a group from which the Hutus descend, who spoke a Bantu language and seem physically to have been strong, short, and muscular. These historians also maintained that roughly 400 years ago a taller, Nilotic people from East African regions came, saw, and conquered the indigenous population. While the victorious forces accepted the language of those whom they defeated, they introduced a new standard of wealth to the region—cattle, which they had brought with them. Over the years, the original inhabitants gave up to the invaders most of their land and their economic freedom. Thus developed a feudal culture in which the taller conquering tribes, from whom today's Tutsis claim descent, gained considerable but not universal control over the earlier Hutu and Twa inhabitants.

To those European writers, the conquerors were viewed as being intrinsically superior in height, intelligence, and capacity to rule; and, not surprisingly, they physically resembled those writing the history more nearly than did members of the indigenous populations. Many writers also believed that the conquering tribes were noblemen who had come from Christian Ethiopia and were descendants of the Biblical figure Ham (a son of Noah). This "Hamitic" theory, however questionable its historicity, was difficult to challenge for those who had neither written records nor traditions of Western scholarship; and it was accepted widely enough in Burundi during the twentieth century to have had a considerable psychological impact on the local population. Schools, churches, customs, and social organization have all continued to the present time to reinforce the idea that the supposed descendants of Ham, the Tutsi, are inherently superior to the Hutu and Twa.

So successful has been this indoctrination that many Hutus today, including those who have immigrated to the United States and begun new lives, acknowledge that they feel inferior and intimidated even when only engaged in ordinary conversation with Tutsis.

Almost all later twentieth-century historians and anthropologists have rejected the Hamitic theory, and, pointing to the similarity in language among all groups in the region, have explained differences in physical appearance as resulting primarily from diet rather than geographical origin. They agree that during most of the precolonial period the taller people whom we today identify as Tutsi generally enjoyed considerable but not universal dominance over the Hutu and Twa in rule, wealth, land ownership, and social standing. They equally agree, however, that between the two main groups existed not only commercial and social interaction, but also, and more importantly, intermarriage. Therefore, the exactness of ethnic classification becomes ever more questionable as time passes and intermarriage increases. All three ethnic groups living in Burundi were governed by kings or leaders called *bami* (singular, *mwami*), who, with their relatives, made up a special ruling class called the Ganwa, who considered themselves to be neither Tutsi, nor Hutu, nor Twa. What may be most important in the history we have received is what is *not* said: the stories received through oral tradition suggest neither constant fighting nor universal ethnic separation and subjugation during the precolonial period. The statement frequently found today in news media—that Hutus and Tutsis have been fighting for centuries—has little basis in historical fact.

The countries today known as Rwanda and Burundi were among the last to be colonized in the great scramble for Africa that occupied European powers at the close of the nineteenth century. King Leopold II, the monarch of tiny Belgium, a country scarcely larger than Burundi itself, had claimed a vast area (around seventy-five times the size of Belgium itself) west of Burundi, named the Congo Free State, as his personal property. There, seemingly endless forests covered lands almost as extensive as all of the United States east of the Mississippi. Within these forests, for a time one of the world's chief sources of rubber, were thought to lie great mineral riches of gold, diamonds, precious stones, and useful metals. Compared to Belgium's lucrative capture, Germany had, by claiming Rwanda and Burundi, arrived in time only for the tailings of the mines, the scraps from the table.

The peoples within the territory comprising Rwanda and Burundi shared languages, customs, and ethnic groups; yet within that territory, the historical patterns of alliances, loyalties, and commerce legitimately defined the two areas as separate colonies. Rwanda and Urundi (as Burundi was then called) were neither created nor separated by the stroke of a colonial pen: well before the Germans arrived, the two countries had existed with individual identities—as twins, though not identical twins.

In Burundi, Germany established a trading post at Usumbura (today, the capital, Bujumbura) and set up a minimal colonial government for about a quarter century. Nevertheless, except for a railroad line from Lake Tanganyika to the port city of Dar es Salaam, Tanzania, a few words of German that made their way into Kirundi, and a scattering of buildings and remote bridges, the Germans left behind few traces of their presence. One can travel the length and breadth of Burundi and never hear German spoken. It is as if the lush tropical vegetation had overgrown what few remains that culture and society might have been left behind. Burundi today is as oblivious of Germany as Germany is unaffected by Burundi.

After Germany's defeat in the First World War, the League of Nations gave Belgium a mandate to administer Ruanda-Urundi, which formed little more than an appendix to the huge body of the Belgian Congo that it already governed. The Belgians, in assessing their new colony, observed that in Burundi the primary ruling group was the Ganwa, followed by the Tutsi, with whom they often shared physical features and family connections. The Ganwa and Tutsi tended to be taller, and to have more prominent noses and angular features, than the shorter, flat-nosed Hutu. In social ranking, while some Hutu were landowners or religious and political leaders, overall they held fewer positions of leadership than the Ganwa and Tutsi; the Twa held none. Since Belgians, like other colonialists, found governance easier if exercised through a fixed, formal, hierarchical social structure, they increasingly awarded positions of authority to the Tutsi (including the Ganwa in that group), and left to the Hutu and Twa the task of tilling the soil. Thus, for example, whereas in 1929 Hutus in Burundi accounted for 28 percent of landholding leaders, by 1937 they comprised only 2 percent, and by 1945, none remained. Hutu landowners and ritualists, or religious leaders, had been stripped of the responsibilities and privileges they had previously enjoyed, and were reduced to the status of the Hutu peasants, who already formed the great bulk of the population.

While codifying a hierarchical social structure, the Belgians managed to combine exploitation with neglect, doing almost nothing to nurture, develop, and educate the general population. In the 1940s in Astrida (today, Butare), Rwanda, they built one school for the sons of chiefs; otherwise, such few schools as existed in Ruanda-Urundi were established by the Catholic Church—and they were so few that literacy was less than 10 percent in Burundi when Belgian colonial rule ended in 1962. In fact, knowledgeable officials today insist that Burundi, Rwanda, and the Belgian Congo had no more than ten university graduates apiece when those nations received their independence in the early 1960s.

Some colonial powers left behind at independence a cadre of indigenous civil servants trained in administration and governance. Not, however, in Burundi and Rwanda. Instead, in these distant, isolated, mountainous kingdoms, the Belgians in the mid-twentieth century left behind an entrenched feudal political and social structure. Under their system in Burundi, the minority Tutsis became rulers. The majority Hutus, and the few remaining Twa, tilled the soil and looked after the Tutsis' cattle. They were peasants, unresisting serfs. Rather than preparing these countries for self-governance, then, Belgium's forty-year rule pushed them back nearer to the Middle Ages. The political and social structure left behind helped provide the framework for the ethnic wars and recurrent genocide that have proven more dangerous to the lives of Burundians and Rwandans than all the land mines left in later years in the soil of their neighbors. The new nation-states that housed this structure were almost certain to fail. And they did.

It may be that the Belgians, having departed from the vast and mineral-rich Belgian Congo amid turmoil, slaughter, and worldwide obloquy, and having never given much attention to Ruanda-Urundi anyway, simply wanted to close up shop and get out of town. And one might have thought that things could only get better. Wrong. What emerged after the Belgians' departure was a society even more stratified, more unjust, crueler, and certainly more murderous under home rule than that under Belgian colonialism. In 1988, one of the few scholars on Burundi and one of the best known, René Lemarchand, testifying before the U.S. Congress, said, "Nowhere else in Africa have human rights been violated on a more massive scale, and with more brutal consistency, than in Burundi."[1] In the following year, Catherine Watson wrote, "Next to South Africa, Burundi is the most polarized country in Africa."[2] While the Belgians had rigidified and codified inequality where some mobility had previously existed, the indigenous rulers who came to power soon after independence—both the Hutus in Rwanda, and the Tutsis in Burundi—went beyond the colonialists in employing murder and massacre to maintain their position.

After the Second World War, Belgium completely failed to see the writing on the wall that read "Independence is inevitable." In 1955, Antoine van Bilsen, a Belgian professor, published a "thirty-year plan" that anticipated a gradual evolution of self-government for the Belgian colonies by 1985. But the decade from 1957 to 1967 saw a tidal flow of independence movements rush across Africa, carrying Burundi with it. In the few months during which Belgian authorities planned for the independence of Burundi, they assumed that, like Belgium, the newly independent state would be governed through a constitutional monarchy. And although they were pulling out, the Belgians sought to influence voters in selecting political parties in the newly forming government.

In Burundi, the Belgians were strongly suspicious of the Uprona political party, headed by Prince Rwagasore, son of King Mwambutsa IV. Rwagasore was a political candidate who had everything. Handsome, articulate, and smart, he was a Ganwa prince, thereby appealing to monarchist sentiment; and Rwagasore's Russian education had made him sympathetic to social and economic policies admired in left-wing political circles. However, viewing Rwagasore and Uprona as too radical, Belgium heavily and overtly favored the rival Parti Démocratique Chrétien (PDC) instead. When Uprona won 82 percent of the vote in 1961, Rwagasore was named prime minister, but tragically was assassinated two weeks later by a Greek immigrant in the pay of opposition political leaders. Thus, political assassination was present at the creation of the newly independent Burundi.

Several years of confused rule followed, during which ethnicity was added to family and party differences in a mad scramble for power. First, in 1965, a Hutu Upronist, Prime Minister Pierre Ngendumwe, was assassinated by a Tutsi who went unpunished. Uprona had won twenty-one of thirty-three seats for deputies in Parliament and twelve of sixteen seats in the Senate. Most of these victorious members were Hutu, as were the members of the Parti du Peuple (PP), which placed second, with ten members. The king, however, offended Hutus, Upronists, and PP members by choosing someone from his own cabinet, who was of neither party nor of the majority ethnicity, but was a Ganwa who had never run for office, and therefore held no parliamentary seat. When some Hutu elements within the army attempted an abortive takeover to restore the victory earlier won at the ballot box, the overwhelmingly Tutsi army responded with military trials and the executions of almost a hundred Hutu leaders, including Gervais Nyangoma, director-general of the prime minister's office; Sylvestre Karibwami, president of the Senate; Emile Bueumi, president of the National Assembly; Paul Nibirantiza, president of the Parti du Peuple; and other cabinet ministers, senators, and high officials. The props were in place and the stage irrevocably set for the first army takeover and the beginning of almost thirty years of military dictatorship when army captain Michel Micombero assumed power on November 28, 1966. He set the pattern for his successors in three respects: he was an officer whose despotic, militaristic rule was supported by the armed forces; he came from the Hima subgroup of Tutsis, who lived in the southern Bururi region of Burundi; and he ruled by terror.

Within a few years, Micombero instituted a genocide of monumental proportions, notable not only for its scale and effectiveness, but also for the silence and indifference displayed by the world. In 1972, Micombero deliberately set out to eliminate all educated Hutus above the age of fifteen so that, as he explained to one Western reporter at the time, Tutsi rule would be safe for at least the next generation. Since boys received preference over girls in education, the victims were mostly male. A Western missionary who had served in Burundi during that period later described to me how army trucks and buses arrived at boarding schools to take away all Hutu schoolchildren, who were delivered to firing squads or buried alive in mass graves. Estimates go as high as 300,000; at least 150,000 Hutus were certainly slaughtered, roughly 10–15 percent of the total male Hutu population at that time and probably 75 percent of Burundi's educated Hutus. During that genocide, any Hutu walking down the street with a pencil in his shirt pocket might be snatched by the military and summarily killed, since it indicated that he knew how to read and write.

The executions were swift, merciless, and virtually without opposition from within or outcries from without the country. As Reginald Kay stated in *Burundi since the Genocide,*

> What may literally be termed as genocide was largely ignored outside the country. The UN only became involved with the enormous refugee problem. The Organization of African Unity (OAU) expressed no opinion of the killings and repeated . . . [the genocidists'] version of events as the established facts of the case. . . . The role of France was not surprising to outside observers. The French Government provided military assistance during and after the killings. . . .
>
> The Catholic Church responded with a series of platitudes. The virtual absence of international protest surely encouraged the government to pursue its discriminatory policies. The immediate result was that the structure of society altered more dramatically in a few months in 1972 than in the decade of independence and the more than sixty years of colonial rule that had preceded them. The domination of the Tutsi, and particularly by the Hima, was now nearly complete.[3]

In 1976, Lieutenant Colonel Jean-Baptiste Bagaza overthrew his misanthropic, drunken, and partially mad cousin Micombero and instituted a dictatorship that added the suppression of religion to the suppression of Hutus. To Bagaza, all Christian churches represented challenges to his dictatorial authority and were therefore enemies of the state. Consequently, he confiscated church properties, banished most missionaries, and directly controlled all religious practices. For example, in 1985 the minister of the interior announced, "Funeral masses may continue to be held provided that they are celebrated at the time of death. Masses which are celebrated at a residence or at the home of 'lifting of mourning' or similar circumstances are forbidden. Home visits to the sick are forbidden." The consequences of his edict extended well beyond religion. Since such little education as existed had often been provided by Christian religious groups, Bagaza's banishing of Christian missionaries and persecution of the church significantly crippled instruction in reading and writing as well.

That suited Bagaza. While Micombero, through mass executions in 1972, had sought to eliminate the existing educated class of Hutus, Bagaza sought to guarantee that education would be so systematically denied to Hutus that they would never develop a group of people capable of participating in government. Under his rule, an estimated 47 percent of children did not attend school at all. Of those who did, only a few proceeded to education beyond the age of twelve. In fact, in 1985 only 4 percent of Burundi's teenagers were enrolled in secondary education. Within that tiny group, the overwhelming majority were Tutsis, not Hutus.

To make certain that Hutus were all but excluded from secondary schools, the examination system was rigged. Only Tutsis were allowed to serve as the regional and cantonal inspectors who determined which students proceeded to secondary education. These examiners arranged for all student examination papers, after their submission, to be identified with an *i* for Tuts*i* students or a *u* for Hut*u* students so that the examiners could ensure only a minimal number of Hutus advanced. In such an educational system it became almost impossible for a Hutu to win—either in secondary school or in the nation's only university, where admission and instruction were totally controlled by the government.

In his government, as in his plans for the future, Bagaza limited Hutus to token participation. Only seven of sixty-five seats in the National Assembly, and two out of fifty-two positions in the Central Committee, were occupied by Hutus. Thus, though making up 85 percent of the population, Hutus generally received less than 10 percent of the positions in the schools, universities, and Parliament.

Bagaza might have been able to get away with simply persecuting the Hutu. However, like Hitler, who thought he could simultaneously conquer Europe and the Soviet Union, he mistakenly chose to fight a war on two fronts. In attacking Christian churches, he made both political and spiritual enemies. That was too much even for Burundi.

Thus, Major Pierre Buyoya, supported by the Burundi Army, was able to launch an effective and bloodless coup in September 1987 against a dictator feared or disliked by Hutus, Christians, and the international community. In comparison, Buyoya, smooth and articulate, appeared to be a promising change, especially when he spoke of Hutu-Tutsi unity. By admitting a few Hutus to his cabinet and appointing a Hutu prime minister, his compass seemed set on the road to reconciliation.

In reality, however, little changed. The Hutu prime minister, Adrien Sibomana, was a cipher; when denied access to the grounds of the military academy by army officers, he resigned in humiliation, as did other Hutu cabinet members. Buyoya refused to accept their resignations, yet he kept an army in which 99 percent of the officers were Tutsi. Similarly, in every other area controlled by his government, Tutsi dominance was near universal: 95 percent of the judiciary, 88 percent of the faculty at the University of Bujumbura, and all thirty-three members of the Comité Militaire de Salut National (or, Military Committee for National Security, which had final authority over national decision making) were Tutsi. While Buyoya initially provided a façade pleasing enough for Burundi to become, per capita, the largest recipient of International Development Agency (IDA) loans in the world, his dictatorship proved increasingly anachronistic in the late 1980s.

The pleasant façade was first shattered in August 1988 when, after a clash between Hutus and Tutsis in the northern town of Marangara, Hutus killed fourteen Tutsis with machetes in a churchyard. In response, the Burundi Army entered the region, enjoyed six days of killing, and in the ensuing violence, used helicopters, incendiary bombs, troops, and armored vehicles to annihilate large portions of the populations of Marangara, Ntega, and Kanyinya, all northern communities. At least 20,000 Hutu lives were taken in exchange for the fourteen Tutsis initially killed, proving again, as colonialists had shown almost a century earlier, that knives and machetes provide little defense against an army that has all the guns. And proving, too, that defenseless women and children, the main victims today, can seldom escape a surrounding army.

The reaction of the international community was muted. Even so, Buyoya found it harder thereafter to attract funds and support for his military dictatorship. Under international pressure, he therefore established a committee to draw up a new constitution, which would allow free multiparty elections. In June 1993, he went confidently to the polls, only to lose to Melchior Ndadaye by a margin of two to one. Buyoya put on a good face. He seemingly accepted the defeat with grace, and Melchior Ndadaye, the first freely elected president of Burundi, was inaugurated on July 10, 1993.

For the tiny mountainous nation, now finally deserving of the title "republic," it was a historic moment. The isolation fostered centuries ago by language and geography, and furthered by indigenous and colonial feudal cultures, seemed ready to disappear like a tropical rain as Burundi prepared to enter the twentieth century during its final years. The hopes of the population were high. It seemed a new beginning.

BURUNDI'S FIRST FREELY ELECTED PRESIDENT

Melchior Ndadaye, who won the presidency on June 1 and lost his life on October 21, 1993, was a genuinely extraordinary man. Had he lived longer, his life and influence might well have followed in the paths of two heroes in the twentieth-century fight for freedom from oppression: Mahatma Gandhi and Martin Luther King. Like them, he was a passionate advocate of nonviolence, spent time in prison for speaking out against injustice, rose naturally to be the foremost spokesman in his nation for those most severely subjugated; and like them, he died at the hands of assassins.

Born in the town of Gitega in 1953 to parents of modest means who recognized the importance of education, Melchior Ndadaye proved capable of meeting the rigorous academic standards imposed on those few Hutus allowed access to secondary school. Growing up, he helped the family with agricultural chores even while attending school. But when Micombero ordered the slaughter of educated Hutus in 1972, Ndadaye fled to neighboring Rwanda, a country where Hutus had wrested control from the Tutsi hierarchy soon after independence in 1962 and were willing to give aid and refuge to their ethnic kinsmen from Burundi. There, Ndadaye was part of a small Burundi diaspora in the National University of Rwanda—Hutus all, and all hoping one day to return to Burundi. Gathered together as students were most of the people who would later form the leadership of the Frodebu Party, several of whom were to serve in Ndadaye's cabinet. The group had various heroes, not all of them nonviolent. The Marxist slogan "From each according to his ability, to each according to his need" appealed to many Africans, most of whom were needy. In fact, Ndadaye nicknamed his first child "Geva" after Che Guevara, and his second son "Tika," in reference to Marxist dialectic.

Yet because of his opposition to all forms of violence, Ndadaye found Marxism too harsh an influence after leaving the university, since his temperament had always been more compassionate than condemning. His fellow Burundian students in Rwanda remember him as more interested in elevating the peasantry than in overturning governments. Intellectually keen, he nevertheless let his head follow his heart, which beat with those who tilled the soil. Thus, after wholesale genocide in Burundi was replaced by mere dictatorial repression, he returned there in 1983 to direct a cooperative agricultural project that brought financial credit to farmers, whom he believed to be fully capable of taking on larger responsibilities if given the opportunity.

Ndadaye equally believed Burundians to be capable of self-government.

Along with other exiles returning from Rwanda with dreams of a democratic future for Burundi, he began forming a political party, Front pour la Démocratie au Burundi (Frodebu). Its existence was kept secret, however, since political parties other than Uprona were banned by President Buyoya. Nonetheless, Frodebu's members did not remain silent, and Ndadaye's outspokenness landed him in jail in 1989.

In 1988, the Burundi Army's indiscriminate slaughter of 20,000 Hutus had prompted international criticism and reduced foreign aid. Therefore, to put a better face on his government, President Buyoya in 1989 initiated nationwide town and village meetings to discuss reconciliation between Hutu and Tutsi. At such a meeting in Gitega, Ndadaye made his political debut. He began his speech, in moderate voice and temperate language, by suggesting that Burundians acknowledge the killings of 1965, 1972, and 1988, and then work to build a democratic society with a legal system of equal rights for all. He next asserted, cautiously, that the time was not yet ripe for general elections, because people continued to hold hostile ethnic stereotypes that perpetuated separatism and conflict. In measured tones he carefully laid before his nervous listeners a modest proposal: Burundi should undertake a ten-year transition to democracy, during which those currently holding power would gradually liberalize the political process, allow multiparty democracy, and open the privilege of military service to all citizens, regardless of their ethnicity. As the audience of Hutus and Tutsis began to glance with discomfort, wonder, and surprise at his boldness, his voice rose in a crescendo of earnestness as he concluded by stating that Burundians' greatest need was to hear diverse opinions without fighting, to recognize that democracy must evolve through an exchange of ideas, not gunfire.

The speech was too much for the government. Three days later, while Ndadaye, his wife, and children were having lunch in their home, security agents arrived to take him away.

He was imprisoned for three months. Rumonge Prison, where he was kept in solitary confinement in a concrete cell that had no windows, bed, chair, or toilet, was considered the worst of the miserable prisons in this impoverished country. To torture the inmates, the authorities sometimes deliberately flooded its cells with water from nearby Lake Tanganyika, causing Ndadaye to stand in water, making sleep impossible and chills inevitable. His freedom was gained only through the intervention of Amnesty International and other international human-rights organizations. He was never brought to trial. President Ndadaye was later to tell his cabinet ministers, "My experience in prison was so horrible that I would never wish anyone else to undergo it." One of his first acts as president was therefore to abolish capital punishment and to grant a general amnesty to almost all prisoners throughout the country.

When international pressure forced the Buyoya government to allow the formation of various political parties and hold general elections in 1993, Melchior Ndadaye, both by his important role in forming the Frodebu Party and by the strength of his vision and character, was his party's unchallenged choice as candidate for president. Although initially he was not well known, as he traveled across the small country, speaking to ever-growing crowds, he awakened the hopes of silent people who, oppressed for most of the century, felt they had finally found a voice for their aspirations.

Before long, it should have been obvious to all observers that if the votes were counted fairly, Ndadaye and Frodebu would decisively win. Although Ndadaye's oratory was not powerful, his presence was. He did not dominate or intimidate his listeners, but rather awakened in them a sense of their own capacities. He could talk to simple people without talking down to them. Even though Kirundi, the native language of Burundi, has little technical vocabulary, he successfully communicated his ideas on complicated topics like taxation, foreign trade, and equal employment to a largely illiterate population. And the peasants who heard him, inspired by his commitment, undertook challenging campaign tasks and consistently performed beyond their own expectations. Someone who later served in Ndadaye's cabinet recalled how, during the 1993 election campaign, he had received political brochures brought to Frodebu headquarters in a small mountainous village in Cibitoke by a crippled but dedicated political volunteer. The man had no legs, no crutches, no wheelchair. But using only his hands, he had propelled himself on a body-length scooter, raised on small wheels only a few inches off of the ground, several miles up muddy mountain roads and footpaths to deliver the materials.

Ndadaye captured the confidence of his crowds, above all, because people believed in his unselfish intent to serve the nation. As the campaign proceeded and people's hopes grew, men and women threw down their coats or cloaks for him to walk upon, both as a sign of respect and to have Ndadaye touch their clothes, which they then cherished like a saint's relics. Sometimes as he was traveling by car from one village to the next, peasants would lie down in the road, forcing his convoy to stop so that they might reach in and touch their hero. While accepting their adulation with courtesy and humility, Ndadaye gained such an expanded sense of mission as he traveled across the country that he became, as one of his cabinet members described, "totally fearless," frequently reassuring his staff, "My security is the population."

As he campaigned, Ndadaye became confident not only of his safety but also of his party's inevitable victory. Yet his first concern was not his party but his nation. In Gandhian fashion, he was prepared not even to seek the office to which his election seemed assured. Therefore, on September 17, 1992, almost a year before elections, he sent Jean-Marie Ngendahayo to Buyoya to deliver the following proposition and promise:

> I understand that you want to go through with having elections, although as you know I suggested in 1989 that there be a 10-year transition period during which you would remain President. What I suggest now is that you present yourself as a candidate above all political parties—not the candidate of Party Uprona. If you will do that, I will not seek the presidency, and the Frodebu Party will campaign for you and not put up its own candidate.

Ndadaye communicated this message just two months after Frodebu had become a lawful party. He added, however, that in the legislative elections, Frodebu would campaign seriously against the Uprona Party and would certainly win.

Ndadaye believed that if Frodebu held a majority in the parliament while Buyoya was a nonpartisan president, the population would gradually become accustomed to seeing different points of view debated and would recognize that political groups from different ethnicities could work together. To Ndadaye, Frodebu's largest challenge would not be to win the election, but to manage change. And to his private friends, Ndadaye also confided that part of the challenge of change would be to see whether the army would accept the election of a Hutu president.

When Ngendahayo's mission failed, Ndadaye sent as his envoy to Buyoya a Tutsi from Bururi province, Gilles Bimazubute, who had previously served under the despotic Micombero. Later, Ndadaye himself went. In each instance, however, Buyoya refused the offer. Whether he could not believe that he could lose, or was unwilling to work with a Hutu Parliament, or already had in mind that the army could reverse the decision if he lost the election is known only to Buyoya.

What events showed, however, is that a nonviolent follower of Mahatma Gandhi and Martin Luther King was chosen by a two-to-one margin by the people of Burundi, only to have their decision reversed by Ndadaye's death at the hands of Buyoya's closest friends and followers inside the confines of an army camp in Bujumbura.

Ndadaye's death made little impact worldwide. In some major capitals the story of his assassination made the front page for one day. After that, a few back-page stories followed, and then the events of Burundi receded into the mountain mists and this isolated, distant country was again forgotten. Indeed, no means existed for continuing news to reach the world, since there was not then, and is not now, a single international journalist permanently assigned to Burundi. A few reporters may fly in at the time of a "story," only to be removed again a few days later. The likelihood that they know much about the country, its culture, or its history is slender. And even if they did, they would be sent on assignment elsewhere as soon as the "story" lost its newsworthiness.

In 1993, only four countries from the developed world had embassies there: Belgium, because Burundi was a former colony; Germany, for the same reason; France, because Burundi is francophone; and the United States, because President Kennedy had promised to put an embassy in every African country that gained independence.

Washington, Brussels, Paris, or Bonn could not have had full awareness of what Ndadaye's death was to mean, for he was little known outside Burundi. Except for two trips to Germany and Cameroon, Ndadaye had rarely left the Burundi-Rwanda region of central Africa before becoming president. At most, only the few diplomats who met Ndadaye when he visited the State Department in Washington, or the slightly larger number whom he met at the United Nations headquarters in New York, might have gotten a sense of his priorities, which he expressed at a New York press conference on October 4, 1993. Asked what he most hoped to achieve as president, Ndadaye answered,

> I don't want any more bloodshed in Burundi: I don't want to see a single drop of innocent blood shed in my beloved country. I want to build a society where equality is embraced as more than just a thought or a slogan: a society where liberty and justice is available to everyone.

In terms of realpolitik, Burundi scarcely matters to the outside world. The United States, for example, has zero economic interest in Burundi: total trade between the two countries in 1993 amounted to only seven million dollars—less than one day's Christmas sales at a large metropolitan department store. We have zero military interest: nothing that Burundi could do militarily could ever threaten the United States or even a small developed nation. We have zero direct political interest, for Burundi's government has neither the clout nor the respect to influence other nations. Burundi matters only if we care about human life—if we believe that it makes a difference when people suffer terribly, when they grow up impoverished and uneducated, or when they see their children and parents fleeing through the forest to avoid being hacked to pieces or shot to death for no reason other than their ethnicity. Only if we believe that all human life has value; that God created all people, not just some; and that in some perhaps mysterious but nonetheless inescapable fashion we are bound together in a web of destiny in which what touches one life vibrates for all—if we believe those things, then Burundi matters. And if so, then the assassination of Melchior Ndadaye affects us as well.

THE KILLING OF A PRESIDENT PROMPTS
THE KILLING OF TENS OF THOUSANDS

There can be no question that the murder of Melchior Ndadaye has had life-changing consequences for Burundi's six million people. After assassinating Ndadaye and his closest Frodebu leaders, the army, Upronists, and allied extremist Tutsis sought simply to proceed with their coup. They intended to install as president François Ngeze, a Hutu puppet whose radio address had been prepared for him several days before the assassination. Thus, within a few hours of Ndadaye's death, Ngeze announced on the radio that in response to the request of the Conseil Militaire (Military Council), which was assuming power, he was taking the position of president and head of state. That afternoon he began making courtesy calls to diplomatic missions. The Burundi Army and the Uprona Party were so accustomed to coups, so isolated in their awareness, and so myopic in their vision that they expected no significant opposition.

According to Lt. Jean-Paul Kamana, who was assigned to serve as Ngeze's aide-de-camp for the next few days, Ngeze's first call on the afternoon of October 21st was at the French embassy. For some years France, which had maintained a larger interest in Africa than any other major power, had assigned twenty to thirty French military advisers to live in Burundi and work full-time with the Burundi Army. Ngeze was therefore surprised when the French ambassador, Henri Crepin-Leblond, told him very directly that the coup was unconstitutional and unacceptable: he, and the army, would have to give back power to an elected government.

His second call was longer, but no better. The head of the United Nations Development Program office, Mrs. Jocelyn Basil-Finley, made it equally clear in an extended rebuke that the international community would not tolerate the putsch.

After these unsuccessful meetings, Ngeze returned to report to Buyoya, Buyoya's former chief of staff Siningi (by then already freed from prison), and the army and Uprona leaders who had planned the coup that the take-over had not yet been accepted. The putschists persisted nonetheless. Ngeze rode in Ndadaye's limousine, accompanied by presidential guards; he made several presidential appointments, including a new director of intelligence; and he appeared on television that evening with all the official trappings traditionally surrounding a legitimate president of Burundi.

The next day, October 22, he met with the diplomatic corps and other representatives of international organizations at Kigobe Palace. Ngeze used the argument put forward by putschists everywhere—that someone needed to take over and restore order amid confusion; hence, he had assumed power with the support of the army. But the international community did not buy it. To cries of "No," "The country has a constitution," and "You cannot take over by force," Ngeze backed down and returned to Buyoya, the army, and Upronist leaders to say that he could not serve: the coup had failed.

On that same afternoon, protests in the capital were beginning. The marchers—at least 5,000, according to one expatriate eyewitness—were peaceful, saddened, shocked, and sober, demonstrating nonviolently, as Ndadaye would have wanted. They had organized on their own, since all their government leaders were necessarily still in hiding or in sanctuary in foreign embassies. Local security forces—the gendarmerie and army—were their enemies, not their protectors. So they had to march protected only by conscience, faith, and a modicum of international scrutiny. As they passed the French embassy, where the greatest number of survivors from Ndadaye's cabinet were gathered, their homemade cardboard signs carried simple messages: "Melchior Ndadaye, we love you," "Democracy yes, putschists no," and the lengthier "Our martyrs have been slaughtered barbarically. At least give us their ashes so we may bury them properly."

The burial came on December 6. No foreign heads of state and very few foreign emissaries outside of those already living in Bujumbura attended. The bodies of the president, the vice president and speaker of the National Assembly, the two deputy speakers, the head of intelligence, a provincial governor, and those of Mrs. Ntibantunganya and Mrs. Katabashinga, now cleaned and embalmed, some bayoneted and all bruised, lay in their closed coffins for the ceremony. The bodies were lowered, the flags flew at half-staff, and all military leaders were present: proper protocol was observed.

The capital was marked not only by ceremonies and demonstrations but also by governmental stalemate. The coup had effectively created a complete vacuum of legitimate political power. The constitution of 1992 had defined the line of presidential succession as proceeding from the president, to the vice president and speaker of the National Assembly, to the deputy speaker. On October 21, all three were assassinated. As one scholar perceptively wrote, those who organized the coup did it with the constitution in one hand and a gun in the other.[4] The constitution had also specified that in the event of the president's death, new elections must be held within three months. But everyone agreed that new elections were impossible. Since Burundi in all its history had held only one set of free and honest elections—in June 1993—it had neither the mechanisms nor the finances in place immediately to hold elections again.

The highest-ranking survivor in government, Sylvie Kinigi, had not been elected. She been appointed to her position by President Ndadaye: the first female prime minister in the history of Africa. As a Tutsi Upronist whose name had not even appeared on a ballot, she had no claim to lead the country. Moreover, her party had been deeply involved in planning the assassination. Present at army headquarters with their Tutsi kinsmen during the early morning hours of the coup were Upronist leaders Libère Bararunyeretse, Alphonse Kadege, François Ngeze, the would-be head of state, and Charles Mukasi, later party chairman of Uprona. They were joined by Jerome Sinduhije, a retired military officer active in plots from Micombero through Buyoya, and by two leaders of Tutsi extremist parties affiliated with Uprona: Terence Nsanze of Abasa, and Dr. Alphonse Rugambarara of Inkinzo. During that night of terror, no Upronist was harmed. Without exception, only members of Frodebu were killed, and with one exception, they were all Hutus.

The surviving leaders of Frodebu were in no position to offer immediate and strong leadership. Many remained in hiding, and none could be certain of where to go or what to do. Unable to seek protection from the army that had killed their president and cabinet colleagues, many sought refuge at the embassy of France, a country that demonstrated its capacity to act more quickly and decisively in Africa than any other. French Ambassador Henri Crepin-Leblond offered protection to Mme. Laurence Ndadaye and her children at his residence, and while other governments hesitated in the wake of the coup, France sent twenty gendarmes from Paris to protect high-level Frodebu parliamentarians and officials, many of whom then went from the embassy to the Hotel du Lac on nearby Lake Tanganyika to formulate plans.

Gathered together there, Frodebu leaders were divided on the best way to preserve democracy—and their lives. The majority hoped for an international military force of 5,000 troops to provide protection. Had such troops come, they might have saved tens of thousands of lives—no one can be sure. What happened instead was that the Organization of African Unity agreed to send 500 African soldiers before December 31, 1993. Extremist Tutsis publicly protested so effectively and threateningly against this announcement, however, that the OAU backed down and sent only eighteen officers, and no armed troops, to Burundi in February 1994. Other Frodebu leaders proposed organizing their own militia, separate from the army. Some of these proponents, including Léonard Nyangoma, would later break away from Frodebu and in exile form a political group, the Conseil National pour la Défense de la Démocratie (CNDD), which joined an existing military force, the Front pour la Défense de la Démocratie (FDD). The FDD was essentially a guerilla force, formed largely by peasants and a few Hutus who had served in the Burundi Army. To this group of fighters, Nyangoma brought the political experience necessary for negotiation.

While the capital was frozen in inaction, the countryside, where 95 percent of the population lives, was burning in anger. Melchior Ndadaye was the only person in the twentieth century ever to give the majority of Burundians the hope of achieving dignity, self-respect, and self-government. To them, the shock was as immediate as the radio waves that carried the message of his death; the outrage as powerful as the volcanoes that had formed their landscape—and it now erupted and flowed across the countryside. The fury was wild, desperate, uncontrolled. Though arms for private citizens were outlawed—and were too expensive for most peasants—machetes, knives, and torches remained effective weapons of violence. Although the postcolonial period had experienced several Hutu uprisings, all had been confined to a single location and all had been ineffectual. Hutus now, for the first time, lashed out en masse across the country, aggressively and pitilessly, against the Tutsis to whom they had so long been subservient and whose political and military leaders had now taken away their greatest hope. Tutsi homes were burned, families slaughtered, and even neighbors with whom their families may have intermarried were killed. The fury was incited by fearful and vengeful political leaders, but it also resulted from years of frustration and resentment.

The army, culpable for Ndadaye's death, must have been surprised. In the great genocide of Hutus in 1972, Micombero's soldiers had gone into the villages to gather educated Hutus and take them away. When a truck could hold no more, they instructed the Hutus to return the next day. And most Hutus obeyed. Having been serfs for generations, they were accustomed to obeying those in authority unquestioningly. If a Tutsi told them to do something, they did it.

But not this time. The violence against Tutsis was real, unselective, and universal. And the army's reaction was the same. Soldiers went out in their blindés, trucks, and helicopters and fired their machine guns indiscriminately at Hutu villagers in the countryside. Peasants felled trees across major highways and smaller roads to interrupt the army's movement. By day, rural peasants sought to hide in the forests; by night, to wreak revenge wherever possible.

The extent of the death toll will never be known, but 150,000 is a generally accepted and probably conservative estimate. If correct, it means that at least 2.5 percent of the population was slaughtered by both sides in a few weeks after Ndadaye's death. That would be equivalent to over 6 million Americans being killed—a number three times as large as all troops who have been killed in all of America's wars in more than 200 years. And yet the Burundi slaughter never made the newspapers in most American and European capitals and towns. The dead bodies spun down the rivers or were dropped in latrines and unmarked graves, outside the focus of television cameras. The lives of Burundian peasants just didn't matter that much.

Fortunately, the United Nations and the international community took some notice. So universal was the condemnation, so clear the threats of being cut off from economic aid, political recognition, or commercial interchange, that the putschists themselves were shocked into catatonic inactivity. An army unaccustomed to any outside onlookers suddenly found itself surrounded by outraged attention. And the nations watching had much bigger armies than their own.

Therefore, amid international pressure and threats to cut off diplomatic recognition and economic assistance, all sides in Burundi recognized that international involvement in shaping their future government was inevitable.

So the putschists backed down. But no one knew how to move forward. In an effort to breathe life into this deadly vacuum of legitimate power, in November 1993 the United Nations secretary-general sent a special representative to Burundi. Ahmedou Ould-Abdallah, a former foreign minister and longtime diplomat from Mauritania, was dispatched to help reestablish a government and, above all, to help Burundi avoid a civil war and overt massive genocide.

If Ould-Abdallah had not been sent, one can easily suppose that a more full-fledged civil war would have erupted. Through his knowledge of African customs and his indefatigable efforts, he brought together the various political parties and a group of African "wise men," or *bashingantahe*, for negotiations. This group, at Ould-Abdallah's prodding, urged that the constitution be amended so that Parliament could itself elect the new president. Thus, Cyprien Ntaryamira, who on October 21 had hidden in the house of his neighbor while she cleverly misdirected the soldiers looking to kill him, was elected and installed as the new president of the Republic of Burundi on February 9, 1994. During this same period, Sylvestre Ntibantunganya, who had walked past his guards on October 21, barefoot and disguised in his gardener's clothes, was elected vice president and speaker of the National Assembly.

The arrival of the United Nations in the person of Ambassador Ould-Abdallah was important in stabilizing a tottering nation. But the UN arrived without troops and without any genuine international commitment for taking decisive action to restore democracy. Its capacity to influence events was therefore tenuous, and trickled away bit by bit, day by day.

THREE

FROM WASHINGTON TO BURUNDI

Like most people, I lived most of my life knowing almost nothing about Burundi. But the events of June 5, 1993, changed all that for me.

On June 5, in a special election, I decisively lost to Kay Bailey Hutchison, a Republican, the U.S. Senate seat from Texas that I had held only briefly but that the Democratic Party had held for over 100 years. As my wife Kathleen and I that night watched our hopes for continuing service in the Senate fade before us in the election numbers on the television screen, we talked about the future and agreed that an ambassadorship, if available, might offer both the privilege of public service and an opportunity for our two young daughters to benefit from living amid other cultures.

Since all ambassadors are appointed by the president, within a week I was talking with President Clinton's chief of staff, Mack McLarty. When his assistant phoned to suggest several countries as possible assignments, Burundi immediately engaged my interest, and I indicated that if an ambassadorship there were offered to me, I would be delighted to accept. Then, after high-level meetings between the president, vice president, secretary of state, and others to decide upon various ambassadorial assignments, and after the months of paperwork and scrutiny that accompany all such presidential appointments, on June 8, 1994, under the chandeliered ceiling of the elegant Benjamin Franklin Room at the State Department in Washington, I was sworn in as U.S. ambassador to Burundi. Determined to work with Burundians to help nurture their fledgling democracy, I suggested, in my remarks on that occasion, that Burundi observe the American motto *E pluribus unum* and recognize the importance of drawing all ethnic groups into one united nation. I also suggested, more prophetically than I knew, that to achieve democracy and peace, forgiveness is as important a principle in statecraft and the life of a nation as in our spiritual and personal lives. It works. The problem with "An eye for an eye, and a tooth for a tooth" is that, when practiced, it leaves both parties toothless and blind.

Within two weeks I was on a flight, alone, to Bujumbura.

Regrettably, I had to leave my family behind: State Department fears that Rwanda's recent widespread genocidal violence would spill into Burundi had prompted an order temporarily evacuating all dependents of U.S. government employees from Burundi. As the plane began its approach in the early morning of June 23, I strained in my window seat for a first sight of Bujumbura, whose very name sounded artificially exotic, as though it had been made up by a Hollywood screenwriter. Through the scattered morning clouds, I could recognize hillsides with tiny terraced farm plots, as green as Ireland, dotted with the grayish brown conical thatched roofs of small houses, clumped together in little villages. Ahead, just before the plane made its final arc, I saw the dark sapphire surface of Lake Tanganyika break into view, a few golden ripples touched by the morning tropical dawn adding movement to its rich transparency. The second-deepest lake in the world, a mile deep and 400 miles long, I remembered from my recent reading. And I smiled as I recalled that this lake was where, in the classic movie *The African Queen,* Humphrey Bogart and Katharine Hepburn had ended their famous river journey by torpedoing a German steamer and frolicking in its blue water. Yet for me this was not celluloid fiction, but real life and a new beginning: formerly U.S. senator from Texas, now U.S. ambassador to Burundi.

Waiting on the airport tarmac was Leonard Lange, the deputy chief of mission (or, second in command), who since February 1993 had been chargé d'affaires in the absence of an ambassador. Joining him were the dozen Americans who together composed the "country team." Having been without an ambassador for over a year, they would have gotten up at 5:00 a.m. to greet almost anyone whom Washington had sent.

Awaiting us outside was a long, white, somewhat bulbous 1993 Chevrolet Caprice, a small American flag flying from its right fender, a blue and white State Department flag from its left. The driver, Bernardin Rwirangira, was a tall, friendly Rwandan who had lived in Bujumbura long enough to have driven for seven previous American ambassadors. His skills were not to be taken lightly. Only the main thoroughfares in the capital had street signs with names; the locations and names of other streets were known only to the initiates, like Bernardin, who had been around for years.

As we headed toward the city, eight miles away, my eyes darted hungrily

Many peasant farming families live in small houses with conical thatched roofs.

from one thing to the next, as though I would have no time to consume the scene later. Our Chevrolet shared the highway with a few other cars, some old, some new, but most often, white four-wheel-drive vehicles owned by the nongovernmental organizations (NGOs) that provided development assistance or relief support to the country. The heaviest traffic was not in the road, but on the roadsides, where most people walk or trot, not ride. Owning a bicycle sets a family apart from its peers, and for most of the population, owning a car is an unimaginable dream. If families had only a few items to carry, the men walked free, leaving the women and children to carry the loads. The women were eye-catching, wrapped in brightly colored cotton cloth, their dark black skin glistening in the morning sunlight. Their carriage was inevitably erect: it had to be, since those items needing to be carried were first placed on their heads. They might be baskets, bundles of firewood, or, often, five-gallon plastic containers filled with water, since most houses in Burundi lack running water at home. Often on a woman's back, held only by an extra cloth tucked into her garment, was her newest baby. In a country where the average family has six living offspring, children are almost always in view.

Belching clouds of diesel smoke came the trucks. Some moved slowly and jerkily, their loads perhaps leaning heavily to one side. Others came roaring by at speeds of seventy to eighty miles an hour. No pity is shown to trucks in

Africa. The driver knows only to make the truck go as fast as it can. Nevertheless, we twice came to a complete halt. Cattle with horns long enough to make a Texas longhorn breeder envious ambled across the road as their handler led them to greener pastures. Cattle were far too valuable to run free, and land was too precious to keep them confined to one pasture. Roadsides in both the country and the city provided grazing rights for cattle, which remain today, as for centuries, ancient symbols of wealth. Halfway toward the city, Leonard pointed to some low rises several hundred yards away on an otherwise flat plain. Little more than grass and shrub brush covered them. No monuments, crosses, or historical markers of identification. But underneath that earth lay the remains of tens of thousands of Burundi's educated Hutus, most of them slaughtered in the Bujumbura stadium in 1972 as part of the massive genocide directed by President Micombero.

Our paved highway gave way to a dirt road, its surface reminiscent of a flattened egg crate. Bernardin wove his way carefully, watching the truck ahead move at a crawling pace between small puddles and potentially axle-bending potholes on this central thoroughfare. Soon we passed the nation's largest single industrial employer, Primus Brewery. Partially owned by the government, it provided almost as much in revenues to the government as did all the taxes collected in Burundi. Nearby we crossed a small stream, where Leonard observed matter-of-factly, "During the worst times, bodies sometimes came floating down the stream, but it emptied into the lake, where crocodiles could devour them."

As we entered the city center, my eyes, ears, and nostrils were vying with one another to store coherently in memory my sensory overload. The overwhelming sensation was of energy—teeming energy—in manifold and unfamiliar forms. In shops with faded and chipped façades were people bargaining over a piece of cloth, a pair of shoes, a rake, or a hoe. Women were weaving straw baskets of intricate design, often with strangely fluted, pointed tops unique to the region. In some sections there were simple, unpainted metal stalls scarcely six feet high or wide out of which someone was selling chewing gum or packaged candies, or perhaps fresh bananas, rich green avocados, or orange-pink papaya. The scent and sight of smoke came from small charcoal fires providing heat for a blacksmith to mend a bicycle wheel or for a hawker to roast ears of yellow corn skewered on narrow sticks and held up for sale. In cobbler's stalls, men stood, or rested on stools, barefoot and waiting for probably their only pair of shoes to be repaired; seamstresses sat outside, some using ancient, foot-powered Singer sewing machines. As we neared the large central market, a high drab enclosure of concrete and steel where one could buy anything from mattresses to freshly delivered produce, I sensed we were at the heart of the capital's commerce.

Most of the men were dressed in shirts and trousers of faded cotton, oftentimes bought secondhand. President Bagaza in the 1970s had insisted that men abandon their loincloths and blankets for more modern dress. But the women remained striking, wrapping their lithe and athletic bodies in brilliant, aggressively colored cotton prints.

The buildings reminded me of the simple two-story shops I had seen in border towns like Nuevo Laredo, Mexico. Some were vividly and newly painted in yellows, pinks, or pale blue, but more often the stucco façades revealed chips, scars, and scuff marks on buildings whose owners lacked money for repair and attention to detail. Burundi's charm and beauty lay not in distinguished architecture or tidiness, but in the vitality of its people.

Streaming down the surrounding hills toward the town center came hundreds of trotting people. Women carried large bunches of bananas on their heads; others balanced sacks of potatoes or large baskets filled high with pale green beans or bright orange carrots. Often their children trotted beside them. But trotting, almost always trotting. For getting down hillsides, trotting is evidently less tiring than walking, and somehow goods perched above one's shoulders or on one's head can in that way be carried more securely. Many of these people had carried their produce from tiny plots of land as far as ten miles away. They would probably sell all of it for only a few hundred Burundi francs (a dollar or two), then head back home before dark.

Ambling or just standing around the corners were youthful gendarmes in grayish blue uniforms — puffy trousers and matching shirts. Each had an AK-47 slung over his shoulder. The demeanor was haughty, the posture and manners undisciplined. But they displayed a sense of power that comes to a youth carrying a gun to be used as he likes, without fear of reproach by his superiors. The peasants pouring down the hills gave them ample room as they passed toward the market, and avoided exchanging glances.

On a hill only a few minutes north of the city center lies the boulevard du vingt-huit novembre, a street of spacious houses built largely by prosperous expatriates in the 1960s, several of which now house diplomatic residences. The American ambassadorial residence is there, flanked on one side by the home of a Belgian businessman, on the other by the residence recently rented to Burundi's foreign minister. Like many middle-class and all larger houses in the city, each is surrounded by walls, and those on Boulevard du Vingt-Huit Novembre were slightly higher than most. I would soon come to realize that my ten-foot stone wall, covered with fuchsia, pink, and amber

The porch of the embassy residence overlooks a carefully manicured tropical garden.

bougainvillea, was all that separated me from the anarchy that ruled every street in Bujumbura. And that my living and dining rooms and bedroom were all within range of an easy grenade toss from the street. At this moment, though, as we turned into the property, the large steel gates opened to reveal a long, gleaming white one-story building with a columned porch extending for most of its length. From there one looked out over an exquisitely manicured and designed front garden framed by three identical traveler's palms, their arches perfectly superimposed over a majestic view of the city and the sparkling azure waters of Lake Tanganyika. Rising several thousand feet above the far shoreline were the silent purple mountains of Zaire.[1]

Beyond the end of the porch, a row of red hibiscus shrubs led through a trellised archway to a *paillotte,* an open seating area without walls, covered by a thatched roof supported by wooden poles, and partly shaded by the large flat deeply green leaves of an avocado tree, hanging richly with fruit. Beyond the driveway I could see a larger open thatched-roof area leading down to an Olympic-sized swimming pool and a tennis court. Not the reason I came here, I thought, but I'm going to enjoy it.

The front door opened off the porch to reveal an eighteen-foot dining table and chairs, with a single, rather plain metal chandelier hanging overhead. Parallel to the porch was the living room area, its furniture arranged so that several different conversational groups might form at even the largest

Traveler's palms shaped like a lady's fan, standing in the front garden.

gatherings. The furnishings, though attractive and serviceable, showed by their wear that the State Department had last refurbished the house twelve years ago, and a plywood ceiling held up by strips of wood negated any sense of opulence. The residence proved useful for my almost daily encounters with members of the Burundi government, who often preferred the relative privacy of meeting there rather than at the U.S. embassy downtown, where visits were more easily observed.

During its sixteen months without an ambassador, the residence had been cared for by Emmanuel Gahungu, a longtime household employee who showed me through the house. That done, I was eager to see my office at the embassy chancery itself.

A five-minute drive away, it was located just off the main street, Rwagasore Avenue, on a dirt road named l'avenue des États-Unis. While awaiting its steel gates to open, I noticed two men standing before a ditch across the street, their backs toward us, facing an empty lot. I soon learned that in a city center without public toilets, that ditch was one of Bujumbura's most popular places for men to urinate and hold brief conversations.

Bernardin pulled up to the door of an unostentatious two-story building. Inside, I was saluted by the marine security guard, our first line of defense. As at most small embassies, the Bujumbura force consisted of only six marines. Nevertheless, they provided a sense of security to the American com-

The American embassy was an unostentatious two-story building.

munity of approximately eighty people. While their official duties were only to protect the documents and facilities, every American felt certain that these marines would fight to the end to save any endangered American. We valued them accordingly.

I was particularly eager to meet the local Burundian employees, or FSNs (foreign-service nationals), as they are called. Whereas most Americans spend only two or three years on assignment in Bujumbura, a few of the FSNs had worked for the U.S. embassy for over twenty years. I hoped to draw on their institutional memory, their knowledge of customs, gossip, and inside news that otherwise might not readily be available to an ambassador. After a brief tour to meet our USAID (U.S. Agency for International Development) workers, it was time to go home.

We pulled into the residence driveway, and as I got out of the car, Bernardin said, "Good night, Your Excellency." And after responding, as I walked toward the house, I understood why the State Department seminar given in Washington for new ambassadors cautioned against expanded egotism. With the American flag flying over your right front fender, marines saluting, clerks standing, employees holding open your door, and people addressing you as "Your Excellency," you could fool yourself into thinking that you really were excellent in a way others are not.

Then, entering the house, I noticed that the eighteen-foot dining table was the only place inside the house to eat. Emmanuel had covered the end nearest the kitchen with a small white tablecloth and had set the table with State Department bone china bearing a gold seal and eagle, sterling silver cutlery, and a crystal wine glass. Beyond that lay fifteen feet of connected tables, each with a laminated top, under a simple brass chandelier. Emmanuel, wearing a white jacket with gold buttons for the occasion, brought me a glass of wine. I felt as though I belonged in a *New Yorker* cartoon. And then, as I toasted the occasion, alone, and looked down the empty expanse of table, I hoped it would not be long before my family could join me, and I thought with amusement of my statement to Mack McLarty a year earlier: "Mack, I'm not looking for white gloves and chandeliers. I'm just looking for a real job."

FOUR

THE EMBASSY AND THE COUNTRYSIDE

Massacres Explored

THE EMBASSY VS. WASHINGTON

My first two weeks were spent getting to know the people I would be working and living with — in the embassy, the government, and the community at large. After presenting my credentials to the president of Burundi, I visited, in a series of meetings, with various cabinet members, parliamentarians, business and religious leaders — and had individual interviews with each member of the "country team," the Americans who headed the various departments and the USAID mission.

They had been through a lot. All had been in Embassy Bujumbura during the hopeful days leading up to the election and inauguration, and all had suffered the disappointment and ensuing chaos of the October 1993 assassinations. Since then, they had been living through the miasma of inaction from a stupefied government and a leaderless nation. Scattered reports of the fighting in the countryside had come in, and while the extent of the killing will never be fully known, Burundi's prospects were grim. Attitudes of helplessness and hopelessness were spreading in Bujumbura. Then, less than a hundred miles away, the horrendous Rwandan genocide, which began in April 1994 and took an estimated 800,000 lives in less than three months, not only unnerved Bujumbura but frightened Washington as well.

As a precautionary measure, the State Department in April had instituted "ordered departure" — the removal of all family members and "nonessential personnel" from both Rwanda and Burundi. Most Americans at Embassy Bujumbura believed that a sound decision at that time. But during the recent weeks after the killing spree in Rwanda, Burundi had been relatively quiet. In particular, not one person among the expatriate community of roughly 6,500 Europeans and Americans had been targeted, attacked, or killed. Yet to live alone in a small, isolated community where one had to boil the water, take malaria prophylaxis, wash raw vegetables and fruit in iodized water, be prepared for electrical blackouts—and then to work with a rudderless government incapable of caring for its people—to do all this without the support and affection of a family was the largest hardship faced by this dedicated and somewhat demoralized group of Americans. They wanted their families back, and were convinced they could safely come.

Once a month, the decision whether to continue the ordered departure was reviewed in Washington. Once a month, the embassy was to offer its recommendation and the rationale for it. The due date came in my second week.

When the country team met for its formal consideration of the topic, the vote was 10–1 to request that ordered departure be ended and families returned to Bujumbura. I told the team that I would draft the cable myself, ask each member to review it so that all views, pro and con, were expressed, and then send it.

Our main argument was that an action that had been prudent in April was unnecessary in July. The deluge of violence from Rwanda, even where it had spilled over the border, had endangered neither Americans nor any other expatriates. In fact, no other foreign embassy had removed any of its people from Bujumbura, and we were concerned that if our example were followed by other nations, the questionable credibility of the fragile democratic government in Burundi would be further undermined. Finally, we thought that the judgment of those with firsthand experience in Burundi, who thought it safe for their families to return, should be respected. To us, the case seemed clear. To State Department authorities in Washington, it looked different.

On July 3, 1994, I made the following entry in a journal that I was just beginning (and never wrote in again):

I suppose, in the privacy of one's private journal, one should record one's disappointment as well as observations, or triumphs. Today I was greatly disappointed to get a cable from [a high-level official in the State Department], saying that the cable I had sent the previous day, reporting that, by a margin of 10–1, the Embassy's Emergency Action Committee was recommending an end to Ordered Departure (or, forced evacuation of Dependents and Non-Essential Personnel), was "not well received" in Washington. He said many things: that, given the problems of Rwanda, the RPF's [Rwandan Patriotic Front's] advances there, the question of presidential succession in Burundi, and the general uncertainty of the region, they could not consider lifting the order. All those matters, of course, the

Embassy staff, which live with these matters daily, had considered. Our point in the cable was that no American had been hurt or attacked, and American dependents were in no special danger.

The real disappointment, as great in some ways as the decision, was when in a conversation that followed between us he said that I needed to protect my reputation, that I would not want my credibility undermined, and that the cable was not well received and I might wish to withdraw it or send another saying that, upon reflection, I changed my mind.

I responded that I could offer my resignation, but I could not withdraw a statement that I believed to be true, and could not make a statement I did not believe. I offered to send a cable next week, referring to our conversation, saying that I understood the rationale they were applying, but I would not alter or withdraw the cable I had written with the policy that I and nine people who had been here for a long period believed to be true.

The conversation ended amicably, but I left it disappointed that the mentality I had known in the State Department years ago, and feared might yet be present, is. That is, CYA—cover your ass—never take a risk. The reality, as we here view it, is that Burundi is a very dangerous place for Burundians, but not particularly for Americans. And I was disappointed that he would recommend that I could *improve* my reputation and my credibility by taking an action that would effectively *deny* my integrity. He wanted me to lie in order to improve my credibility. I said no.

ORPHANS OF WAR

My second week in Burundi provided my first opportunity to go into the countryside. Chris Reilly, our seasoned security officer, had learned that seventy-two orphans from a convent school in Rwanda were waiting by the bridge that crosses the narrow stream separating Rwanda from Burundi, hoping to be taken to Bujumbura by two trucks provided by the United Nations and Médecins Sans Frontières (MSF, or Doctors Without Borders). He suggested that we drive to the border to make certain the children were rescued. So we climbed into a 4x4 white Toyota Land Cruiser and headed directly north on Highway 1 for the Rwandan border.

Highway 1 itself is narrow, winding, and dangerous, but paved and well constructed. As the road rises, one notices the communes sprinkled among the thick foliage of bananas, palms, and other tropical trees that cover the hillsides so thickly that one only occasionally gains glimpses of the people moving within. Towns and villages are surprisingly few. Hence, the small groupings of families found on almost every side of every hill seldom have services that people in the developed world take for granted. Most Burundians live without electricity, telephones, running water, sewers, or personal transportation. School buildings are scattered, school attendance haphazard. Almost half of Burundi's children have never attended school. Tilling their small, often terraced plots of land, 85 percent of the population lives by subsistence farming. Parents hope to provide enough for their own families, which average six children. If lucky, they may get two, or occasionally three, crops a year. Bananas, manioc, beans, corn, and potatoes form most of the staples of the diet; meat is rare, and vegetables requiring more attention, such as green beans, broccoli, lettuce, or tomatoes, are most often raised for sale and carried on the heads of trotting women and children into Bujumbura or the nearest market town.

A few people raise rabbits for sale. As Chris and I whisked along the highway, our windows open and the fresh air flowing, on several occasions young children came running out into the road, waving their arms in an effort to stop us, while a brother on the roadside held by the ears a live rabbit, kicking painfully as it was offered for our Sunday dinner. Farther ahead on the road, a competitor might be holding a large brown hen or rooster by the feet, its feathers puffed out by gravity, its would-be seller shouting and smiling at every passing car. Traveling the highway were the ubiquitous white 4x4s of NGOs or United Nations agencies. Large trucks pulling extended trailers slowly climbed the steep and twisting gradients. Inevitably, they were providing transportation for hangers-on. Literally, hangers-on. Boys and men, from teenagers to old-agers, and on rare occasions women too, if they can find a projecting piece of wood or steel to stand on and a handhold of any sort within reach hang onto the backs of huge trucks for a free ride. Uphill, the ride is usually slow, yet faster and easier than walking. But the hangers-on are no fewer when the trucks go careening downhill at fifty to sixty miles an hour. Those going uphill wave politely to passers-by; those barreling downhill smile broadly, cheer, and scream giddily. It is a roller coaster for people who have never seen a roller coaster or an amusement park, and seldom, if ever, the inside of a private car.

After driving for several hours, we arrived in the late afternoon to find a large group of children, from infants to teenagers, gathered between the river and the road. A few boys were kicking a homemade ball of twine, but most of the children were seated on the ground beneath tall eucalyptus trees, the mottled, white and tan bark peeling off the trunks and the pale green leaves quivering in the breeze. The strong fragrance of eucalyptus oil overpowered

Eighty-five percent of the population lives by subsistence farming, done largely by women. Photo by Judy Walgren, 1994. Courtesy of the Dallas Morning News ©.

the fumes from the waiting diesel trucks about to cross the little bridge that joined Rwanda to Burundi.

These were orphans of war. The Rwandan genocide that for a brief time filled our newspapers and evening television programs had filled this river and many others with bodies floating like timber down a logging stream. When households were attacked, the most frequent response was for families to flee into the forest if they could. Since attacks most often came at night, family members often became separated from one another. For this group of survivors, the whereabouts of their parents was unknown. The most the world could do was to give the children temporary shelter and relief. Médecins Sans Frontières would provide care in Bujumbura, learn their names and villages, and seek to reunite them with relatives or friends.

My eye was drawn swiftly, then fixedly to an angular, fine-boned Tutsi girl who looked to be six or seven years old. She seemed to have stepped out of the pages of a children's storybook. Dressed in a white and apparently starched pleated dress laced with pink ribbon, she might have just come from a christening or birthday party. How she came to be so attired, and to look so immaculate in those circumstances, was beyond me. Perhaps she had been told that she was going to meet strangers who would look after her, and she wanted to look her best. Or perhaps she had had to leave all other clothes behind, and so chose to wear her finest dress. More remarkable than her doll-like appearance was that in her lap she held a younger brother, aged perhaps eighteen months, bouncing him, cooing to him, cuddling him, helping him stand up and rock from side to side as she held his hands. Here was a child, without parents, forced to become a mother before she could even fully become a girl. She was so beautiful that, whether just or not, she undoubtedly would be one of the first children taken by anyone who came seeking to adopt a child. But what heartaches and memories she carried with her were beyond my comprehension or imagination.

Burundian children entertaining themselves with simple homemade toys, such as balls of twine. Photo by Judy Walgren, 1994. Courtesy of the Dallas Morning News *©.*

Just at sunset, the noisy white UN trucks arrived. Whatever paperwork was required had already been done. In large worn leather-bound ledgers, the names had been recorded of those crossing the border; ink had been rubber-stamped onto various papers; and the children were allowed to proceed. Everything seemed in order; we could go home. Visiting the Médecins Sans Frontières camp in Bujumbura three days later, I was told that the young girl and her brother had been reunited with relatives and that their parents might still be alive.

MARIE: THE MADONNA OF RWANDA,
A SURVIVOR OF GENOCIDE

Roughly two weeks later I made my first visit to a United Nations camp for Rwandan refugees, situated in a northern province of Burundi near the city of Kayanza. The terrible cruelty that had been inflicted by Hutus against Tutsis in Rwanda, like the harsh conditions under which refugees from that genocide were living, was staggering.

As I approached the refugee camp, roughly one hundred kilometers north of Bujumbura, I descended a long hill on a narrow and winding section of the highway. The road, no longer paved, was flanked on each side by tall eucalyptus trees, their patchwork of white and tan bark glowing in the morning sun. The reddish soil by the shoulders of the road gave way to green ferns and lush grass as we descended the hill to a bank by a narrow stream, bouncing and rippling in its long descent toward Bujumbura. On the left hillside I could see the glint of the sun against bright blue plastic, which projected from a glistening orange background of damp clay soil.

Those thin sheets of blue plastic bearing a white United Nations seal marked the only protection that 2,000 people had from torrential tropical rain or, at an elevation of almost 5,000 feet, the cold mountain air. Each piece of blue plastic formed a small rounded semicircle, spread in an arc over slender branches that had been cut from nearby trees, creating shelters shaped like miniature Second World War airplane hangars less than four feet high. The ground was slick with wetness. Such few possessions as the refugees had carried with them on their trek from Rwanda were either piled inside in a corner of their hovels or left open to the elements. Small communal fires serving every four or five families held sooty black pots where beans or manioc or rice was boiling. I saw no trenches around the tents; what they were like when it rained I did not wish to imagine. People had blankets, and some sat huddled in them, even on this temperate and comfortable day. Many of the people were dirty, since bathing was difficult and refugees sometimes had only the clothes they wore. The one person who stood out to me from this mass of humanity was Marie, whom I met at the nurse's station during my tour of facilities with the camp supervisor.

The nurse's station was a simple windowless enclosure, its sides formed by staves tied tightly together, with an overhanging tin roof raised high enough above the walls that there was an easy flow for ventilation. Standing with her back to me as I entered was a tall woman, clad in the long wrap of cloth customary in the region, but with a dull green shawl pulled over the top of her head. As she turned partially toward me, I could see a profile of her left side, and was reminded of the Madonnas of the seventeenth-century Spanish painter Murillo and their endearing sweetness. But as the nurse came toward me and the woman faced me, I saw the stitch marks surrounding a huge scar, beginning at the upper right corner of her forehead, crossing her right eye, which had been stitched permanently shut, then extending into her cheek. The stitches throughout were large x's, as if designed for a horror movie.

With her right arm and hand, she was holding her infant child, but the hand had only a palm and a thumb. Her four other fingers had been deliberately sliced off with a machete. Long, slender fingers are an attribute of beauty for which Tutsi women are known. Her Hutu assailants had been determined to deface her permanently, to make her a living reminder to people who saw her of the threat they too faced. It is more terrifying to leave behind a living, walking memorial to cruelty than simply to dispatch a person and allow her baby to rot in an unmarked grave. Both Burundi and Rwanda had left behind ample evidence of mutilation and humiliation, tools of terror to keep fear in the forefront of Tutsi and Hutu minds alike.

As the camp supervisor translated her story for me, I learned that her village had been attacked at night—surrounded and torched by marauding Interahamwe (Hutu thugs working with the Rwandan government) during the April genocide. Her husband and three of her children had been murdered, but she had escaped with her baby. The attackers then captured her in the forest, and chose to disfigure her so horribly that she would never marry again. Miraculously, with hands and face bleeding profusely, she had managed to survive, preserve her infant daughter, and walk over fifty miles to safety in Burundi. I wanted to ask how she managed to avoid bleeding to death, where she had gone for medical care, how she had found this refugee camp—but I could not bring myself to do so. Her suffering had obviously been immense, and I was not sure where well-intentioned compassion became indecent curiosity. Seeing the consequences of her suffering was enough. Yet I couldn't help feeling, as I looked at this disfigured but benign and taciturn mother holding her child to her breast, that this, not Murillo's painting, was the Madonna of Rwanda, a survivor of genocide.

I asked whether I might do anything for her. She responded that she simply wanted to go home to her village. By now, it was safe.

"What prevents you from going?" I asked.

"I have no money for a bus ticket," she replied.

"What does a ticket cost?" I asked.

"About 750 Burundi francs," was the reply.

I was stunned. She was saying that for just $3 she could go home.

At that, I asked the camp supervisor, who had been translating, to step aside and chat with me. Had he any reason to object to her returning, I asked. None, he replied. I reached for my pocketbook, remembering regretfully that I had not brought much cash for the day. I found a bit over 5,000 francs, and giving that to the superintendent, asked him to buy her a ticket and give her the remaining funds. He promised to do so, but would have to tell her privately, later. Otherwise, he and I would be swamped with requests, and some would be resentful that they had not been the lucky ones.

When I returned two weeks later, Marie and her child were gone, but through the generosity of a friend, I brought along 100,000 francs. Jim Sale, a stockbroker in Dallas, Texas, had telephoned to see how I was doing, and I had related Marie's story. He spontaneously offered to send $500 if that would help other refugees get home. I brought the money, separated into envelopes containing 2,500 francs and a slip of paper with the following message:

> *Ce don vous est offert pour vous aider à retourner chez vous au Rwanda et il vient de la part d'un citoyen américain qui croit que tous les peoples sont les enfants de Dieu, et que tous sont frères et sœurs. Il s'appelle Jim Sale et son adresse est la suivante:* 200 Crescent Court, Suite 500, Dallas, Texas 75201.

> (This donation is given to assist you in returning to your home in Rwanda from an American citizen who recognizes that all people are children of God, and all are brothers and sisters. His name is Jim Sale and his address is 200 Crescent Court, Suite 500, Dallas, Texas 75201.)

I left the distribution of funds and selection of recipients to the camp director. By that time, the Tutsi-led Rwandan Patriotic Front (RPF) had driven out the Hutu-dominated Rwandan Armed Forces (FAR) and the Interahamwe; Tutsis could safely return to Rwanda; and the camp was closing down.

As I walked back to the Land Cruiser, I reflected on how even a small amount of money in a country of such poverty could alleviate great suffering. And I recalled the lines from Wordsworth's "Tintern Abbey":

> . . . that best portion of a good man's life,
> His little, nameless, unremembered, acts
> Of kindness and of love.

Thanks, Jim Sale.

A MASS GRAVE AND A MASSIVE COVER-UP

While the situation was improving for Tutsis in Rwanda, allowing their return, it was becoming horrific for many Hutu peasants in Rwanda, who, innocent or guilty, were suffering in a cycle of revenge as the Rwandan Patriotic Army (RPA), successor to the RPF, drove thousands of them daily to seek safety in Burundi.[1] By mid-July, over 100,000 Hutu refugees had crossed into Burundi. In fact, one camp at Magara at times contained over 50,000 people, giving it more residents—all housed in four-foot-high blue plastic hovels—than any town in Burundi except the capital.

The camps that sheltered Hutu refugees from Rwanda were established and administered by civilians from the United Nations, but Burundi Army units (which, like the RPA, were manned entirely by Tutsis) were encamped alongside to make certain that Hutu refugees did not maintain arms or threaten Tutsi hegemony in either country. And frequently, although their cooperation was never publicly acknowledged, the Burundian and Rwandan armies joined in the vengeful slaughter of helpless, unarmed Hutu refugees.

One such massacre occurred in July 1994 in Burundi's northeast province of Kirundo. Amnesty International and Physicians for Human Rights, an international organization based in Boston, had received from members of the UN High Commissioner for Refugees (UNHCR) well-substantiated reports that several hundred refugees who had sought safety by crossing from Rwanda into Burundi were waiting at a temporary encampment near Kiri, in Kirundo, to be taken to shelter. During the night, armed men in uniform, identified as being from both the Burundian and Rwandan armies, abducted at least 120 men, trucked them to a location by the shore of a nearby lake, and slaughtered them with guns, machetes, knives, and clubs. However, three captives had escaped into the darkness of the lake and swum to safety, ultimately making their way to a safe haven provided by the UNHCR in Bujumbura.

A group from Physicians for Human Rights and Amnesty International, after confirming the existence of a mass grave near the lakeside, came to ask for the U.S. embassy's participation in a public exhumation of the bodies, to be followed by forensic examination. Would we help? My response was that we should go immediately, before the bodies were taken away or someone prevented our visit. However, they wanted to proceed in a manner less likely to provoke official criticism. The completion of the necessary arrangements then delayed our visit until August 1.

Early that morning, I took the driver's seat in an embassy Land Cruiser, accompanied by a USAID staff member and Cosmas Vrampas, a Burundian citizen of Greek parentage, who acted as navigator and translator. I preferred employing someone of European descent for translation from Kirundi because ethnic suspicions are generally so deep-seated that if one interviews a Hutu, he or she might not trust a Tutsi translator (and vice versa), whereas people of both ethnicities are always delighted to encounter that rare white person who speaks their native language.

The organizers had cleared the intended visit with the Ministry of Justice, the Office of the Procurer General (attorney general), and the provincial governor of Kirundo, Philippe Njoni, in whose office we were to meet. The governor's headquarters were located in a simple two-story white stucco structure on the edge of the town of Kirundo. Upstairs, dressed in suit and tie, Governor Njoni waited in a spacious but plain office with windows wide open to allow a breeze to pass through. Hanging on the wall, the standard-issue photograph of former President Ndadaye, with a green background that represented Frodebu's colors in the election campaign, told me that he was a Hutu governor and a member of Frodebu.

Before long the international organizers arrived, along with a military commandant and two truckloads of thirty or more armed Burundian soldiers dressed in camouflage, to escort us to the burial site. We departed the town along a dirt road, the red dust rising in the air prompting me to roll up the windows and put on the air conditioner. Kirundo is not part of the mountainous, green, and lush portion of Burundi. Lying on a flatter, more arid plain, part of the gradual downward slope leading to Tanzania, it is covered by scrubby and pale vegetation. After driving for several miles through a colorless and unpopulated landscape, our convoy stopped, and people began parking their vehicles wherever they could alongside the road.

A solitary yellow stucco house could be seen about a hundred yards beyond, but a cleared area on our left revealed the reason for our visit.

With scrub vegetation and small trees forming a backdrop, we saw there a mound of earth perhaps fifty yards long; it had been recently turned, and was free of grass or immediate cover. Obvious to eyes and nostrils was that someone had come in the night and poured some petroleum product—perhaps diesel fuel or crankcase oil—in rows a foot or two apart, running the length of the mound. Evidently the hope was that the smell of the petroleum would somehow overpower the stench of decaying human carcasses. It didn't. But it added an even more surreal dimension to an already surreal scene. How could the perpetrators of the massacre possibly believe that trying to lessen the smell would somehow mitigate the horror of the deed or prevent its discovery?

As I looked across the uneven grayish earth, my eyes stopped on the tallest object there. Projecting eighteen inches from underneath the soil was a single leg, its yellowed decaying flesh largely gone, a soiled white canvas tennis shoe still clinging to the foot. Nearby was a ribcage, picked clean by dogs or vultures, I suppose, as were a spine and pelvis that I sighted. Then, after testing the earth for firmness, I walked slowly out onto the stench-ridden mound to attempt a closer inspection. Someone may have been calling to me in a language I did not understand; I wasn't sure, and chose not to look. But then, as I was silently trying to grasp the scene in my consciousness, I heard a loud argument in French beginning behind me.

Apparently, as the volunteers from Physicians for Human Rights were beginning to remove the tools and equipment necessary for excavating the bodies and examining them forensically, the army commandant had stopped them. They would not, he explained, be allowed to dig up the bodies. Doing so would, in Burundian culture, constitute a sacrilege resented by the families of the deceased and the people living nearby, he claimed. When I joined them to ask whether he had come with us only to prevent the group's doing its work, he replied that his troops had come "to protect you from the villagers who might be angry if they knew that foreigners had come to intervene in their lives." Disgusted, I asked Cosmas to walk with me to the nearby house. There I learned that its inhabitants had no concern about foreigners digging up bodies—they just wanted to be rid of the corpses. The bodies themselves had been brought to this location a week or more earlier, they explained, by Burundian and Rwandan soldiers. They did not know to whom the land belonged; it had never been cultivated. But they wished the bodies could be taken away.

Returning to the group, I heard, as the passionate argument continued, the governor explaining to the commandant that he had granted his permission, along with that of the procurer general, for them to engage in this exhumation. They had the authorization, and had brought along documents to prove it.

No matter. The commandant had made his decision, and his troops, by their posture, looked ready to enforce it. The governor was perspiring profusely and stammering a little. Accustomed to Texas governors like Ann Richards or John Connally, who in emergency situations could mobilize and give orders to the National Guard and direct all law enforcement officials in the state, I felt sorry for the governor's embarrassing position. It wasn't his fault. He wasn't weak. He had courageously sought to help his people. But with one side in a contest having only words, and the other words and guns, it was clear who would win.

As the experts would obviously not be allowed to examine the corpses, I asked the civil procurer responsible for handling the case how we could be sure of the identities of those buried there. To that he replied that since theirs was the only mass killing in the area, they must be the group of refugees executed at Kiri. In other words, civilian law-enforcement officials acknowledged the existence of a massacre of defenseless refugees at Kiri. But the army was unwilling for outsiders to prove the victims' identities and thereby confirm the murders that everyone present knew had taken place.

As I put the car in gear and began the long drive home, I realized I had been given a graphic lesson in what life is like in a country where an army can both engage in murder and scornfully reject any inquiry or directive from the civilian authorities.

The next day I followed up with an hour-long, private meeting with Colonel Jean Bikomagu, chief of Burundi's armed forces. The meeting was an example of the military's exercise of evasive tactics, which I was to witness frequently in the months ahead. He refused to take any responsibility, to conduct an investigation, or to reprimand the troops. All such investigations in the Burundian system, he claimed, must come from the procurer general, with whom he would cooperate. Beyond that he would not go.

On my part, I let fly one of the few arrows in my quiver. Having explained that I was certain he could not be proud of heading a military that engaged in the slaughter of defenseless victims, I indicated that it would be my responsibility to report to my government and to the international community at large the events I had seen. If his forces could not cooperate, then they must be content with whatever report I made.

HOMELESS HUTUS, HOMELESS TUTSIS

Having interviewed in my first few weeks both Tutsi and Hutu refugees who had fled genocide in Rwanda for safety under blue UN plastic sheeting, I came to realize that they were the recent arrivals, and formed the smaller portion of refugees in Burundi. Two larger groups had preceded them and set up squatters' communities made of corrugated tin, straw, cardboard, leaves, and whatever might give some modest protection from the elements and their neighbors' curiosity.

The first homeless group was composed of Hutus, often called *dispersés,* or "dispersed people." These homeless were formed in three ways. First, during the presidential campaign of 1992–1993 and after his election, Ndadaye stated that Burundi could never be whole until those who had fled the country during the attacks against Hutus in 1965, 1972, and 1988 were allowed to return to their lands. After his election, many returned, but most had not yet recovered their old lands or found new ones. Second, some Hutus who had fled the violence after Ndadaye's assassination were now trickling back home, only to find their lands or houses occupied. Third, Hutu refugees from Rwanda, fleeing the vengeance of the RPA, were filling refugee camps along the northern border of Burundi at the rate of over 1,000 people a day. All these homeless dispersés were considered refugees by the United Nations, since they had lived abroad and then crossed international borders to enter Burundi. All were therefore entitled to receive limited UN benefits.

The second homeless group consisted of displaced Tutsis (called *déplacés*) who had been driven from their homes in Burundi during the vengeful aftermath of Ndadaye's assassination, and had sought refuge inside Burundi. Tutsis, innocent and guilty, had often been attacked by their Hutu neighbors, and had therefore fled for safety to civic locations, especially schools, which had generally been run by Tutsis. Their being gathered together made protection an easier task for the army, which often established adjoining encampments in order to safeguard Tutsis, whom they considered to be their kin, against possible Hutu attacks. These Tutsis, being displaced inside their own country, had not crossed international borders and therefore were ineligible for the UN benefits given to refugees.

Thus, many Hutus received modest international assistance, but most Tutsis did not. And in a world where daily life was customarily viewed through the prism of ethnicity, Tutsis saw Hutus as the group favored by the international donor community, whereas Hutus saw the Burundi Army as protecting Tutsis and slaying Hutus. Moreover, the proximity of army camps to déplacé centers fed the fears and hatreds that the army and déplacés shared.

Under these circumstances, the déplacés frequently became surrogate killers and thieves for the army. A common pattern developed nationwide: the army provided trucks and transportation to déplacés, taking them to a Hutu commune that was to be attacked. After surrounding a household or commune with troops, the army set fire to the thatched-roof huts, leaving the déplacés, armed with machetes, to deliver the coups de grâce to the terrified residents. Together, army troops and déplacés then loaded any stolen property onto the army trucks and returned to the déplacé encampments, where the spoils were divided.

TRANSCRIPT OF TERROR: ONE DAY'S VISIT

To explore the extent and intensity of the conflict between the homeless and the surrounding communities, I toured the northern province of Kayanza, accompanied by the embassy refugee officer, Julie O'Reagan, and Tharcise Nsavyimana, head of ITEKA, a human rights group with Hutu and Tutsi members. Here are several excerpts translated from Nsavyimana's report on our inspection tour:

> Commune Muhanga. This commune has been profoundly affected ever since the month of June and the situation has not been stabilized up until now: tens of persons (between 100 and 200) have been killed, hundreds of houses pillaged, burned, or destroyed. All of the schools are closed.
>
> In the province of Muramvya, the hillsides where houses have been burned or destroyed include the following: Ndava, Gashibuka, Rushemeza, Masama, Gaharo, Ngoma, Mibazi, Nyamwera, Jimbi, Ceyerezi, Muhanga. The destruction and pillaging were essentially the work of the military and the *déplacés* of Muhanga. . . .
>
> In zone Muogora, all the houses on all the hills have been pillaged, set afire, or destroyed. We have been able to observe the destruction of houses on the hills Gasara, Gatumbori, and Masama. . . . Some persons have begun timidly to return during the past two days. . . . At Gasara, at the home of the Barakobotse family, a military person there showed us a great hole capable of holding up to 20 people, which served as a supply depot for the *bandes armées* [Hutu rebel forces]. Food, munitions, and documents of the assailants were discovered there as well, asserted the Army.
>
> Wednesday, 26 August, 1994: on colline [hill] Nkango in the commune of Butaganzwa where many people from the zone of Mubogora had come to seek refuge, military forces encircled the hill very early in the morning.

Near the home of Jean Mawangari, military killed about 40 people—
men, women, and confused children including Mrs. Mawangari and her
5 children. Military troops then immediately buried the bodies inside the
latrines.

After pointing out that the major commercial section in the community
of Rango had been pillaged, burned, or destroyed, the head of the human
rights group made the following observations:

- The action of the bandes armées, Hutu rebel groups, has contributed to destabilizing the communities which we visited, attacking
both the military *forces de l'ordre* [forces of order] and also the civil
population.

- The military have destabilized the commune Muhanga by pillaging
and destroying its central commercial area. Under the cover of pur-
suing the bandes armées, they have killed many innocent people,
including women, the elderly, and children, and have destroyed
the houses of many innocent people. This abuse has not been repri-
manded by the military hierarchy and risks aggravating the climate
of distrust between the population and the military itself.

- The déplacés have equally contributed to instability through their
killing, destruction, and pillaging, performed with the complicity of
the military. Because of the instability, the population has let three
months pass without sowing any new crops. They will therefore require assistance to avoid dying of starvation.

- Food assistance must be given to the déplacés if they are to avoid
the temptation to pillage others.

- The civil administration needs to collaborate with the military authorities and the population in order to study appropriate mechanisms for restoring the confidence of the population that security can
be provided.

This is but an excerpt from a longer report based on a single day's visit by
three people to half a dozen villages near Bujumbura. Most of the killing,
burning, looting, and destruction had been performed in recent days or,
at most, in recent weeks. Yet none of the hundreds of lives and houses destroyed had been reported in local or international media. Nor had anyone
been charged with a crime. The victims who survived were completely with-

out any recourse to justice. With the military forces de l'ordre responsible for most of the disorder in society, it was hard to see where the people might turn for hope.

MURDER IN THE CATHEDRAL

For many people worldwide, hope is found through religion—at church. So it is in Burundi. Although there are long-established Muslim communities in Gitega and Bujumbura, a majority of the population is Christian—primarily Catholic, although Seventh-Day Adventists, Southern Baptists, Plymouth Brethren, Mormons, and other denominations, to name but a few, all have missions and members.

The Catholic Church during and after the colonial period was closely aligned with Belgium, and its hierarchical structure reflected values and practices similar to those of the ruling colonial power. Thus, just as Tutsis were identified in Brussels as those deserving education and positions of leadership in secular society, so, in Rome, Tutsis had been similarly identified as the natural leaders of the church in Burundi. Tutsis therefore composed most of the priesthood, especially its highest positions. Even so, by the 1990s the times were a-changing in the church as they were elsewhere, and the Vatican began naming Hutus as bishops. Among the first was John Berchmans Nterere, whose elevation to the bishopric of Muyinga was announced in late July 1994.

To some Tutsis, naming a Hutu bishop was seen as a direct and intentional insult—yet another indication of the outside world's ignorance of Burundi and its hostility toward the Tutsi. They were determined to teach the Hutus a lesson and to send a message to the Vatican. Bishop Nterere related to me how they did so during one of his earliest celebrations of the Mass as bishop.

The date was September 4, 1994; the location, the town of Muramba, province of Muyinga, near the border of Tanzania. There, just as the Host was being consecrated, several army trucks arrived. On board were uniformed troops armed with rifles and automatic weapons, and, in civilian clothes, Tutsi déplacés transported from the encampment just outside Muramba.

The events which the bishop narrated to me are described in translations of a public letter from the bishop and in a more extensive, private report prepared by someone who came to assist the next day and interviewed clerics, parishioners, and the wounded. First, the bishop's letter:

Sunday, 4 September, 1994, as I was presiding at the Eucharist in the course of a baptism and confirmation, an armed group entered the church at Muramba. One of the assailants entered by the lateral door and commenced to shoot into the assembly of at least 3,000 of the faithful. The people rushed headlong toward doors too small to allow them to exit rapidly. I could see another assailant in military uniform, armed with a gun, shooting in the direction of the high altar. Unfortunately, the other assassins were armed with machetes and large knives, and were waiting outdoors in order to kill. . . . At the same time, at the marketplace in Muramba, the same drama was proceeding. People say that the attackers disembarked from a military truck, throwing grenades into the marketplace. People fled in the stampede. There were many dead and wounded. The preliminary count, one day later, shows 71 dead, 23 gravely wounded and hospitalized, and others wounded who have returned to their homes.

Many people were able to identify, among the assailants, certain *déplacés* who are natives of Muramba, now residing in Muyinga. They cite, "Tharcisse et Xavier," son of Bampoyiki. The soldier Berchmans Nteziriba is equally identified.

A longer, private, eyewitness report that I received from an expatriate priest who assisted the wounded on the same occasion conveys more fully the horror of the moment and the extent of the confusion. A translation from the French original follows:

While the Mass was being performed, it appeared that buildings in the marketplace had caught fire. While efforts were being made to calm the people, a military truck arrived and persons in uniform got out. Entering the church through the lateral door, they began firing. In the group of assailants were undoubtedly some Twa, Tutsi Rwandan refugees from the refugee center nearby, and members of the group "Sans Échec" [literally, "Without Failure," an extremist Tutsi youth group] who though arriving from Muyinga actually came from Bujumbura, and several people in uniform presumed to be members of the Burundi Army. They threw grenades, fired weapons, and created chaos. One catechist was killed on the spot. Many people tried to throw themselves to the ground and hide; others fled for the exterior. The people were aggressive, above all those who waited outside the church for the people. Being armed with machetes . . . they tried to hit above all at the face or the base of the neck. By the next evening, one learned that in the attack there had been at least 72 persons killed, 24 wounded and transported to the hospital in Muyinga. Among the dead were 36 women, 15 children, and 21 men. . . .

Bishop Nterere succeeded in hiding first in the sacristy and then in a rear bathroom. Following that, he took flight by foot toward Muyinga, traversing among banana groves, always avoiding the main roads. A priest who was performing the services with the Bishop was successful in finding a bicycle, and rode to Muyinga in order to appeal for help. Bishop Nterere finally arrived at Muyinga at around 5:30 p.m., safe and sound.

It seems that no one from the HCR or the Red Cross came to Muramba to evacuate the wounded because it is said that the HCR and the Red Cross do not have the right here to proceed into a region that is directly in a state of war. Thus . . . some old missionaries were invited to evacuate the wounded from Muramba to Muyinga. Various expatriate missionaries worked at the hospital in Muyinga with members of the Red Cross until 4:00 a.m. in order to wash and care for the wounded who had been brought to the hospital. The next day they continued to take care of the sick, and other missionaries searched for additional wounded. At this time, those who went to Muramba have later found where the fires had been, the bodies of burned people.

After our arrival in Muyinga on Monday, we visited the hospital. What a horrible situation. There were wounded of all kinds. Some had been wounded by grenades, others by machete, and others by bullets. [The victims] were all Hutus. It's clear that [the attackers] were trying to kill anyone without distinction of sex or age because, among the wounded, there were tiny infants who were probably only 4 or 5 months old. The young infants all had grave wounds at the level of the head, and others cut at the ear. I was stunned to see a great number of people who had wounds resulting from blows from the machete over the entire body.

It was atrocious. We have spoken with the wounded who have entirely confirmed, in a fashion unanimous and independent, the version according to which the attack at the church itself, during the liturgy, was by people in uniform. For us, that it was the military is clear. Other persons have told us that they were attacked in the market as well. No one can explain the attack. To respond to the questions, people say simply, "*C'est comme cela*" [That's the way it is].[2]

FIVE

GOVERNMENT AT A STANDSTILL

INACTION, THE UN, AND THE CONVENTION OF GOVERNMENT

Although I was making frequent trips into the countryside during the weeks after my arrival, I spent the majority of my time in Bujumbura, where government activities were concentrated. Unfortunately, those activities were few.

After the assassinations of October 21, 1993, when the government had been brought to a near standstill, the UN within a month sent Ambassador Ahmedou Ould-Abdallah to Burundi to help prevent massive warfare and to develop a functioning government. In February 1994 he succeeded in gaining agreement from all parties that a Frodebu member of Ndadaye's cabinet, Cyprien Ntaryamira, would be Ndadaye's presidential successor. But, unfortunately, only two months after his inauguration, Ntaryamira had the misfortune to accept a plane ride back from a summit meeting in Dar es Salaam, Tanzania, with Rwandan President Juvénal Habyarimana. That plane was shot out of the sky with a rocket on April 6, 1994, and its fall signaled the start of the historic genocide in Rwanda, new fears, and a search for yet another president in Burundi.

Upon Ntaryamira's death, one would have supposed that the vice president, Sylvestre Ntibantunganya, would immediately have inherited the full powers of the presidency. But not in Burundi. Not in a country where the Tutsi had dominated for most of the century. A combination of Tutsi intransigence, street violence by its youths, boycotts, an uncooperative and long-established Tutsi bureaucracy, sheer effrontery—and army and gendarmerie complicity in murder and mayhem—meant that the Tutsi power structure was willing to consider Ntibantunganya as only an "interim president." These Tutsis insisted on a new agreement to establish a new and legitimate president and government. And they got their way.

Once again, Ould-Abdallah was to play a key role in shaping Burundi's government. A diplomat with many years of experience in Brussels, Paris, Washington, and New York, Ould-Abdallah was urbane and witty, a lively conversationalist with the manners of a born aristocrat and the cleverness and experience to see through façades. He saw that Frodebu and the Hutus had the population and the votes to win elections, but that Uprona and the Tutsis had guns, education, and the experience of ruling. In a country that had never known the democratic experience, Ould-Abdallah believed that there could not be a simple and effective handover of power to the majority. As he later explained,

> I felt . . . Burundi was unprepared for majoritarian democracy; majority rule simply could not be sustained given the realities of Burundi's political and security situation. Indeed, I believe that in many African countries the introduction of democracy should be allied with a ten-to-twenty-year transitional period of constitutional power sharing.[1]

In his view, Burundi might have "one man, one vote," but the feudalistic system had been too long established to be overturned overnight.

In an effort to find a compromise, Ould-Abdallah conceived the idea of bringing together all political parties and the principal power groups to form a Convention of Government, which, by meeting together, might agree upon a fully empowered president and upon how governance should proceed. For Uprona and the Tutsi-related parties, it meant legitimacy and paid positions in government after having been rejected at the polls. For a frightened and frustrated Frodebu Party, it meant an opportunity to participate in the government it had been elected to lead, in spite of the continuing assassinations of its members. For a country needing to replace near anarchy with a governmental structure, it meant a chance to move forward. But for democracy, it resulted in a further crippling of the will of the people.

The convention consisted of face-to-face negotiations between Uprona and its politically allied parties versus Frodebu and its allied parties. The official chairperson was Antoine Nijembazi. A prominent Tutsi businessman, he joined representatives from the church and the general community as referees who could give community support to whatever agreement was reached. Nijembazi was considered by both sides to be fair—a considerable achievement, since he confided to one negotiator that the army leadership had informed him that if it was not happy with the results of the negotiations, Nijembazi's factories and offices might be burned. As one foreign diplomat said to me, "Government in Burundi is like government by the Mafia."

The more protracted these negotiations, the more Frodebu appeared incapable of governing. Therefore, it benefited Uprona and its allied parties to drag out the negotiations as long as they could, which they did. Thus, Frodebu negotiators found themselves caught in a vise. Delay meant more assassinations of its members. But Ould-Abdallah's search for prompt compromise seemed to come at their expense. Frodebu recognized that, as Ould-Abdallah later admitted, he did not believe Burundi was capable yet of democratic government. Consequently, members of the majority party, Frodebu, felt they were being forced to give away at the negotiating table what they had won at the polls. In particular, they thought Ould-Abdallah was diluting democracy by insisting on including in the cabinet several representatives from minority parties, thereby giving 20 percent of the cabinet positions to parties that had failed to elect a single member of Parliament and had received support from only 2 percent of voters in the elections.

Throughout this period, the "Group of 5" (the ambassadors of Belgium, France, Germany, and the United States, and the representative of the European Community) met twice weekly with one another and with Ould-Abdallah and used whatever influence we had with whatever persons we knew—whether within or without government—to press for an end to negotiations, the preservation of democracy, and the beginning of a functioning government.

On July 29, 1994, we succeeded in getting the United Nations Security Council to make a tepid pronouncement, which included the following statement:

> This Security Council supports the ongoing political dialogue in Burundi aimed at reaching an early agreement on presidential succession. It calls on all parties to reach rapidly a settlement based on democratic principles . . . the Council demands that all parties cease immediately any incitement to violence or ethnic hatred. The Council encourages all those who support a peaceful solution to persist in their efforts.

But privately, Ambassador Ould-Abdallah said to our Group of 5: "If the international community is not willing to introduce armed forces, then we have to accept appeasement. Our people [i.e., the international community] ran away in Rwanda; therefore we must get the best we can here."

The wrangling among the political parties continued throughout September. Then, on October 1, 1994, Sylvestre Ntibantunganya, who had been serving as interim president since April, was confirmed by Parliament as the new president by a vote of 68–1. Uprona gave Ntibantunganya this landslide in exchange for a series of concessions that weakened the presidency:

• All legislation and decrees would now require the signature of both president and prime minister (who, it was privately agreed, would be an Uprona Tutsi).

• Fifty-five percent of major appointments would go to Frodebu and its allied parties; 45 percent to Uprona and its allied parties.

• A National Security Council was established, which had unelected members and was to be a group of *bashingantahe,* that is, "wise men," to advise on governmental policy and disputes.

While the powers of the presidency, the majority party, and the largest ethnic group were all significantly lessened, many participants looked after their own short-term, selfish interests. The Convention of Government turned out to be essentially a division of the political pie: which parties and which persons got positions in the cabinet, ambassadorships, top posts in the civil service. According to Ambassador Ould-Abdallah:

Those negotiations, which began in late April [1994] were centering on the distribution of positions in the provincial and central governments, not on the country's long-term or even mid-term interests. Frankly, I found the politicians' greed in fighting for these lucrative positions objectionable.[2]

Disappointing as the self-serving nature of these negotiations was, the scramble for government positions was not surprising. Because most African nations are so poor, and entrepreneurship so foreign to their experience, the path to economic security—a decent job—is more often through government than through private business. That is especially true for a country as poor and war-torn as Burundi. And poverty breeds corruption.

Given the questionable motivation of a number of the participants, and the intense suspicions, fears, and desire for revenge among many at the negotiating table, the document that emerged could not have been a brilliant or lasting document, as history was immediately to prove. It may, however, have been as much as could be papered together at that time. And for the moment, it gave the country a sense of positive direction again.

Burundi's minister of defense, Firmin Sinzoyiheba, an obligatory guest at the annual U.S. Marine Ball, with the authors, 1994.

INVITING MURDERERS TO DINNER

The signing of the Convention of Government and the installation of the new president thus brought some new hope to the citizens of Burundi. And to Americans, it brought a return of families: "ordered departure" was lifted. We were elated.

I felt confident that our families would be safe. But I did have one, minor apprehension, and it would require very careful, diplomatic presentation to Kathleen: inviting murderers to dinner.

During my first week in Bujumbura I realized that, for the first time in my life, I would be host to killers. To further democracy in Burundi, I could not ignore those people, good and bad, who directly affected the course of events in Burundi. Some were assassins, putschists, torturers, baby killers, and *genocidaires*. But I remembered the 1960s and 1970s, when many Vietnam protesters considered people heading the U.S. government to be "murderers," and yet those protesters wanted contact with leaders whose policies they sought to influence. Civil discourse, even with murderers, is an inevitable part of diplomacy. If enjoying baked Alaska or strawberry charlotte at the American ambassador's residence was that spoonful of sugar that might make the medicine of democracy go down, I was ready to provide it. Over

Kathleen and Bob dancing at the U.S. Marine Ball, 1994.

the months that followed, Kathleen and I would invite to the residence more times than I cared to count former President Pierre Buyoya, Colonels Biko-magu and Daradangwa, the various defense ministers, Uprona Party chairman Charles Mukasi, and no doubt more putschists than I knew. That simply came with the territory. Fortunately, upon her arrival, Kathleen understood. It did not lessen her zest for the new life our family was beginning together.

SIX

CHRISTMAS IN BUJUMBURA

Grenades, Gunfire, and Curfew

The days back in Texas had turned to weeks and then to months. Living alone with two small children, with Bob eight thousand miles away, began taking its toll. At night Sarah sometimes cried for Daddy, and her four-year-old conscience pricked her as she remembered times when she had run away rather than let Bob give her a hug. More than once, as she tried to understand his absence, she asked, "Are you and Daddy getting a divorce?" A State Department evacuation order was a concept she couldn't comprehend. Mariana showed less concern as she prepared for first grade in a new school with friends from kindergarten. In late night phone calls to Burundi, she would cheerily ask Bob to describe the crested cranes that lived in his lush gardens on a hillside so remote from her world it might as well have been on another planet. These frequent, almost daily, phone calls were invaluable to the children and me and well worth the thousand dollars a month that they cost us personally.

For my part, I lived in thirty-day segments, anticipating each month's State Department review of the ordered departure. Independent and relatively self-sufficient from growing up as one of eight children, I did not flounder during this period, but as two months turned to three, I too began to feel the empty space that his absence created. It was almost as if I were holding my breath until we could be together. I was desperate to breathe, and my hopes rose on the first of every month as the State Department review approached. After the fourth month, the news that we could join him was met with jubilation and a flurry of activity.

We were told, "Do not take anything that you would not be willing to leave behind." The pillaging of the U.S. ambassador's residence in Rwanda after Americans fled that country resulted in the loss of numerous cherished personal items belonging to Ambassador and Mrs. Rawson. I was careful to heed the warning.

With six large suitcases bulging with clothes, a few books, and Barbie

Four-year-old Sarah trying hard to understand the separation from her father in Africa.
Photo by Judy Walgren, 1994. Courtesy of the Dallas Morning News ©.

dolls, we left amid tears from the San Antonio airport. After an overnight stay in Brussels, as the guests of U.S. Ambassador and Mrs. Alan Blinken, we arrived in Burundi twenty-four hours later. I peered through the window of the Belgian airliner at the lush green mountains below us as we made our final descent over Lake Tanganyika to Bujumbura and into another world. Fears that had dogged me since the first call from the White House a year earlier—of machete warfare, language barriers, and tropical diseases—melted from my psyche as I viewed my new home from above. I had never felt happier or more enthusiastic in my life. Little did I know the challenges that awaited us.

My two little girls were the center of my universe. Ensuring their happiness and well-being was my first priority as we settled into life in this enchanting and distant land. In addition to the threat of warfare was the threat from the invisible enemies of bilharzia (also known as schistosomiasis, a disease caused by parasitic worms), dysentery, and malaria. Drinking water was boiled and filtered at our house. We were even told not to brush our teeth with the tap water there, so jugs of purified water stood next to each sink in the bathrooms. (Often, our water supply went out altogether, along with the electricity.) All fresh vegetables, including lettuce, had to be washed in a bleach-like solution to kill dangerous bacteria. We became used to the slightly antiseptic taste of our salads over time. Saturday nights were set aside for the ritual of taking the antimalarial medicine prescribed by the State Department. I had to hide the mefloquine, which came only as tablets, in a chunk of chocolate for the girls to chew, since they did not yet know how to swallow pills. Fortunately, their dosage was small, only a sliver of a full-sized tablet. Dr. Brooks Taylor, the very competent regional embassy doctor in Nairobi, warned us against swimming in Lake Tanganyika, a popular pastime for many expatriates. We ignored his advice only once, since our first swim resulted in a leech attaching itself to Bob's leg, in an episode both bloody and hilarious.

Soon these precautions and inconveniences became such a normal part of daily life that we no longer noticed them. The larger question of the girls' schooling and the growing warfare around us displaced the more mundane challenges quickly. Nevertheless, within weeks I felt completely at home in my new environment, and established a daily routine not very different from that in Texas. At 7:45 each morning I buckled Sarah and Mariana into their car seats for the short drive in our four-wheel-drive Mitsubishi Pajero (known in America as the Montero) down the mountainside to the L'École Française (the French School) in the center of Bujumbura. I always took my walkie-talkie with me as a direct line of communication with the marine on duty at the embassy and with other Americans carrying radios. We all had code names, some based on U.S. rivers. Mine was "Medina," for the clear-flowing stream in my home county of Bandera, Texas.

The first several weeks passed with relative calm, and Bujumbura in particular remained mostly peaceful. Life in a tropical paradise was not so bad after all. The morning of December 20 seemed no exception.

Making our way to school, we encountered the usual vibrant and enchanting African scene that greeted us every morning. Passing endless streams of mostly barefoot Burundians walking or trotting up and down the steep hills of the city, we dodged potholes and, sometimes, herds of long-horned cattle, even in the middle of town. It was the last day of classes before Christmas vacation, and the girls were particularly cheerful that morning as we drove along, singing our made-up song, "We're bumpin' along the roads in Bujumbura!" I pulled into the dirt parking lot of the school and walked through the narrow wrought-iron gate of the high-walled compound. Set in a valley near the center of town, against a backdrop of high green hills, the school consisted mainly of single-story red brick buildings arranged around a barren field. The simple cement-floored classrooms were clean and adequate, and the school, which educated children from kindergarten to age nineteen, was justifiably proud that, despite its modest appearance and remote location,

Giselin and Mariana at L'École Française, 1994.

many of its graduates were accepted at the Sorbonne and other famous European universities.

Holding hands, the girls and I made our way across the open schoolyard. Soon Mariana, as always, let go of my hand and ran up the hard-packed dirt track to join her friends forming a line outside their room. I will always remember the sight of my little blonde-haired girl, her ponytail and lunch box flapping in the wind, rushing to join her classmates as they all chattered gaily in French. In a school with 400 students from thirty different countries, and only a handful of Americans, communication could be difficult. Mariana's earliest friendship came during her first week when she and Giselin, a French-speaking African girl in her class, both traced their names in the dirt during recess to introduce themselves. Sarah quickly learned to laugh at herself as she struggled with a new language. One day, when the teacher said in French to come sit down, Sarah thought she said "take off your shoes"—which she obediently proceeded to do! Although initially anxious about putting my daughters in a French school, I was overjoyed that they both had adapted so quickly and seemed so happy. Returning to my car, I contentedly headed home to wait for the noon hour, when they would be finished.

At 10:00 a.m. the phone rang. It was Caroline Pitterman, an Italian whose American husband was head of delegation for the United Nations High Commissioner for Refugees in Burundi. Having grown up in Bujumbura, and therefore accustomed to the ebb and flow of violence in the country, she matter-of-factly told me that her husband's office had just called to warn that there was gunfire and rock-throwing in a downtown area near the school and that both United Nations and European Economic Community employees had been advised to avoid that section.

I gripped the phone as I dissolved into brief, sobbing panic. I didn't fear for my daughters' safety at that moment, but I was terrified that I would be unable to get through the riot to retrieve them. I immediately called the U.S. embassy, which verified that fighting had just broken out because of a murder in the downtown marketplace. An angry crowd had then pursued, captured, and beaten the killer right next to the American embassy. Now, because of pent-up tensions, the violence was apparently spreading. I asked to use the ambassador's official car because it was partially bulletproof. Within a few minutes the driver arrived.

I jumped in and asked Bernardin to go quickly to the French School so that I could bring Mariana and Sarah home. I had calmed down, but my maternal instincts were at full strength.

Bernardin decided to take an alternate route, on streets skirting the edge

Sarah at L'École Française, 1994.

81

of town. We saw heavy streams of people briskly walking or running *away* from the center of the city—which was unusual for that time of day. Nearing the school, we saw no indication of trouble. Nevertheless, at the front gate, the director, shirtsleeves rolled up, was pacing anxiously outside. We had not been able to communicate well before, since he speaks French and I speak English, but in that moment we both drew upon unknown abilities to express ourselves in the other's language and be understood. He urged me not to take the children away; they were "secure." His firmness and confidence convinced me. Later I learned that he had turned all parents away. Perhaps, to ensure stability at the school, he could not disrupt classes for every spasm of violence in the city. Accurately reading the threat level to the school during such episodes was a skill probably not listed in his job description as headmaster.

When I returned at noon to pick up the girls, the scene was very different from usual. Several French military officers—mostly fathers, rather than the usual group of mothers—were picking up their children. Almost everyone was carrying walkie-talkies or cellular phones. Children who lived in certain areas of town were being held in their classrooms until military personnel could escort them to their homes; by now, violence threatened several parts of the city. Gathering the girls, Bernardin and I immediately drove home. Once inside our ten-foot-high garden walls and gates, I breathed easier, thankful that this was the last school day of the semester.

Concerned about American families in Bujumbura, I spent the afternoon telephoning them to make sure that they all knew of the trouble, and to hear their assessment of the danger. Even though some reported hearing gunfire in their neighborhoods, none felt directly threatened. We knew we were not targets of the violence. The fear and hatred were between Tutsi and Hutu. Even so, for those of us new to the country, the situation was frightening. That evening it got worse. It was not unusual to hear grenade explosions or machine-gun fire at night in Bujumbura, but on this night it seemed endless. Bob and I tried helping the girls fall asleep in their own room. Then, during my bedtime story, one explosion was so loud and so close that I said, "How about everybody sleeping in Daddy's and my room?" For once, Bob didn't object.

Crossing the hallway to the master bedroom, we pulled back the mosquito netting that hung like a canopy from the ceiling around our king-size bed, and all climbed in. A few seconds later, Mariana snuggled up to me and asked, "Mommy, why are they having a war out there?"

I lay awake virtually all night. Staring into the darkness of our room through the gauzy haze of the mosquito netting, I listened to the rhythmic breathing of my husband and children sleeping next to me and cringed at the sound of each explosion. The next morning the marines reported that they had counted forty grenades detonated during the night. It was small comfort knowing that in Burundi the army sometimes tosses grenades in the air simply to intimidate the people.

The next day downtown Bujumbura was as vacant as a cemetery. Sans Échec, Sans Défaite, and other armed Tutsi youth gangs had declared a *ville morte* (literally, a dead city) and had erected roadblocks in various parts of the city to shut down commerce and keep people from coming to work. American embassy personnel all went to their offices, as did UN employees to theirs: a deliberate effort not to surrender to those who wanted to paralyze the city and had often succeeded in doing so. The diplomatic corps joined forces in trying to convince the government (and army) to assert authority over Sans Échec and similar groups responsible for the shutdown. In addition, with the embassy's regional security officer, Chris Reilly, Bob drove throughout the city, the American flag flying on his white Chevrolet, to learn firsthand the extent of the damage and violence. He wanted a strong and visible American presence in all quartiers of Bujumbura; in a sense, to let the thugs see that the United States was watching. Afterward, he spent much of the afternoon at the embassy in telephone conversations with both sides. Returning home, he continued to receive calls from the State Department in Washington late into the night.

Another night of grenades followed, and another and another, although the explosions became fewer each night. During the day, commerce and activity had almost stopped. In addition, the Burundi government imposed a citywide curfew from 7:00 p.m. to 5:00 a.m. I was worried about a variety of things, including how to complete Christmas shopping for my children. Finally, on Friday, December 23, I heard that a few stores were open (mind you, there were few to begin with!), so Bernardin came with the bulletproof car and we ventured out. I dashed quickly into three shops and went home feeling that Santa Claus would be tolerably well represented.

Earlier, Bob and I had planned a Christmas party for the American community, and then considered canceling it. But so many people asked us not to, saying it was the only good thing they had to look forward to, that we simply rescheduled it from 7:00 p.m. to 4:30 p.m. to comply with the curfew. The violence had generally calmed down during the day, so two days before Christmas we began to celebrate.

Our exceptional and reliable Burundian household staff—Marcien, Jean-Marie, and Emmanuel—came down from their hillside villages to help set up the long buffet table inside and a bar on the gleaming white veranda outside.

The tranquil and beautiful gardens surrounding us belied the bloody violence beyond our high walls. The sun shone brightly as we made final preparations for our guests. Then the phone began to ring. From different sources Bob was told that an overthrow of the Burundi government was being planned for that evening by elements in the Tutsi military. Unusual movements of troops were reported as evidence of a coup in progress. The news made me jittery. As I greeted arriving guests, I thought, "This is a bizarre life!" Bob remained on the phone, utterly calm. He assured me that rumors of this type are not unusual. After checking a variety of reliable sources, he concluded that there was no coup imminent and joined the party.

The potluck buffet lifted our spirits. Most of the American community in Bujumbura came: embassy staff, workers from USAID and NGOs, including the Jane Goodall Institute, American missionaries, and of course, all their families. Graham and Sarah White, British citizens who had been in Burundi for twenty years, played the piano and flute in our spacious living room. Their five young sons joined the rest of us as we sat on couches and on the floor and sang Christmas carols at the tops of our lungs. Everyone enjoyed it so fully that we lost track of time, and at 6:45 Bob had to urge our guests to leave so that they would get home before the newly imposed curfew.

The next day was Christmas Eve. A religious service and a play organized by the American missionaries and others at the nearby Novotel Hotel was to go on as planned, but the starting time had been moved forward to comply with the curfew. My girls and I dressed up and drove alone down the mountain to attend. The small plain meeting room was filled with people. A makeshift stage was in front; standard gray folding chairs accommodated the audience. Dozens of children were milling around in homemade traditional Christmas costumes as we were handed a typed program and took our seats.

The missionaries I met in Burundi impressed me as the quiet heroes of Africa. Their genuine self-sacrifice and compassionate assistance to the poor and suffering were offered with no thought of material reward or public recognition. On that afternoon, on a small stage crowded with children and adults, and with their radiant faces, uplifted voices, and unshakeable faith, they presented a Christmas program that will long remain in my memory. For one glorious hour we could all forget about the killing and focus on the spirituality and hope of the season. A chair I had saved for Bob remained empty next to us. Even though it was Christmas Eve, he felt compelled to continue holding the forceful face-to-face meetings with those suspected of being behind the violence and with others in positions of influence. I regret-

Christmas 1994 in Bujumbura: Kathleen,
Mariana, and Sarah.

ted his missing the service but knew that he was where he should be. I thought of him as I remembered Jesus' words "Blessed are the peacemakers."

Santa Claus came before 5:45 a.m. on Christmas morning. I know because that was when Mariana woke us and, with Sarah, dashed into the living room. They were so excited and pleased with what Santa had brought. (Thank goodness for African crafts!) We spent a quiet and happy day together, one seemingly far removed from the warfare and tragedy surrounding us. Although the city had become calmer, tensions were by no means resolved. A few grenades exploded Christmas night—sounds we were becoming accustomed to.

The day after Christmas was an embassy holiday. Since daytime life had basically returned to normal in Bujumbura, Bob and I took the girls to Ruzizi National Park, just outside the city. After a brief search we found a lone attendant who took our money and opened the dilapidated gate. We seemed to be the only people in the entire park as we began our drive down the narrow red-dirt roads, finding our own way, since there were no signs or maps to guide us. Just ahead, we saw a log lying across the road. Only when the log suddenly moved did we realize that it was actually a python. Turning south, we reached the Ruzizi River and drove along its banks until the dirt tracks ended and the vastness of Lake Tanganyika lay before us. A crude wooden bench stood on a small bluff overlooking the mouth of the river. The four of us sat there, sharing binoculars, and watched seven large crocodiles lying nearly motionless on a sand bar in the middle of the stream. A family of hippos, in a slow and deliberate journey upriver, slipped quietly and effortlessly through the brown waters below us, pausing only occasionally to snort noisily and shake their heads. The sun glistened over the tranquil blue waters of Lake Tanganyika, and the towering mountains on the distant shore in Zaire looked particularly clear and beautiful. With the shade of an amatete tree shielding us from the African heat and a gentle breeze caressing our faces, I felt a sense of peace and contentment that we were all together again and in Burundi.

SEVEN

QUIET HEROES

With the New Year, calm returned to Bujumbura and to the countryside. The 7:00 p.m. government-imposed curfew continued, bringing Bob home from the office earlier than usual. No more diplomatic dinners or late-night meetings. All communication was by phone after dark. But most enjoyable to me was the uninterrupted family time that these evenings provided—a rare pleasure in public service. Still on school vacation, Mariana and Sarah spent their days swimming, playing tennis, and drawing.

The director of the United States Information Service, Gordon Duguid, and his wife, Noreen, hosted an afternoon backyard barbecue at their home near Lake Tanganyika. Our small American embassy community was becoming closer as warm friendships were formed. Just as we were about to leave the Duguids to comply with the curfew, Sarah looked up to see a seeming black cloud crossing the sky. With her little four-year-old face illumined by the evening light, she said excitedly, "Look, Mommy, it's fruit bats going to Zaire!" Making their homes in palm trees near the Duguids, thousands departed each evening across Lake Tanganyika to the mountains and forests beyond. We all stood in wonderment as they passed.

On the last free weekend before classes resumed, we decided to drive to the remote Baptist mission we had visited before, high in the mountains near the Rwandan border. Founded in 1949 by Swedish missionaries, the post was now led by a Danish couple, Knud and Jytte Hansen, who had lived in Rwanda and Burundi since 1961. It was a magical place. To visit there was to step back to a special place in time. A time when there was little electricity, no paved roads, when you ate only what you grew in your own garden. A place where the night sky, free of artificial lighting, revealed a profusion of bright stars. A place where there were virtually no mechanical noises—only the sound of voices echoing across the valleys, the wind blowing through the

Tall eucalyptus trees, like great sentinels, towered over the road to the Baptist mission at Rubura.

trees, or chickens clucking nearby. It was called Rubura—and it will live in my heart forever.

The first two hours of the drive north from Bujumbura proceeded along a surprisingly well-maintained paved road. Or perhaps its smoothness was simply the result of how few cars existed in this poorest of countries. From the shores of Lake Tanganyika we climbed higher, up steep and winding mountain grades. Burundi's lush landscape surrounded us with dense groves of banana trees and thriving tea plantations. Eucalyptus trees towered above us, lining each side of the road like great sentinels, their long high branches forming a canopy above us. Beyond the trees were sweeping valleys, deep ravines, and carefully tilled fields dotting the hillsides. The scenery was refreshingly beautiful; the January air clear and crisp. And as in all of Burundi, we never lost sight of people walking or standing alongside the road.

Soon we came to a wide spot in the highway called Bugarama. Natural springs moistened rock cliffs on the left side of the road. As we pulled over, a dozen vendors rushed over and shoved broad platters made of woven straw and overflowing with vegetables through our car's open windows. Grown nearby, the broccoli, cauliflower, carrots, and cabbages were fresh and colorful. Gigantic vibrant bouquets of tropical wildflowers, many more than our Pajero had room for, were thrust in our faces in this maelstrom of activity. All the sellers spoke rapidly and loudly in Kirundi as they pressed forward to sell their goods. With the Hansens living so remotely and on such meager salaries, we liked to take along food and flowers when we visited, so we bought what we could pack into our car and proceeded.

Soon after Bugarama, we passed through the first of three military checkpoints. My heart rate always rose slightly as we approached these roadblocks and rolled down our windows to speak briefly to the tall slender Tutsi soldiers. Sometimes they smelled of locally brewed banana beer. I always found the combination of alcohol and machine guns, which the soldiers casually slung over their shoulders, unsettling. But they never gave us any trouble, and with our clearly marked diplomatic license plates and American flag decals on our windows, they often waved us through quickly.

One hundred seven kilometers (around sixty-six miles) from Bujumbura, past the town of Kayanza, was the left-hand turn onto the winding copper-colored dirt road to Rubura. The Hansens had provided simple and straightforward directions: "From Kayanza, north towards the border to Rwanda. Very close to 107 or 108 kilometer marker there is a stone/dirt road on the left hand side. Take road 6–7 kilometers and then on top of hill turn right 1/2 kilometer to Mission station. Rubura U.E.B." Once off the paved highway, we entered deepest rural Africa. But in this, the second most densely

*Sarah, Kathleen, Bob, and Mariana at a village market near Bugarama,
on the way to the Hansens, 1995.*

populated country on the continent, we never escaped the Burundi people. Nor did we want to. Our drive through these back roads presented a lovely and peaceful scene. There was no urgency to the gentle stroll of the women along the well-worn mountain paths that day. Their colorful native dress was strikingly beautiful against the green backdrop of the mountains and forests around them. Balancing bundles of twigs and branches for their cooking fires on their heads and carrying hoes, they stopped and stared as we drove past. Barefoot children with ragged clothes and bright smiles ran happily beside our vehicle, laughing and calling until they grew weary and came giggling to a stop. Old men sitting on stone walls beneath the shade of eucalyptus trees stopped their conversation to silently watch us pass.

As we drove deeper into the mountains and forests, I felt a stirring within my heart and an unexplainable sense of coming home. Eight thousand miles from Texas, in a world and a culture so different from my own, I never understood that emotion, yet never failed to experience it as we drew nearer to Rubura.

As the afternoon drew to a close and the shadows from the tall trees grew longer, I opened the car window to "feel" what was around me. The air was pure and fresh, the waning sunlight warm and golden as it filtered through the branches. I looked into the faces of those we slowly passed and felt from them a sense of tranquility after a day's hard work done. It was a glimpse into the Burundi that could be. A Burundi where tilling the soil, rather than killing one's neighbors, was the substance of one's life.

We turned down a final high ridge, which, through a clearing, afforded us the first glimpse of the Hansens' compound across the valley: a cluster of simple yellow and rust-colored brick buildings lining the crest of the adjoining hill. Passing by the first building, a mission health clinic currently vacant, we suddenly found ourselves surrounded by large numbers of people. Their expressions suggested not anxiety, but quiet resignation. Small children scurried to and fro, their tattered, filthy clothing hanging like rags from their bodies, their bare feet encrusted with dirt and mud. Water poured from a small outdoor pump as women rinsed their laundry and draped it across shrubs and trees to dry. A square of blue plastic sheeting that lay on the ground must have been brought from a United Nations refugee camp. On top of it, articles of clothing were spread to dry in the afternoon sun. A man to the left of the road was vigorously chopping wood with a large crude axe. Near him, small black kettles with lids were set upon piles of hot coals, sending a haze of smoke into the air. At least a hundred people had gathered there. It was apparent that they had just arrived and were settling in. They

*Jytte Hansen watching our daughters play with
her rabbits, 1995.*

looked at us with solemn faces as we slowly drove by. Soon we would learn
the details of their sad fate.

One hundred yards beyond stood the simple bamboo-and-wood gate
marking the entrance to the Hansens' home. Ahead, standing on her small
brick porch, was a beaming Jytte Hansen in a bright pink and purple dress,
her soft, wavy white hair framing her kind and cheerful face. She always
knew when we would arrive because she could hear our car coming miles
away. Just behind stood her husband, Knud, a gentle man who speaks nine
languages. While farmers in Denmark, they had decided almost forty years
ago to serve in Africa as missionaries. We thought of the Hansens, both
in their sixties, as our children's "African grandparents." Visiting their small

farm and church aroused in my girls the same curiosity and excitement that visits to my own parents' ranch home in Bandera, Texas, always did. At this remote African outpost, however, life was lived far more simply.

Drawing on their agricultural experience in Denmark, the Hansens had planted an array of fruit trees and vegetables in small plots around their mountaintop home. A native *amapera* (or, guava) tree stood at one corner. Mrs. Hansen boiled the seeds from this fruit down to a thick sugary syrup that she added to the porridge made for local villagers and refugees. Opening a simple wooden cupboard on her front porch, she proudly showed us her large passion fruit and papayas recently picked nearby. At Rubura, as everywhere in Africa, little is wasted. Although the Hansens went monthly to Bujumbura for supplies, they came as close to living off the land as any friends I had.

For my children, the greatest excitement came from seeing the chickens and rabbits. During times of crisis, as when armed skirmishes after President Ndadaye's assassination made it dangerous to leave the mission, the eggs and meat from these animals became important to the Hansens' survival. But for the most part, the animals were treated as pets. Mr. Hansen, in his thick Danish accent, patiently introduced the girls to his rabbits, lifting them up to see inside the hutches and taking the tamest animals out of their cages to be petted. The Hansens later brought two young rabbits, one black and one white, and a beautifully constructed hutch to Bujumbura for Mariana and Sarah to keep.

Just before dusk, Mr. Hansen walked with us down the rocky road, past the large simple brick church, to the weary refugees we had passed earlier at the bottom of the hill. Crossing the border from Rwanda, bringing their children and little else, these Rwandan Hutus had secretly traversed the mountain paths, hiding among trees and bushes to escape the Rwandan Patriotic Army. Six months earlier, horrifying images of an estimated 800,000 people, mainly Tutsis, slaughtered by Hutus had filled television screens around the world. By now much of the world had forgotten about central Africa's suffering. But inside Rwanda, the Tutsis remembered, and their army, the RPA, wanted revenge.

These Hutu survivors, mostly young men and women with small children, had run to a place where they had been told they would find shelter, food, and safe transport to UN refugee camps in Burundi—the Baptist mission at Rubura. Pastor Hansen told us that hundreds had arrived just that week, prompting the United Nations to designate the Hansens' mission as an official transit point for refugees from Rwanda. It wasn't the ministry that the Danish couple had envisioned in their last year before retirement, but

Pastor Hansen speaking softly to the Rwandan refugees in their native language, 1995.

they assumed it with dedication, compassion, and efficiency, organizing a strict feeding and aid program, the food and medicine carefully distributed, and a requirement that those desiring additional supplies must do chores to earn them.

Holding Sarah on my hip, I watched with awe as Pastor Hansen moved through these sad and quiet families that evening, speaking softly to them in their native language. Bob lifted Mariana above the curious children, who were intent on touching her flaxen hair. He stood at Pastor Hansen's side, asking for translation and mentally recording the details of abuse, intimidation, and murder. The melancholy faces of those lost souls remain etched in my mind.

Their prospects were not good. Running from the Rwandan Tutsi military on one side, they were now subject to harassment by the Burundi Tutsi military on the other side. As if caught in a grotesque game of human ping-pong, they lurched from one predator to the other. Now, in desperation, they had sought refuge on this remote mountaintop. If not transported to the safety of a UN camp soon, they would probably be killed. It was as simple and as frightening as that.

We hurried back up the narrow dirt road to the Hansens' home, now dimly glowing with the light of kerosene lamps. There was a slight chill in the air as the sun disappeared behind the mountains and the blackness of night descended. Having no phone, Pastor Hansen sought help for the refugees by ham radio. Although transmission at Rubura was scratchy and unreliable, he carefully located the proper shortwave frequency and made his call. In the half darkness of a narrow storage room, he hunched over his small black radio, diligently and repeatedly sending greetings in Danish to the Nielsens in Bujumbura, fellow Baptist missionaries from Denmark.

Minutes passed as I silently watched one of Africa's quiet heroes at work, knowing that at the bottom of the hill, huddled by their wood fires, the lives of a hundred people depended on this decent, unheralded man and his radio.

Finally, through the irritating static, came a faint response. Unintelligible to me, Pastor Hansen responded enthusiastically in Danish, obviously understanding every word. I remembered learning that the U.S. military during the Second World War had used Navajo speakers to communicate with military posts overseas because the Japanese could not understand their obscure language. To the Burundian or Rwandan militaries, Danish would be equally unknown. Pastor Hansen's urgent plea for help was received. A UN truck should arrive in the morning. Now all we could do was wait.

Meanwhile, we couldn't escape the delicious aroma coming from Mrs. Hansen's kitchen. After a long and emotional day, we suddenly realized how hungry we were.

Mariana, Sarah, and I joined Mrs. Hansen as Bob and Pastor Hansen sat by a roaring fire in the living room for a quiet discussion. No one we knew was more trustworthy in discussing Burundi than Knud Hansen. His more than thirty years of experience in the country, keen intellect, and spiritual foundation, which left him free of bias or self-interest, made him someone whose judgment Bob knew he could rely on. And he did.

Meanwhile, Mariana, Sarah, and I were learning from another master. Trained as a nurse, Mrs. Hansen showed as much culinary skill as she did medical expertise. And on that remote African mountaintop, she did both with only the barest of tools.

Her small kitchen was a study in simplicity. Sitting in the corner was a large black wood stove brought from Scandinavia decades ago. Pots of various sizes simmered on top, lids covering their contents to keep them warm. A small pile of neatly chopped wood was stacked next to the stove. A wood-handled push broom and red dustpan were leaning against a bright yellow wall. Plain, smooth concrete formed the floor. Nailed to the wall was a simple varnished board, creating an open shelf where jars, bowls, and salt and pepper shakers were neatly lined. Dishtowels, tea strainers, and a fly swatter hung on small hooks below. Next to the stove was an old-fashioned iron such as my great-grandmother might have used. With no electricity other than that provided for two hours a day by an outside gas generator, the heat for the heavy metal iron came from placing it on the wood stove.

I stood next to Mrs. Hansen and helped her slice the delicious white potatoes for which the Kayanza region was known. While Mariana and Sarah set the table, Mrs. Hansen turned to her one "modern" convenience, a tiny butane stove, to cook a final dish more quickly. The butane had to be conserved, since it was expensive and difficult to get.

But before sitting down to dinner, Pastor Hansen invited us to step outside with him. I have never seen a deeper or brighter night sky. The stars were piercing in their brilliance and detail, and far more numerous than I had ever seen. For as far as my eyes could see, there was no artificial light: no cities, no homes, no streetlights. I had not realized how faded the night sky became when assaulted by the neon and fluorescence of our American cities. Surrounded by the darkness and the light, I felt an intoxicating sense of peace and of being in my rightful place. I did not wish to be anywhere else in the world at that moment.

Lowering my gaze from the sky, I soon noticed, below a small ridge twenty yards away, the sparks and smoke from a campfire rising with the gentle sounds of Kirundi, murmured quietly by the Hansens' night watchmen. They had come from their huts in the hills to stand guard. Pastor Hansen went to talk with them, and then, having guests, he decided to turn on the gas generator to provide electricity for two hours. As the whirr of the generator started up, we returned from the chill night air to a dinner of pork roast, potatoes, fresh vegetables, and homemade bread. At the close of the evening, as the candlelight flickered off the Hansens' warm and inviting faces, I thought again of how fortunate we were to be there.

The next morning we were up with the sun. We had slept well in the small one-room brick guesthouse next to the Hansens' home, where we had read books to the girls by candlelight before burying ourselves under heavy quilts against the cold mountain air. During the night, I slipped out of bed several times to pull the covers back over Mariana and Sarah in their little cots. I will never understand why children kick their blankets off at night, even when it seems freezing to me.

With the morning sun came the warmth of a typical Burundi day. Rubura was buzzing with activity. Across the narrow valley to the green mountains that marked the border with Rwanda, the daily tasks of chopping wood, hauling water, and cultivating fields by hand were already underway, little changed for centuries. Sitting on the ground near the Hansens' front door was an elderly man, cutting the grass with a small sickle. He gathered the tops of the grass with one hand, and, clump by clump, cut them with the other. I then noticed that he had no legs. Wanting to work despite his handicap, he earned his meager wages and a simple daily meal in the only way he could.

Mrs. Hansen was working in her kitchen, rolling out dough, sorting and rinsing fresh fruit, and putting a kettle of water on the wood stove for tea. Through open windows that had no screens, she cheerily poked her head out to bid us good morning. "Would you like to gather eggs this morning?" she called to the girls, knowing it was a favorite pastime.

"Yes, yes," they responded delightedly, and off they went.

As she and I followed to the chicken coop, she spoke lovingly of the natural beauty that surrounded her. On one side of their simple stone house, the delicate white blossoms of a passion fruit vine, in intricate and perfectly symmetrical patterns, hung like Belgian lace over the small porch. Nearby, huge lemons, green like our limes in the United States, dangled heavily from their branches. Avocados, camouflaged by dark green leaves, bulged with ripeness. A small field of sweet potatoes, which Pastor Hansen cultivated carefully, was protected by a low fence.

More important to her than the bounty of nature was the unaffected goodness of the people. She spoke of the farmer who faithfully, for over thirty years, had walked three hours daily to deliver them one liter of fresh milk from his cow. As she good-naturedly scolded her two dogs, frisking at her feet, we walked back to the house, the girls proudly holding the eggs they had gathered. Life at Rubura seemed so simple and peaceful, where one rose with the sun and went to bed by candlelight, where the gentle rhythms of the land and the air and the sky created a fuller, slower pace of life than most of us in the "developed" world experience. Jytte Hansen understood well the richness of her experience.

At breakfast, Pastor Hansen reminded us that life at Rubura was not always as harmonious as it seemed that beautiful January morning. He told us that in October 1993, after President Ndadaye's assassination, "if a Hutu saw a Tutsi, that was an enemy. When a soldier (Tutsi) saw a Hutu, that was an enemy." One morning during that period, Mrs. Hansen's kitchen routine was suddenly interrupted by the sound of machine-gun fire. Looking out, she saw Burundian soldiers just a hundred yards from her home, on a knoll beside the church, shooting across a narrow ravine and into the open marketplace filled with Hutus on the opposite hill. The hoes of the local people were no match for the Kalashnikovs of the Burundian military. By the time the soldiers left at noon, over forty people had been wounded or killed.

Pastor Hansen explained how his wife, trained in nursing, had rushed to help, applying bandages and administering first aid. "My wife is very good in such situations," Pastor Hansen remarked. "She has very strong nerves." Throughout the afternoon and into the night, she had moved from one injured person to another, calmly and forcefully doing what she could to save their lives or relieve their pain. "I'm amazed to see how you can survive with a bullet through your body," Pastor Hansen observed; most of the wounded had survived.

As we were finishing breakfast, a local Burundian employed by the church to help care for refugees arrived at the door. His thin frame looked nearly skeletal beneath faded tan overalls that had been cut off jaggedly at the knees. An oversized white shirt hung off one bony shoulder. His bare feet looked as tough as leather. Speaking rapidly in Kirundi, he delivered a morning report.

During the night, Burundian soldiers had arrived and begun threatening the Rwandan refugees camped at the bottom of the hill. While we had slept peacefully in the guesthouse a hundred yards away, the soldiers had stealthily taken five people, whose bodies were soon found floating in the river. The soldiers had warned the refugees to be gone by 6 p.m. or be driven out. Thus, their only hope was for the UN trucks requested in last night's radio call to arrive before that time. Without hesitation, Pastor Hansen got back on his ham radio to contact the nearest UN office, now open, and urge an immediate rescue of the unarmed refugees at his mission.

Two hours later, lumbering down the narrow dirt road came two large white trucks with pale blue UN emblems on their doors. At the wide point in the road where the Rwandans had been washing their clothes, the trucks turned around, backed up the hill, and parked one behind the other. Then, with small bundles under their arms, the refugees climbed or were hoisted into the backs of the huge trucks. Mothers with outstretched arms reached for their children to be lifted up to them. The truck bed, with its high sides and covered top, was quickly jammed with people. It was a noisy and rough process, with no particular organization and no particular concern for comfort. Nevertheless, I felt I was witnessing a profoundly humanitarian act. Far from any television cameraman, and unknown to the rest of the world, a hundred lives were being saved, even if only temporarily in some cases, by the United Nations. What chance would those families have had, in that remote part of the globe, without help from such an international organization expressly dedicated to alleviating such suffering?

Within a half hour, every refugee was gone. The shrubs and trees were bare of laundry, the arched brick doorways were vacant, the numerous wood

UN trucks being quickly loaded with Hutu refugees, 1995.

fires, which provided warmth last night, were now small piles of cold white ashes. No wood was being chopped, no food being cooked, no children running to and fro. I stood in the stillness of that moment and said a prayer for the nameless families whose paths had so briefly crossed mine. Chased from their own country and threatened in this one, what would their futures hold? I turned and walked up the rocky road to join Bob and the girls.

Later, Mrs. Hansen served afternoon tea, a European ritual faithfully observed at Rubura. Spreading a pretty Burundian cloth over the wooden table on her small side porch, she laid out china cups and saucers, a pot of tea, a thermos full of cold water that she had boiled and filtered against disease, and plates of delicious Danish pastries and cookies baked in the oven of her wood stove. It was a cool and shady spot in which to sit and enjoy the fresh air and the lush greenness around us.

As we were drinking our tea and the girls were coloring at the other end of the table, two French-speaking UN workers appeared and joined us. Before their teacups could be refilled, however, the Hansens' Burundian assistant arrived again and asked us to come quickly. Halfway down the steep rocky road near the church we could see a young man walking slowly in our direction. He clutched his body with folded arms. I stood nearby as he told Pastor Hansen in Kirundi what had happened. Throughout the conversation, he made gestures of being kicked and hit. During the night he had been among

Unknown to the world, a hundred lives were being saved by the United Nations, 1995.

the group of Rwandan refugees taken away by the Burundi soldiers. His five companions had been killed. He was left alive, though beaten severely, because the soldiers wanted him to discover which mountain route the Rwandan refugees were using to enter Burundi, then report back. Because the boy could speak Kirundi, they had incorrectly concluded he was Burundian and had allowed him to live, yet demanded he be an informant. His life was obviously in peril. Learning that the boy's parents had been part of the group of refugees just evacuated on the two UN trucks, the UN workers radioed the trucks to stop, and then drove away to deliver the boy to his family. "Well," said Pastor Hansen calmly, "at least he has a chance now." On such a narrow thread often hangs the difference between life and death in Burundi.

It was by then late afternoon, and as the sinking sun was bathing the green landscape in a golden glow, I asked Bob if he would watch the girls while I took a walk. Opening the bamboo gate, I stepped outside the Hansens' yard and strolled down the road to the church below. No manicured lawn surrounded this Baptist mission, only rocks and dirt and native grasses that melded into the countryside beyond. No fancy steps or elegant entrances led in, just a pair of faded wooden doors standing half open. From within, beautifully haunting voices filled the mountains with song. I stepped inside. There, illumined by fading sunlight streaking through the broken windows stood fifty children practicing hymns for the next day's service.

One young boy was playing a guitar; another pounded a large homemade drum of tightly stretched cowhide. Clapping their hands, they sang loudly in Kirundi with high-pitched voices that seemed quaintly off-key. Among the Kirundi words, I recognized a chorus of "alleluia," sung as they lifted their faces and hands toward the exposed wooden beams and vaulted ceiling high above them. I sat alone amid the empty pews for nearly an hour, entranced by their enthusiasm and joy.

Soon the Saturday evening practice came to an end. I stood outside the church as musicians and singers began leaving. The children were running and laughing; the women, singly or in groups, made their way down the steep mountainside back to their homes, some miles away. A young man continued practicing his accordion as he disappeared through the trees, the music growing fainter and fainter. It was near nightfall and the sky had grown very dark. Lightning bolts crisscrossed the sky beyond the mountains in Rwanda as the sound of thunder rumbled in the distance. A storm was coming, and with it strong gusts of cool air. Once again I turned toward the inviting glow coming from Mrs. Hansen's kitchen windows. Already I could see the smoke from her woodstove rising about the roof.

But as I climbed back up the rocky red-dirt road, I met Bob and Pastor Hansen, and we were joined, once again, by the tireless Burundi messenger who assisted refugees. He reported that fifty more Rwandan refugees had arrived and were encamped at the bottom of the hill in the brick buildings just vacated by the UN trucks. With him were a neatly dressed woman and her husband, Vital Senkindi, a secondary-school administrator in Runyombyi, about ten miles across the border. Originally built by the UEB (Union des églises Baptistes), the school had been taken over by the government. Pastor Hansen had met this couple on a visit there a week earlier. Because of continuing violence, the school was not currently offering instruction. Instead, it now housed a small contingent of twenty to thirty UNAMIR (United Nations Assistance Mission for Rwanda) troops drawn from Mali and Ghana. Nonetheless, the administrator and his wife continued living there: that way they could look after the buildings, and since the school was surrounded by UN troops and guarded by a white UN tank, it seemed like one of the safest places in the area.

About three miles from their school, near Nishili commune, was Camp Busanze, which fed 9,000 Hutus daily. Many lived within the camp; others, in the immediate area. All had been displaced from their homes elsewhere in Rwanda. According to Senkindi, at about 9:00 p.m. on the previous night, Friday, January 6, RPA soldiers surrounded the camp, took up positions, and began shooting directly at the people inside. Senkindi's mother, who lived next to the camp, had described to her son what she had seen. Total chaos, she said, broke out as RPA soldiers began firing and using bayonets and knives to cut up the men, women, and children. They then shoved the body parts down the latrines—a gruesome practice widely used by both sides to terrify and humiliate their enemies, make decent burial impossible, and hide their cowardly deeds from the outside world. The shooting and killing continued until daybreak on the 7th. By then the camp had been completely destroyed.

The UNAMIR soldiers, Senkindi reported, stayed in their school compound throughout the night. The commander of the UNAMIR contingent contacted his regional headquarters when the attack began. Yet in spite of his having troops and a tank, he was instructed to do nothing to stop the slaughter, but to wait until morning, after the killers had left, before entering the camp. Only then did UN helicopters arrive to transfer a few of the wounded to a hospital in Kigali. Senkindi said that the UNAMIR soldiers that morning had estimated that as many as 750–1,000 people may have been killed. The attack was so terrifying and the UN response so pitifully weak that Senkindi, living in the same walled compound as the UN soldiers did, felt obliged to flee.

We had heard and seen helicopters earlier during the day at Rubura, but had not known their purpose. And although Pastor Hansen had heard gunfire during the night, he had no knowledge of its source. At this point, with evening fast approaching, there was little any of us could do. So we trudged soberly up the hill toward the house, wondering what the morning would bring.

The next morning, Sunday, we walked with Pastor Hansen down the hill to the site where the refugees had gathered. Overnight, their number had swelled from fifty to three hundred. Pastor Hansen moved through the group slowly, quietly speaking with many of them. Bob was at his side, recording on a notepad their tales of Friday night's cruelty and slaughter. In each instance, the details were almost identical. The number of dead cited, including the figure from the school administrator, was almost always around 750. And they recounted the same horror: the troops who surrounded them and fired upon them throughout the night; their attempts to hide; the slaughter with bayonets as well as bullets; the bodies mutilated, some thrown in latrines; their defenselessness; their fear as they fled through the forest; their relief to be in Rubura. We had not heard a more horrible story of mass killing directly from the victims since arriving in Burundi. Having learned of their suffering and its cause, we now had to wait for Bob to get back to the embassy telephones and communications network to see what could be done.

Pastor Hansen's church, with pews carved in Denmark, 1995.

After talking with the refugees, Pastor Hansen, Bob, and I walked back uphill to the church, where we joined the girls and Mrs. Hansen, seated in pews near the front. These plain but sturdy pews had been carved, donated, and sent years earlier by a church in the Danish town where Hans Christian Andersen had once lived. The clanging mission church bell was calling across the valley that services were about to begin. Already, the large, airy building was half full of people, some of whom had walked two or three hours to attend.

Sundays were always the most vibrant day in Burundi, since the women wore their best, most colorful native garments and equally bright cloths wrapped around their heads. We took our seats as I watched the families, virtually all of them barefoot, file in. Quietly walking down the aisle, they then slid across the wooden pews to their seats. To my surprise, the babies remained happily bound to the backs of their mothers, who leaned only slightly forward in their seats to keep from crushing them. Burundian children are remarkably quiet. I don't remember hearing a baby cry the entire time I was in their country.

A plain brick altar covered with a white cloth bearing hand-stitched words in Kirundi graced the front of the church. A vase with wildflowers was the only adornment. A simple, bare wooden cross hung on the wall. A lectern, also covered in a white cloth, was on the left. A poster with a painted rainbow and white dove was attached to the wall as a display for the congregation. Pastor Hansen had told us that morning as he retrieved the poster from his study that his sermon was on love and reconciliation, teaching that people of different faiths, of different tribes, of different colors should live peacefully as one.

After Pastor Hansen had preached his sermon in Kirundi, the choir that I had heard practicing the night before began singing. A messenger entered the church and whispered in Pastor Hansen's ear that UN officials had arrived with several trucks. We slipped outside, and I listened as Bob and Pastor Hansen, speaking in French, described to them what the refugees had been reporting.

Once again, the large UN trucks were loaded with refugees. Once again, the brick buildings at the base of the hill became deserted. We returned for the close of the church service and then went back to the Hansens' home to help prepare lunch.

With a long drive ahead, and a 7:00 p.m. curfew, we packed the car for an early start home. It had been an extraordinary weekend, different from anything the State Department seminar for ambassadors and spouses had taught Bob and me to expect, and different from the relaxed family visits that we had earlier enjoyed with the Hansens. Little did we know of the dramatic experiences yet to come.

EIGHT

NO WHITE HATS FOR THE
RWANDAN PATRIOTIC ARMY

Driving back from the Hansens' mission on Sunday afternoon, my mind was churning with memories of ragged Rwandan refugees pushing forward to recount to the patient Pastor Hansen tales of their Friday-night massacre. Anxiety was etched across their faces, their words reflecting a battle between desperation and hope. At that moment hope meant an escape to a new refugee camp, where they could again break off small branches, bend them, bind them together, and cover them with blue plastic, all the while hoping that the white UN seal would offer them better protection in Burundi than they had received from the UN troops in Rwanda.

My challenge was how to tell the simple truth about RPA actions in Rwanda, as reported by witnesses and victims, in a manner that the U.S. government and the United Nations would accept. I felt caught in a vise between State Department notions of propriety regarding what an ambassador is allowed to say and my own experiences during the past forty-eight hours. The longstanding and almost immutable practice is that one ambassador never comments on the events and policies in another ambassador's country. The practice is understandable: it reflects good manners and basic good sense not to presume to do another person's job. At the same time, the fates of the twin countries of Rwanda and Burundi were inextricably intertwined. The daily influx of Rwandan refugees, who by now numbered over 200,000 in Burundi, certainly affected the nation to which I was assigned. More importantly, however, at gut level I was unwilling to let notions of good manners and proper procedure assume more importance than an effort to save human lives. This was not my first time to face this problem.

In the first weeks after my arrival in Bujumbura, I had repeatedly visited northern Burundi's ever-expanding camps for Rwandan refugees. Unlike some camps in Zaire and Tanzania, these offered no military training for former Rwandan Armed Forces (FAR) troops planning to return and challenge the victorious RPA forces. All refugee camps in Burundi were under the watchful eye of Burundian Tutsi soldiers stationed there. The camp dwellers had no weapons and consisted mostly of women and children. Over and over, whenever my translator asked them the question, "When will you return to Rwanda?" their response had been, "When the RPA stops killing our people." It was both U.S. and UN policy to get the Rwandan refugees in Tanzania, Burundi, and Zaire voluntarily to go home—soon—immediately if possible. Unfortunately, that policy, besides seeking to avert instability in the surrounding countries and registering a belief that people usually thrive best when living in their own homes, also expressed a desire among developed countries to avoid the financial cost of feeding and housing refugees. Saving money was sometimes as important as saving lives.

The Tutsi-dominated Rwandan Patriotic Front (RPF), the political face of the Rwandan Patriotic Army (RPA), which had defeated the genocidal Hutu government forces in Rwanda, was broadcasting messages over the radio, encouraging Rwandans to return home. Indeed, its representatives went into the camps and claimed that the innocent would be accepted and safe on their return. Unfortunately, this was false. First, there was no system of justice in Rwanda to guarantee their safety; second, a volcano of revenge was bubbling all across that mountainous nation and erupting in countless villages.

The truth was that the refugees would not voluntarily return until they felt safe in doing so. In interviews, they repeatedly reported incidents of refugees returning from the camps to their homes and then disappearing, slain in revenge in their own villages. Still others had returned home, observed, and, realizing they would find no safety there, fled back to the camps in Burundi. Some had found their homes and farms burned or destroyed—or, more often, occupied by Rwandan Tutsis who had been living in exile for years while the Hutus were in power.

Knowing what I did, I could not remain silent. Equally, there was no point in broadcasting a message that would find no listeners. So I sought advice.

On October 21, Deputy Secretary of State Strobe Talbott and Assistant Secretary of State for African Affairs George Moose stopped in Burundi for a brief airport visit while refueling their airplane. They suggested that I prepare a cable with my observations, refer it to David Rawson, U.S. ambassador to Rwanda, for his clearance and comments, and then send the cable out more broadly.

Having already sent several cables critical of the RPA, I decided to telephone the desk officer responsible for Burundi and Rwanda in the State Department's Office of Central African Affairs. Bright and capable, he was also somewhat overloaded with the challenges of dealing with two impoverished countries, one that had experienced the largest genocide of the decade, and another that seemed precipitously close to collapse. Even knowing that, I was astonished at his response to my first-hand report: "Well, Mr. Ambassador, we get all sorts of numbers of dead from Rwanda and Burundi. However, the United Nations office in Rwanda reports that twelve people were killed, not 750, as you have been told." I replied as follows:

> Look, I've been in Africa long enough to understand that African peas-
> ants are not trained in quantifiable accuracy. However, these are not just
> peasants giving this report, but a school administrator responsible for the
> salaries and directing the operations of over twenty people—a man known
> to Pastor Hansen, who began living and working in these two countries
> over thirty years ago. And the school administrator himself, as well as the
> UNAMIR soldiers stationed there, approximated the dead at 750. I'm not
> saying the number is 750; it may be less, it may be more. But I am damn
> well certain that there were more than twelve people killed. This is simply
> a whitewash by the United Nations, which was unwilling to come to the
> aid of helpless people and now is unwilling to take responsibility for its
> inaction.

I was sufficiently outraged that, after one or two further conversations, the State Department agreed that Pastor Hansen and I could accompany Ambassador Rawson later that week to investigate together the site of the massacre.

When Pastor Hansen and I arrived at the designated meeting point in Rwanda on January 14, we were joined by the U.S. Defense Department attaché from the embassy in Kigali. Together, we all received a briefing from officers at the UNAMIR regional headquarters, and then boarded a heli-copter, which I had understood would take us to the site of the massacre, Camp Busanzwe. Once airborne, however, I found I had been deceived. The pilot circled the site, but had been instructed not to land. All that I could see below were some twigs and scraps and a bare spot on the hillside, where, until one week ago, some 9,000 displaced people had been encamped. I had, of course, expected to conduct a first-hand, feet-on-the-ground, visual in-spection, assisted by Pastor Hansen, who knew many people in the commu-nity, having ministered there only a few years ago. But obviously the United Nations and the U.S. Defense Department attaché did not want such an in-spection. I was unavoidably reminded of my experience a few months earlier with the Burundi Army, which had prevented an Amnesty International group, of which I had been a member, from investigating a massacre site at Kiri. Like the Burundi Army, the United Nations had something to hide—complicity (by inaction) in murder. But I wondered what the U.S. military had to hide.

Our group proceeded to a border location on Lake Kivu, where an RPA officer lectured us on their problems with Interahamwe (gangs of Hutu thugs) and former Rwandan Army troops crossing from Zaire into Rwanda, but refused to acknowledge any wrongdoing, or even involvement by the RPA, in the Busanzwe slaughter.

Equally unwilling to acknowledge any failure by his troops was the acting UN commander in Kigali, to whom I raised two concerns: one, that UNAMIR troops had failed to assist defenseless refugees under their protection; two, that the resulting deaths were far greater than the United Nations acknowledged.[1] The lamentable but unavoidable inference is that both UNAMIR and the RPA were seeking to hide a massacre that one committed, and that the other was unable to stop and unwilling to acknowledge.

On the first point, I had not only the testimony of refugees whom we had interviewed in Rubura, but also a handwritten report prepared for Pastor Hansen by Juvenal Nshimiyimana, the former rector of the college near Busanzwe, who visited the refugee camp on the day after the attack. His report confirmed that UNAMIR forces knew of the onslaught while it was underway but failed to respond to desperate pleas for assistance from camp residents. Only the next morning, he wrote, did UNAMIR forces go to the campsite. There, the RPA blamed the Interahamwe for the attack, a statement the rector called ridiculous: "*C'est une histoire à dormir debout!*" (It's a story that could make you fall asleep while standing.)

On the second point, I did not assert that the number of dead was 750, although that was the estimate most often repeated by the survivors. The rector's report, however, stated that the dead who had been *found* numbered 60 persons, killed by machetes, bayonets, and firearms, plus 17 bodies recovered from latrines during an inspection by resident UNAMIR troops, the UNHCR, the Red Cross, and other groups. His figures were therefore roughly a tenth of the estimates given by those who had fled to Rubura—yet they were over six times those of the United Nations. Regarding those numerical discrepancies, Pastor Hansen made two interesting observations. First, he mentioned that the resident UN commander had been staying in Nshimiyimana's house during the attack. (So possibly Nshimiyimana did not want to report the full extent of the slaughter.) And second, Hansen observed that the RPA often takes away the dead and buries them: "In the words of the Red Cross, they 'disappeared.' That's their way of saying they were killed and their bodies hidden. Tutsis are more clever than the Hutus in this. They hide the bodies."[2]

I realized with a certain sense of irony that I was witnessing the opposite of what reportedly happened during the Vietnam War. Then, U.S. military commanders were accused of exaggerating the "body count," that is, the number of Viet Cong and North Vietnamese we had killed. Here, the UN commander sought to underestimate the dead.

Unsatisfied as I was by his unwillingness to acknowledge any UN failure, I also felt sympathy for the UN commander's impossible task, since the international community had consistently denied him the mandate and the troops to defend the Rwandan populace. I knew then, and was to learn more fully later, that six months before the Rwandan genocide began, Brigadier-General Roméo A. Dallaire of Canada, the first head of UNAMIR, had requested the authority to use active military force if necessary, a request to which the UN Security Council declined to respond. At the very time that my own country learned, in mid-April 1994, that over 200,000 people had been killed in two weeks (a number of dead equal to approximately half the total number of U.S. lives lost in four years of fighting during the Second World War), the United States had sought to withdraw *all* United Nations forces from Rwanda. Meanwhile, the UN Security Council, stubbornly unwilling to acknowledge the extent and intent of the killing lest it then be obliged to take action to reduce it, continued its refusal to call this colossal slaughter "genocide." I was to learn later that in May 1994 a United Nations reconnaissance mission had recommended sending 4,500 troops to Rwanda, and the U.S. delegation to the UN had been instructed instead to suggest cutting that force by 98 percent and sending simply a symbolic contingent of 100 troops. The response from the rest of the international community was generally no better. Regrettably, when a population is poor, isolated, uneducated, uninfluential, silent, and largely unknown—and black—foreign governments can easily consider their lives unimportant.

In April 1994, at the height of the Rwandan genocide, it is indisputably documented that UN soldiers who had been protecting thousands of largely Tutsi civilians at Amahoro Stadium and the École Technique at Gicukiro simply abandoned their charges to waiting Hutu *génocidaires*. What happened at Nishili displayed a similar attitude of UN indifference or helplessness. The difference was that this time the dead numbered in the tens or hundreds, not thousands. And this time the killers were vengeful Tutsis in the RPA instead of murderous Hutus in the FAR.

In all this sorry experience there was one additional dimension evoked by the RPA slaughter that I found particularly galling: the attitude of the U.S. military toward the RPA and its leader, Vice President and Minister of Defense Paul Kagame, the military strongman who was the real head of government in Rwanda then and who today has achieved the title of president as well. I had been given the opportunity to meet Kagame a few months earlier, and left that meeting convinced that for those who hoped for an expansion of democracy and justice, he was one of the more dangerous leaders in the region.

During a visit to Burundi in September 1994, Ambassador Rawson and Tim Wirth, my friend and former congressional colleague, who was by then undersecretary of state, knowing my reservations about the RPA, had invited me to join them in a suddenly arranged visit with Vice President Kagame the next day. I immediately accepted. And my first trip to Kigali, Rwanda's capital, was revealing. After landing at the airport, which seemed to be run entirely by expatriates, we drove into town. Along the streets, more than half the buildings were without windows, their shattered glass often still lying on the streets and sidewalks. Everything about the city—the unavailability of water; the uncertainty of electricity; the sometimes-cratered streets, grounds, and buildings—revealed exactly what Kigali was: a war zone just beginning to rebuild.

Arriving for our appointment with Kagame just at twilight, we were ushered through a variety of military checkpoints into a large, somewhat shadowy, spartan office with cement floors and walls. The only striking thing in the room was Paul Kagame, whose appearance suggested Svengali or perhaps Mephistopheles—some magician or sorcerer. He was wearing a dark, almost black, suit that hung from his body as though both the coat and trousers were three sizes too large. He might have resembled a scarecrow, except that he looked less robust. He appeared to be about six feet tall and weighed perhaps 135 pounds. His exceptionally slender frame reminded me of photos I had seen of earlier Rwandan royalty. His shirt collar, like his suit, was too large, causing his tie to hang loosely, and his exceptionally long fingers emerged from the end of his too-large coat sleeves to gesture and reinforce the twenty-five-minute monologue with which he responded to Tim's opening remarks.

Kagame was shrewd, well spoken, and careful. He acknowledged that vengeful killing was underway, but indicated that it would take a long time to allay the suspicions that permeated Rwandan society; nevertheless, he deftly assured us, the perpetrators of injustice would ultimately be brought to account. But when it came to responding specifically to Tim's questions, he resolutely avoided taking responsibility for RPA misdeeds, and at one point said, "About the HCR report of bodies in the river, no one else has seen them. Nor have there been any sightings of bodies going into Uganda. Who has seen these things?" I was tempted to respond, "Millions of people around the world have seen television footage of these bodies floating into Lake Victoria in Uganda," but I waited until it was my turn to speak.

Then, when I asked about reports of Rwandan troops entering Burundi, he did not deny the charge, but excused it by saying they may have been prompted to do so by foreign troops. When I reported that his countrymen in refugee camps had indicated they would not voluntarily return to Rwanda as long as the RPA indiscriminately slaughtered Hutus, he did not directly deny the slaughter; nor did he admit it. Instead, he suggested that such killing could result from the troops desiring vengeance rather than from their acting under orders. While I did not challenge that possibility, I pointed out that the RPA had decisively defeated the FAR partly because, unlike its opponents, the RPA was known to be strictly and powerfully disciplined:

> One European ambassador told me that the former Government of Rwanda troops were like Pancho Villa's ragtag army, often drunk and always wild. Yours, by contrast, he described as being like the Khmer Rouge: merciless, well trained, and Stalinist in discipline. If they were that disciplined before, it's hard for me to believe they would not follow your orders now.

Kagame demurred, but he did not deny. He was more honest with me than the UN had been. Yet as we left his office and walked down the concrete steps into the darkened streets of Kigali, I knew there would be no equal justice for all, no democracy, and no liberty as long as Kagame was the country's strongest leader.

How U.S. military leaders had become so enamored of him, I could not fully fathom. Yes, I understood that he had won a classic military campaign, taking a small, disciplined, well-trained guerilla force and winning a swift victory over an undisciplined and often better-equipped national army several times its size. And he was one of the U.S. military's own people: he had been trained at Fort Leavenworth, Kansas. I knew too that Kagame was clever and spoke English well, and therefore could communicate effectively and convincingly with Americans and many other Westerners. But I was appalled that these skills had so successfully overshadowed his obvious preference for dictatorship over democracy, and his tolerance, or perhaps appetite, for vengeful ethnic slaughter. Yet he was invited to the United States to be feted at the Pentagon. In time, I was sure that the truth about the RPA would come out. But how many lives would be lost, how much suffering endured, how much fear and despair would be borne in the interim?

I did not know then that the carnage wrought by Kagame's RPF and RPA had been well documented, nor that, unfortunately, the documentation had been suppressed.

In September 1994, I first heard that a report being prepared by Robert Gersony for the UNHCR documented massive slaughter by the RPA of defenseless civilians. When I asked to see the report, two very high-level officials at the State Department replied that it was thought to be unreliable, and hence would remain undistributed. A truer explanation is that the report was squelched and buried because it conveyed truths that the United Nations in particular and the international community in general did not wish to be known. Alison Des Forges, in *Leave None to Tell the Story: Genocide in Rwanda,* recounts what happened:

THE GERSONY MISSION

The first convincing evidence of wide-spread, systematic killings by the RPF was gathered by a UNHCR team dispatched for another purpose. When the team and the head of the UNHCR attempted responsibly to bring the information to the attention of the international community, the UN decided to suppress it, not just in the interests of the recently established Rwandan government but also to avoid further discredit to itself. The U.S., and perhaps other member states, concurred in this decision. . . .

After the RPF victory, the UNHCR sent a three person mission headed by Robert Gersony to find ways to speed the repatriation of the nearly two million refugees. . . . Gersony remarked that he had begun the work with high regard for the RPF, which he believed to be the most highly disciplined force he had encountered in years of fieldwork in Africa. . . . Although he and his team did not set out to gather information on RPF abuses, they became convinced . . . that the RPF had engaged in "clearly systematic murders and persecution of the Hutu population." . . . They found the information provided by witnesses detailed and convincing and they confirmed the most important parts of accounts by independent sources in other camps or inside Rwanda. . . .

They reported massacres following meetings convoked by the authorities, murders committed by assailants who went from house to house, and . . . ambushes and massacres of persons trying to flee across the border to Burundi. They stated that the victims were killed indiscriminately, with women, children, the elderly, and the handicapped being targeted as well as men. They concluded that "the great majority of these killings had apparently not been motivated by any suspicion whatsoever of personal participation by victims in the massacres of Tutsi in April 1994." . . .

Gersony himself reportedly estimated that during the months from April to August the RPF had killed between 25,000 and 45,000 persons. . . . Gersony reported the results of his mission to Madame Sadako Ogata, the UN High Commissioner for Refugees, who in turn informed the secretary-general. Boutros-Ghali and some of his subordinates were concerned not just about the extent of the abuses alleged and the eventual impact of the information on the still fragile Rwandan government, but also about the negative publicity for UNAMIR and other UN agencies. . . . He directed Kofi Annan . . . (to) go to Rwanda. . . . Annan, apparently at Boutros-Ghali's direction, reportedly informed the Rwandan prime minister that the UN would do its best to minimize the attention given to Gersony's findings. . . . In the meantime, the information would be treated as awaiting confirmation—that is, it would be kept confidential. . . . Gersony was told to write no report and he and his team were directed to speak with no one about their findings. . . . When the representative of the [UN] special rapporteur tried in April 1996 to obtain more information about Gersony's findings from the UNHCR, he received a curt reply stating: "We wish to inform you that the 'Gersony Report does not exist.'"

Faced with full and horrifying information about a genocide where the moral and legal imperative to act was overwhelming, major actors at the UN and in various national governments had failed to intervene. Burdened with the guilt of this failure, they confronted a more complex situation when Gersony revealed the apparent extent of RPF killings.[3]

What we have, in simple terms, is guilt and cover-up. The United Nations and the United States bear the major responsibility for burying the Gersony report and hiding the horrors committed by the RPA. But nations everywhere—in Africa, Europe, Asia, and the Western Hemisphere—watched with disbelief and denial as one of the largest genocides since the Second World War proceeded in April 1994. Thus, indifference to genocide in April spawned a series of cover-ups of RPA massacres for months thereafter. Not wanting to help those in anguish led to not wanting the world to know the truth: there were no white hats for the Rwandan Patriotic Army.

NINE

TELLING THE TRUTH DRAWS
THREATS OF ASSASSINATION

During the week of January 7–14, 1995, amidst planning with Pastor Hansen for our trip that Saturday to the massacre site at Camp Busanze, I was visited at my office by Niels Nielsen, a tall lean man with graying hair and quiet manner whom I had met briefly at the Bujumbura Airport a few months earlier. He seemed familiar now because his was the Danish voice that had answered Pastor Hansen's radio call asking for UN trucks to evacuate the Rwandans from Rubura. Together, these two Scandinavian missionaries had knotted a lifeline that had rescued several hundred refugees.

Nielsen's request was simple: could I help the people of Butaganzwa, a commune (or region) forty miles north of Bujumbura, where the local Burundian Baptist minister had reported terrible killings of peasants living on the hillsides? They had contacted the provincial governor, but nothing had been done. Would I see what I could do?

I listened closely, then responded, "Pastor Nielsen, I have gone into the countryside many times—and heard of many massacres. I have then returned to meet with the army chief of staff or the minister of defense, to relate what I have heard. And their response is always the same: '*Ah, Monsieur l'Ambassadeur, c'est la rumeur.*' (Ah, Mr. Ambassador, that's just a rumor.)

"I will go to Butaganzwa if you want me to. But if I go, you must find someone who is from the region, speaks Kirundi, and is trusted by the people, to accompany me. I will take a camera to photograph the bodies. I will take a tape recorder, and we will interview people, find witnesses, get the names of the dead, get facts and dates so that no one can say to me again, '*Monsieur l'Ambassadeur, c'est la rumeur.*' If that's acceptable, I'll do it."

"That's absolutely acceptable," he replied.

Only two days later, he had found the person I required—a Burundi University professor of physics. Knowing that I needed to go soon, before bodies and witnesses disappeared, we set the date for Tuesday, January 17.

So, Tuesday morning, promptly at 6:30 a.m., a battered blue Toyota showed up at our home, and the guards admitted Prosper Mpawenayo. Waiting with me to greet him was Chris Reilly, our security officer, who wanted to look over the person who would be joining us. Stepping from the car with a broad smile of gleaming white teeth breaking from his round black face, his hand extended toward mine, was one of the most remarkable people I was to meet in Burundi. "Good morning, Mr. Ambassador," he said in accented English. "Good morning, *amahoro*," I replied. But that ended my use of Kirundi, and I was greatly relieved to realize that he would be translating from Kirundi into English, not French.

We walked over to the paillotte at the end of the garden, where Marcien had set the table with a white damask tablecloth, gold-seal china, sterling silver, embassy crystal, and fresh flowers. After a glass of rose-colored, freshly squeezed guava juice, Marcien offered us, from a silver tray, golden rings of fresh pineapple, brilliant orange mango diced into small squares, and freshly cut small bananas, which he followed with superb eggs Benedict. We hardly seemed dressed for his elegant table, each of us in khakis, a short-sleeved shirt, and shoes with thick soles and rubber cleats for the hillsides that lay ahead.

By 7:00 a.m. I was behind the wheel of the Toyota Land Cruiser that had the biggest engine and the strongest two-way radio of any embassy vehicle. Prosper sat at the right front so that I could be briefed and directed, and Chris sat behind. With an American flag flying on the Toyota's front fender, we left Bujumbura on the familiar Highway 1 North, then at Bugarama turned off the paved highway and onto a red-dirt road that continued over mountain streams on rough log bridges. The green hillsides, sometimes grassy, sometimes forested, were by now familiar, but as we moved deeper into the commune of Butaganzwa, I was struck by the absence of people.

"Where are all the people?" I asked Prosper.

"They are hiding; they are afraid. There are very few cars or trucks in this region. When the peasants hear one, they fear it is the army coming to hunt them, so they hide behind the trees and watch," Prosper said.

I decided to change the subject, and learn more about Prosper.

"Prosper, how old are you?" I asked.

"Forty-four," he replied.

"You're a Hutu, aren't you, Prosper?"

"Yes," he said, smiling.

"Prosper, how can you be forty-four, and highly educated, and a Hutu? I've been told that in 1972 Micombero killed almost all the Hutus age sixteen and above who were educated. And people at the embassy told me that almost all Hutu leaders in Parliament and elsewhere are therefore age thirty-eight or less. How could you be forty-four, educated, a Hutu, and alive?"

"I was lucky. There were 200 Hutus in the University of Burundi in 1972, when the massacre began. Only four of us survived," he said. (Four out of two hundred—2 percent survived, 98 percent killed, I automatically calculated.) "Can you tell me about it, Prosper? I mean *all* about it. Tell me your story. I want to know."

Prosper grew up in the green hillsides of Butaganzwa, barefoot, in a simple mud house with hard cow-dung floors and, of course, without running water or electricity. His life was impoverished according to the standards of the world, yet as the son of a schoolteacher, he had more food and more opportunities than most of Burundi's children, and he managed to be on the very small list of Hutus who comprised about 10 percent of the student body at the nation's only university.

While Prosper was studying at the university, the mad misanthropic dictator Micombero devised his plan for continuing Tutsi hegemony in Burundi. As recounted in Chapter 2, the plan was brutally simple. He would kill all Hutu intellectuals—i.e., anyone who could read and write, above the age of fifteen—and thereby guarantee a generation of Tutsi rule. Since almost all Africans hold education in high esteem, perhaps because of their tradition of venerating the wisdom of elders, they tend to look to those who can read and write and have received formal education as their natural and appropriate leaders. In executing the Hutu intellectuals, Micombero was thereby effectively decapitating the Hutu body politic.

When the massive killing began, Micombero had the army gather Hutus from villages all across the country. Some were told that they were being taken to defend the king against usurpers. Others were told nothing, except to board the army trucks. And such was the docility of people who had long thought of themselves as obedient serfs that most obeyed unquestioningly. They were then driven away, executed, and buried in mass graves. They simply "disappeared."

In 2003, I interviewed Leonce Hakizimana, a former Burundian Hutu refugee, now an American citizen living in Chicago, who recalled that period in 1972: "I was seven years old, living in a village in northern Burundi. I was going to church with my mother on Sunday morning. As we approached the church, she saw a truck, where two soldiers were telling the young boys to get into the truck: they would be taken to play games. My mother stopped, turned around, and said we were going home. I didn't know what was happening, but she did. I never saw any of my friends again."

"Do you know how they died? Were they shot?" I asked.

"I don't know, but I don't think so. I think they were dropped into a trench and covered with rocks and earth," he said.

"But didn't anyone resist?" I inquired.

"Probably not," he answered. "As Hutus, we were trained to think of ourselves as being less than Tutsis. Even after I had a university education and was head of an organization, whenever I had Tutsis present as part of the group, I always felt intimidated, always felt inferior. That's just the way it was. We all felt that way."

The largest slaughter was in Bujumbura itself. There, in the evenings, massive numbers of Hutus were brought into the stadium by trucks, lined up before firing squads, and killed. A European expatriate who used binoculars to watch the killings from his balcony, and a Burundian who was saved at the last minute, both related a particularly gruesome story: at one period, to save scarce ammunition, the army tied the hands and feet of its victims, then drove heavy army trucks over their bodies to crush them to death. Their bodies were then taken away, many to be buried in mass graves near the present airport.

Prosper, after four consecutive nights of killing in Bujumbura when the genocide began, escaped from his University of Burundi dormitory in the early morning hours, when all were asleep, and made his way to his aunt's house in the city, where he hid in her attic for twenty-five days. To enable his escape from Burundi, he managed to obtain a forged Zairian passport. But a problem remained: the Zairois of this region spoke Swahili, as did some Burundians, but Prosper, being from the north, knew only Kirundi and French.

The Zairian border town of Uvira at the broad head of Lake Tanganyika was only fourteen miles away. He needed to get there without being picked up by the soldiers, who, if they realized he could not speak Swahili, would know that he was Burundian, not Zairois. So his aunt found a Zairois to accompany and speak for him as they walked toward Uvira. Three times en route they were stopped and questioned by soldiers. Three times the Zairois spoke, in Swahili, for both of them, while Prosper pretended to be deaf. Three times he was successful. His life depended on it.

From eastern Zaire, where much of the population identifies itself as Hutu, Prosper gained safe passage to Rwanda, where the government and university were headed by Hutu leaders. There he formed part of the tiny diaspora of Burundian Hutus who had escaped Micombero, and who began through their discussions, frustrations, and hopes to form plans to return to Burundi one day and establish democracy. Many of the later Hutu leaders, including future presidents Ndadaye and Ntibantunganya, and future prominent parliamentarians and cabinet members, emerged from this group.

Prosper was more given to physics than politics, and from the University of Rwanda won admission to the University of Turin, in Italy, where, writing his thesis in Italian, he earned a doctorate in physics. He then returned to the University of Rwanda, where he taught for over a decade, until the day after Melchior Ndadaye was elected. On that day, the newly elected president phoned to say, "Prosper, it's time to come home. Your country and your people need you. Please come back to teach at the University of Burundi." Prosper returned home the next day.

It was an awesome pilgrimage—from deaf and silent to doctor of philosophy in physics—and now, vice rector of the university. And I didn't want to be responsible for ending his journey. Pausing, as his story sank into my consciousness, I said, "Prosper, you know that there may be some risk in what we are doing. I am the representative of the world's most powerful country, and the risk for me is not very great. But for you it must be much higher. I won't ask you to do anything you don't want to do. But, very simply, are you sure you want to undertake this?"

"Mr. Ambassador," he replied, "my name is already on the death lists. They may get me or they may not. But if I can do something to end the murder and injustice in this country, I want to do it."

"Fine, that's all I needed to know."

After driving for twenty minutes or so without seeing a single person, we sighted a man near a hand pump, drawing water from a nearby stream. As he heard our approach, he turned to walk quickly away, but we stopped and Prosper called to him. As Prosper, speaking in Kirundi, explained our purpose, showed the man the American flag flying on the front fender, and assured him that we posed no danger, the tension in his body visibly relaxed, and he soon began to speak animatedly. I got out, pocket notebook in hand, ready to learn whatever I could. He took us to the nearby stream, where the day before he had seen several bodies floating slowly amid the reeds, but at the moment he did not know their location. As we spoke, mysteriously, as if they had emerged from the ground itself, four more people appeared, having come out of hiding. Recognizing that we were not the army, they had willingly come forth.

We then proceeded to our appointment with Gabriel Wakana, an administrator appointed by the national government to serve as an examiner of schools in the province of Kayanza. Wakana reported that during January 4–5 there had been widespread, indiscriminate killing by the military throughout the region. He first showed us the small abandoned farmhouse of an elderly couple killed the previous week; their bodies had been thrown into a latrine to make a proper burial impossible. I explained that I needed, where possible and appropriate, to take photographs of bodies so that I could refute the charges that I was responding only to rumor. He therefore took me to a spot nearby, where a local peasant dug up and unearthed the legs and trunk of a body from which the head and arms had been cut off by the soldiers two weeks earlier. Next followed our interview with Claver Nuruhasanzwe, whose father's body still lay unburied among some banana trees; he had been slaughtered earlier that morning.

The school administrator explained that on January 1 the *bandes armées* (Hutu rebel groups), who make guerrilla attacks on the army but also act as self-appointed vigilantes, had come into the area, captured one Tutsi civilian, and taken him to a nearby commune, where he very likely had been killed. The military then came, and for "two long days (January 4–5) started to kill whoever was around." After their departure, he added, "The governor of the province came for a popular meeting, what is commonly here in Burundi called a pacification meeting, and declared that in this zone, whoever is living here, young or old person, is to be killed. And he said we are expressing ourselves against [i.e., we are opposing] the governor. But we are expressing against his administration because we do not want to respond to his call for any pacification meetings because whenever he is holding such meetings, killings do always follow."

I was told that the *conseiller* (a local administrator) had run away but was killed, and his body buried only yesterday.

In one hour, Prosper had entered the names of ten people in one group (including two small children), plus an elderly couple, a local administrator, and two farmers, totaling fifteen people who had certainly been killed during the army's two-day spree. That was our introduction to the hellish experience that the people of Commune Butaganzwa had so recently undergone on Colline Ninga.

From Colline Ninga we drove a mile or so farther to the Catholic mission at Buraniro. As we came down the hill, before us appeared a perfect African sylvan scene. Poplars, sycamores, and eucalyptuses, shedding their mottled white bark, sent lofty limbs skyward, swaying with quivering leaves. Below, a small clear swift-running stream cut through the heart of the village. On this side stood a substantial redbrick sanctuary with smaller church offices set alongside. Just across the stream stood a one-story redbrick school building, its glass windows suggesting a prosperity unusual in Burundi. The area was quiet except for a few children playing on the mission grounds. Father Dominic, an Italian priest who had served in Burundi for twenty-two years, greeted us, and he and I walked inside together, arm in arm, to a plain cement-floored office, where Father Dominic had gathered several people from the community to assist and augment his narration of events during the past two weeks. Although the weather was warm, I noticed that he deliberately closed the door. If those present were going to relate the truth, they should at least be protected from inquiring ears and eyes.

Father Dominic began by acknowledging that after President Ndadaye's assassination, the Hutu majority perpetrated terrifying massacres against the small group of Tutsis in the region. When their killing was complete, the Hutus composed, by his estimate, 96–98 percent of the remaining regional population. And since Commune Butaganzwa had always been overwhelmingly Hutu, those Tutsis who remained, approximately 200–250, were placed in a déplacé camp near the river. For a year after the presidential assassination and the attendant killings, the region had been essentially quiet. However, late in December 1994, Tutsi déplacés from Buraniro and other regions had been brought into an area adjoining an existing military camp just across the stream. The priest estimated the number at 2,000, but others called out, "No, not that many."

By January 4, violence in which the army and déplacés cooperated had already begun. Father Dominic explained, "They [the déplacés] were armed with machetes and were stopping people who were passing by, and they tried to kill two persons, and the others had to pay whatever they had on their own, let's say money or watches, everything they could get . . . but stealing started later, they started going around looting, and we could see people coming with everything they could steal from the houses."

"Is there some way that you know these are the déplacés that are doing this?" I asked.

"Certainly, because the mission is just in front of the camp and we could see the people coming to the camp from those houses . . . and on the 8th we could see the military lorry . . . bring everything they could take from the Bumba market to the camp. And if you go there now, you can see they took two classes to stock everything they had stolen from the houses."

"Two what?"

"Two classrooms, yes. Because the camp is just close to the primary school, and they didn't have anywhere to stock all these things that they have stolen. They went into the classrooms to stock their things there that they had stolen."

"Do those classrooms still have the goods there?"

"Yes, they are still there."

"Good. Maybe tomorrow we can go and have a look at those after we have looked at some other things."

The local people shouted, "Yes, yes, yes."

In spite of what I had already seen, this was hard to swallow: children driven out of classrooms and denied their education so that goods stolen from these children's homes, by their own nation's army and its accomplices, might be stored there.

Father Dominic concluded by saying that he and his assistants had visited every house in Buraniro Parish and he could offer an accurate accounting. On Kigwandi Hill, 263 houses had been looted; on Bwiza Hill, 101 houses—all in the period from January 4–8. Some houses had been burned afterward, but most had not. Yet, during those four days, the priests had buried thirty-one people from these two collines alone. I painstakingly recorded the names of the dead, the collines on which they had lived, and when I could, a few minor details about the people themselves.

A tour past the déplacé and military camps, and both a walking and driving tour to view a selection of the 364 houses that had been looted was enough for the moment. I needed to get home before curfew. But we promised to return the next day.

Father Dominic added, "We have been waiting [for] somebody from Bujumbura since last week because we couldn't stop the killing. It was going on, and we were asking if there was somebody coming from outside so as to see, because they [the killers] don't like to see people coming from outside and to see what they have done [laughter from those present]. This is the only way to stop them."

"The only way to stop them is to have someone coming from outside?" I asked.

"Yes."

"And to have the events reported?"

"Yes, yes."

The next morning, Prosper, Chris, and I were on the road early, heading toward Province Kayanza, Commune Butaganzwa, Zone Ninga, Colline Kigwandi. Overnight, without radios, telephones, or any modern means of communication, word had spread through the commune of our visit. Whereas people had hidden from our car on the day before, today, with our small American flag flying as we barreled down the red-dirt road, peasants ran toward us. Waiting and waving to us by the hand pump at the stream was a small group of residents. We stopped, and speaking excitedly in Kirundi, they took us to the stream to show us the bodies of two men caught in the reeds; we photographed them, although we did not know their names.

We proceeded to a spot near the top of Colline Kigwandi, where we expected to meet the provincial administrator whom we had seen the previous day. But after waiting forty minutes, we struck out on our own. Whether because of intimidation or inconvenience, Wakana did not show up. Our immediate problem was that there was no road leading all the way into the areas we wished to reach. So I put the Land Cruiser into four-wheel drive, and by following a cattle trail, we made our way through the stones and underbrush across the mountaintop and down the hillside. Twenty minutes later, in an otherwise clear and grassy section, we came to a large, forty-foot tree that had fallen across the track. The cows could get around it. We couldn't. The incline sloping down from the cattle trail, though grassy, was too steep for our car to avoid overturning, and the tree was far too heavy for us to lift, nor did we have cables and a winch to pull the tree out of our path. We felt stumped, stopped, and discouraged. And then, on the trail ahead, a group of hillside residents appeared, one with a crude axe, another with a machete. Already familiar with our mission, they immediately set about to chop through the tree, almost two feet in diameter at the point it fell across our path. In forty-five minutes, after paying a modest sum, we were once more on our way along the cattle trail, with one of the local woodcutters acting as our guide. But as we made our way down from the broader uplands, the undergrowth got higher, the path narrower, and as we twisted our way down for another fifteen minutes, we finally came to a halt, got out, and began to walk. By this time, a group of seven or eight people, including children, wanted to take us to the first site. This was not an area of terraced farms, but of hillsides covered with scrub, small trees, and grass. We had seen some cattle above, but here there was no evidence of crops or animals to support the population. How these people sustained themselves, I could not fathom.

After picking our way down the mountainside for an hour (a distance of about two miles), we found the first cluster of mud-brick huts, our destination. I spoke into my hand-held tape recorder: "I am approaching a spot high on a hill in Banga, and the smell of death is already beginning. I just saw a dog run away. Very likely it's been chewing on bodies. Soon I'm sure we will be upon the bodies. We have gone down a very steep descent to get here. Somebody had to go to a lot of trouble to kill these people."

We got closer, and the stench of human flesh that had been rotting for ten days was as powerful, unique, and odious as I had often been told it was. Even the locals were standing back. Before me, in a slight clearing, was a simple rectangular thatch-roofed house. Lying outside, covered with once

A forty-foot tree fallen across the track, preventing our car's passage, 1995.

brightly colored, now soiled and stained, blankets, were two bodies—the head, hands, and feet covered with straw.

As everyone stood back in silence, I took a deep breath, expecting the stench to become even worse as I walked closer to the bodies. I walked about twenty yards across the hard-packed earth to stand over the body of a man who had been killed on January 8. One man joined me to pull back the blanket.

I then spoke into the recorder: "We have just pulled back the straw covering the body of a man with most of his head gone. I guess the head had been attacked, and the name of the man is Ngayabosha. . . . You can see his head is entirely broken apart, and it is obviously a horrible sight."

I was standing over and staring down at a bare skull, which looked, except for the fractures, like the skulls I had seen years ago in a college science class, and occasionally in museums. Yet the death of this peasant, Ngayabosha, was much more real to me. When looking at other skulls, I had thought of history, anatomy, or science. Here, viewing the yellowing skin stretched over the bones of his arms, hands, bare legs, and feet, my nostrils battling the stench from the still-decaying flesh on his trunk, it was not history or science but mortality that I saw and sensed before me.

Once the straw was removed, the villager who had assisted me stepped back. How long I stood over the body, simply contemplating it, I do not know. But it must have been at least a couple of minutes, because when I looked up, I saw all the group, gathered in a little semicircle, gazing quizzically at me.

From there I walked over to the body of a child, and recorded the following: "We have just looked at a father and child. We have pulled back the blankets; their bodies are still lying in front of their house. The man standing here is from this area. He is going to give his understanding of what happened.

Following is Prosper's translation: "It was Sunday, the 8th of January, when soldiers came from Buraniro and started shooting in the air. The population was afraid, and started running away, according to Bukuru who has just given this in Kirundi: 'When they run away, some people [were] left in

Local peasants guide us to a massacre site, 1995.

A villager removing straw and blankets with a long stick because the smell of decaying human flesh is so repugnant, Butaganzwa, 1995.

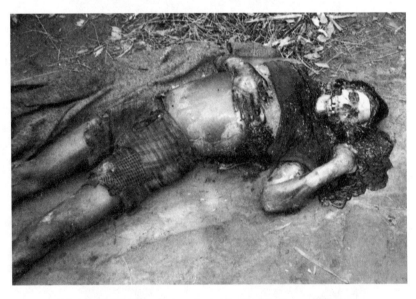

Ngayabosha's decaying body, unburied for ten days, Butaganzwa, 1995.

Bob contemplating Ngayabosha's body, Butaganzwa, 1995.

their homes. Soldiers, accompanied by the déplacés, entered the homes and killed whoever was still around.'"

As I was led behind the house to the body of a woman, I spoke into my recorder: "I am standing by the body of a woman who has had her skull cut away . . . a woman from the area is going to give her understanding of what happened. . . . Did she see this herself . . . with her own eyes?

Translator: Yes.

By this time, ten more people had gathered around. Two young women, Primitive Itangishaka and Cecile Ndayirukiye, both barefoot and wrapped in traditional cloth skirts that nearly touched the ground, came forward with their stories: "It was on January 8 when, at 4:45 a.m., a group of fifteen militaries came with déplacés from Buraniro. Four of them blocked the rear entrance of the house of Primitive, and four others stopped the front entrance of the same house. Seven others were some ten meters above the house, and when those militaries came, they shoot and those people afraid went out. And the militaries said they should remain outside. They [the soldiers] denied them the right to go back in their houses. And they started killing the persons. . . . They attempted to kill her [Primitive] before she run. She was bearing her baby in her arms. And she was asked to put down her baby and take off all clothes. She is at the time with pregnancy. . . . Primitive tried successfully to escape, but militaries made fire [fired guns] behind her, after

A log bridge of questionable strength. Photo by Judy Walgren, 1994. Courtesy of the Dallas Morning News ©.

her, but she succeeded to run away. The militaries attempted to kill her, but by chance, as people were moving around, the militaries went and did not continue to pay attention on her and she run away."

"Was she able to take her child too?" I asked.

"No, the child has been killed. When she run away, she left the child, and that is the child who has been killed, Micheline."

During the attack, Prosper explained, the soldiers had been standing by to protect the déplacés, who with their machetes and hoes were killing the people.

After a two-mile uphill walk to our Toyota, we descended the mountain slowly, grateful for six-ply tires that made it without a puncture. Finding a two-track road, we drove to a stream only ten yards wide but with high banks, spanned by a bridge hewn out of logs. We got out, examined the bridge, jumped up and down on it, but wondered if it would hold the car's weight. If not, we would be in a mess getting the Land Cruiser out of the stream. With everyone else out of the car, I inched the Toyota across, listening, as I passed over each log, for the splitting sound of a tire falling through. But there was no problem, and we continued on to a small village of thirty or forty people.

As they pressed forward to tell their stories, my attention focused on

*Cuts from a knife or machete all across Louis Ntawarushwashaka's scalp,
still unhealed, Butaganzwa, 1995.*

Louis Ntawarushwashaka, whose name translates as "nobody wants to be
miserable." Appearing to be in his seventies, he was stooped and wrapped
in only a blanket, his lean and sinewy shoulders and upper body partially
exposed. His head was bald, except for a bit of short curly black hair glistening in the morning sun. Around his head flies were buzzing, for all across his
scalp were cuts, still unhealed, from someone's knife or machete. What could
have prompted an attacker to hack this harmless man and leave him for dead
I did not know, and Prosper never asked. We did learn, however, that he had
received no medical attention, so we took Ntawarushwashaka and his teen-
age companion to a nearby hospital at Musema.

There we were greeted by a young physician, Dr. Isaac Minani, who promised to treat Ntawarushwashaka, and gave an account of the last two weeks.
Three or four members of the bandes armées had passed through the area
two weeks ago, robbing and threatening several families while demanding
food and shelter. The terrified villagers knew that if the army learned of the
bandes armées' presence, the revenge would be merciless. And indeed, once
the army learned and sent troops, the search for rebels was negligible, but the
vengeful burning and looting was fearsome, and quickly filled the hospital
with wounded survivors.

We met one victim outside: an eight-year-old boy whose arm had been snapped like a tree branch by the boot of a soldier. As a crowd of perhaps thirty peasants pushed forward to view these white strangers, I saw several boys whose hands, necks, or arms still showed dark red wounds where slices of flesh had been taken away.

The hospital, a simple but spacious brick structure without screens to seal the open windows from insects, had single iron beds lining its bare walls. As the doctor introduced me to a twelve-year-old girl, he closed the door behind us, leaving the onlookers outside. Hakizimana and her mother delicately lifted her brightly colored cloth wrap to show me where she had been bayoneted in the abdomen. Nearby lay fifteen-year-old Mpawenimana, who had bayonet wounds in her back and breast. Both spoke impassively, respectfully: they were African children talking to their elders and strangers and did as they were asked. Perhaps that is why they allowed us to photograph their wounds—I don't know. What was immediately evident, however, was that most victims were women and children, probably because men can usually run faster and women are often slowed down by carrying children on their backs or in their arms. I took the names of those whom Doctor Minani knew to have been killed by the army and déplacés, but sought no count of the wounded, doubting that the hospital would have accurate records.

Less than two weeks later, on January 31, Dr. Minani came to my office to ask my help in finding him a new location in which to practice. Two nights earlier, a small band of armed Hutus had passed through Butaganzwa and coerced the headmaster of the secondary school, Hilaire Niyibizi, whose home adjoined Minani's hospital, into providing them overnight lodging. On January 30 the army had learned this, and at 6:30 a.m. on the very day we spoke, January 31, troops arrived and killed Niyibizi in his home. As one of the most educated Hutus in the area, and an active member of Frodebu, Niyibizi was already a likely target, and under scrutiny. His providing shelter to a member of the bandes armées provided sufficient excuse for his execution, if any were needed.

But as another among the few educated Hutus in the community, Minani felt also at risk. That same morning a group of soldiers had commandeered the hospital ambulance from Minani's driver and sped away. Observing helplessly, Minani and his pharmacist (Prosper's brother) escaped into the hills for safety. Meanwhile, having heard the gunfire from the attack on the schoolmaster, the thirty-six patients in the hospital panicked and fled into the woods. Those incapable of moving themselves were carried away by others. And thus the only hospital in the area had been abandoned and shut down, and the only physician and pharmacist were seeking new employment.

My two days in Butaganzwa included numerous interviews, corpses, and

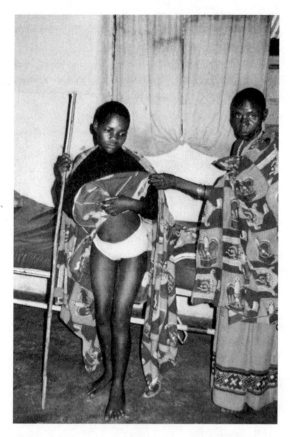

*Hakizimana, a twelve-year-old girl who had been bayoneted
in the abdomen, Musema, 1995.*

exhumations. My conscience was tugged from side to side. On one hand, I wanted irrefutable factual evidence of slaughter. On the other, when told that six people had been killed and buried in a mass grave, did I need to ask a young man to remove the earth covering the yellowed flesh and bones of his aunt and uncle, buried behind their house? I thought I did, and the survivors did not seem to mind. Violent death is so inescapably a part of their everyday life that they do not object if someone is trying to delay their experience of it. The ceremonies surrounding death in Burundi are very simple. Except for the very wealthy, the people are too poor to have embalming, wooden caskets, or gravestones. They simply dig a shallow grave, wrap the body in cloth, and cover it over with the earth—dust returns unto dust very quickly.

The cruelest example of ethnic revenge came late during my final after-

*A young man removed the earth covering the yellowed flesh
and bones of his aunt and uncle, who were buried behind
their house, Butaganzwa, 1995.*

noon. We approached a farm, more prosperous than most, where the farmhouse had four or five rooms and a bright tin roof that reflected the afternoon sun. The farmyard pens were formed with sturdy logs, and contained protective sheds for the animals; about twenty yards from the house, a sizeable pigpen was filled with a dozen or more grunting sows and boars and an ample number of tiny piglets scurrying after their mothers. The pigpen was located near the edge of a bluff about twenty feet high. The fronds of several tall banana trees growing at the base of the bluff reached above the pen and shaded its feeding troughs. A local resident took me to the edge of the bluff and pointed below. There, white maggots chewing away at their eyes and black features, the bodies of three small children were heaped next to those of their mother and grandmother. The ground around them was covered with green vines and growing foliage, but their bodies were rotting away where their attackers had dumped them. The pigs had been left to live, while the children had been left to die. I was told that this was the family of Savimbi, the code name for someone believed to be a leader of the FDD (one of the bandes armées). The army doubtless wanted to send a message of terror and overwhelming revenge. To me, it was a message of unbridled barbarism.

I had seen enough. In two days we had put together a list with the names and addresses (by hillsides) of fifty-nine people who had been slaughtered within a radius of perhaps five miles. Nothing had been reported in the press, locally or internationally. Indeed, little had been reported anywhere to civilian authorities. But then, it was increasingly evident that the civilian authorities had no authority. The authority was the authority of the gun, the machete, the bayonet, the army trucks, the blindés; the authority of a minority over a majority that in the past thirty years had run so wildly amok that peasants were faced with a killing machine, out of control, which was one of the few things that could be counted on to work in this otherwise very primitive society.

The task, then, was how to bring some modicum of relief to people who, as Father Dominic had said, felt their only hope was for someone from the outside to observe and then report what had happened. For me, the first task

The pigs had been left to live, while the children had been left to die, Butaganzwa, 1995.

Maggots chewed away at the children's features, Butaganzwa, 1995.

Bob recording survivors' tales, Butaganzwa, 1995.

was to convince the State Department that such horror should not go unacknowledged, that diplomatic immunity did not mean we should be immune from caring about human life, and that diplomatic courtesy did not mean looking the other way when children were slaughtered like pigs.

In all my elective offices—whether in the U.S. House of Representatives, the U.S. Senate, or the Texas Railroad Commission—I had been free to speak when I chose, knowing that my ultimate judge would be the voters, who, if they did not like what I was saying and doing, could replace me. Working in an appointive position with bureaucratic lines of authority is very different. I had learned after my initial press conference in Bujumbura, in August, that the State Department liked to grant approval before an ambassador held a press conference, and liked it much better if you never asked to hold one. Ambassadors are allowed to respond to inquiries from the local press (but preferably not from the international press), but should request approval before holding a press conference.

But as I was driving back, too outraged by what I had witnessed to feel that, in good conscience, I could remain silent, I decided upon a plan. RTNB, the national TV station, had inquired about interviewing me on the selection of a new prime minister. I could accept the interview, expand the subject matter to include national security, and thereby fall within State Department guidelines. So upon my return to Bujumbura, I sent a "front channel cable" (one receiving wide distribution) to Washington, and opened with a quotation from Martin Luther King: "Those who remain silent in the face of injustice become a party to that injustice." Clearly, I continued, my country would not wish its representative in Burundi to remain silent in the face of injustice; indeed, in a recent letter sent to all U.S. ambassadors, President Clinton had indicated the importance of human rights and of America's longstanding commitment to promoting democracy and justice around the world. So, marching with Martin Luther King on one arm and President Bill Clinton on the other, I informed the department that I had agreed to give a press interview that would reveal what I had discovered, and I would provide a list with names of the dead—who by that time numbered seventy—accompanied by photographs of some of the dead and wounded. The front-channel cable worked. No one called to say I couldn't give the interview.

After getting the photographs developed, the State Department's concurrence, and my speech translated into French, I held a press interview on January 27, 1995. While trying to be forthright about what I had seen, I nonetheless sought to take no sides in a political battle, and never mentioned political parties or ethnicity. But when asked by reporters whom I considered to be responsible for the attacks, I responded, "The people say it was men in uniform."

I acknowledged that murder occurred on both sides:

Most victims were women and children.

But these tiny children were not members of any bandes armées. They were neither concealing weapons nor firing them. They were too small even to have held them. And yet their skulls were split open and their throats bayoneted. Such actions are not bravery and they are not manly. They are pure cowardice.

Fortunately, the overwhelming majority of Burundians, both civilian and military, reject such actions.

There are bandes armées. These extremists are dangerous and destructive of peace. They attack the military, their families, and other citizens. Such violence and vengeance are absolutely wrong, and will postpone peace and understanding. These bandes are resented by most people. They know that when small bandes attack security forces, they inevitably provoke a larger counterattack. Then, it is not the bandes armées who suffer, but those, such as the ones I have photographed, who live in the path of the military response.

The bandes armées must be stopped. But they cannot be stopped by killing women and children. The military leadership must take full control of its troops, and make clear that those who violate international codes of human rights or of military behavior will be held accountable.

I concluded with an appeal to their recognition of what democracy should bring them:

You ask why I talk about this issue now. There are two answers. First, because what I have reported is true . . . second . . . because I believe in Burundi's democracy, and I therefore make a democratic response: that is, I call public attention to injustice. Then the people can tell their leaders that such actions are unacceptable. . . . The people have freedom of speech. It is a fundamental part of faith in democracy that, as the Bible says, if people know the truth, the truth shall set them free. Burundi has the institutions in place. It has elected government. It has substantial representation from many parties so that all views may be expressed. Now Burundi must use that democratic framework, which grants mutual respect and equal treatment under law to all, to bring its people the quality of life that they deserve. . . . Democracy is not a solution to problems. But democracy provides the best means of *finding* a solution to problems of any form of government, because it draws on the talents of all its people. In this worthwhile task, my nation stands ready to work with yours, to see that the potential of *all* its people is fulfilled.

In my judgment, there were consequences to this press conference. Of immediate importance, the military commander for the Butaganzwa region was changed two weeks later. The new commander, from the president's protective staff, was more trustworthy and temperate; therefore, some lives would be saved. I was finding that murderers do not like to have their identity revealed. Although going to the minister of defense and chief of staff of the army in private had done nothing, giving a press conference did.

The national radio and television gave significant but selective coverage to the conference: no pictures of the dead, no comments about the army, only my criticism of the Hutu bandes armées. When my public-affairs officer and I discussed this slanted coverage with the heads of the national TV and radio networks, they acknowledged that Tutsis had complete control over what was broadcast.

A high-level State Department person telephoned to congratulate me privately on the speech, calling it a "masterpiece." Then the same person wrote a cable, which would be part of the State Department public record, cautioning me against being seen as taking sides. For Burundi, that comment was entirely fatuous. If someone in the 1940s had spoken out about gas chambers, pogroms, and ethnic cleansing in Poland, everyone would know that the Nazis were the perpetrators and the Jews the victims. In Burundi, if one talks about slaughter by "men in uniform," everyone knows it is Hutus being slaughtered by Tutsis. True, the bandes armées are there—wicked, cruel, ineffective, and useless in bringing about worthwhile change—but the number of their killings was tiny compared to those of the army. Thus the only way to avoid offending the guilty would have been to say nothing: Chamberlain's policy of appeasement that served Hitler so well.

Although those who engage in murder do not like having their identities revealed, they nevertheless think in vengeful, murderous terms. The governor of Kayanza said in a public meeting, "If Ambassador Krueger returns to this area, he might very well have an accident on the road." The national radio station, in a Kirundi-language newscast, reported the following threat a few days later: "Governor Barazingiza said that Ambassador Krueger and company like to go to communes where there are gunmen, and if ever something happened to him, it will be the responsibility of those people who take him there."

Within two weeks, two Tutsi extremist, pro-Bagaza newspapers carried front-page stories saying that I deserved to be killed. In one, I had the company of my good friend UN special envoy Ahmedou Ould-Abdallah. *La Nation,* under the headline "Abdallah and Krugger [*sic*], Two Diplomats to Beat or Shoot Down" made the following statements:

> From time to time, diplomatic immunity is useless, particularly at a time of war—and we are at war. . . . The UN Secretary Dag Hammarjold [*sic*] was killed in Katanga in 1961. Reactions were fierce. Yet his death had no consequence whatsoever. The French Ambassador to Kinshasa was assassinated by the Zairian Army last year. France was outraged [but] the threats were stifled.
>
> Both foreign personalities were not killed for [nothing]. . . . It followed their interference in the internal affairs of Zaire. Today, Burundi risks being put on fire by these two diplomats [Ould-Abdallah and Krueger]. . . . In brief . . . [they] have not come to represent Boutros Ghali or Clinton in Burundi. They rather constitute a lobby of the Frodebu designed to demonize the opposition forces [i.e., the various Tutsi political parties] and above all mute them.
>
> The best piece of advice from Burundian patriots would be [for them to] leave as soon as possible. Otherwise, they should be shown—through demonstration or otherwise—that Burundi's honest citizenry doesn't want such . . . diplomats . . . a word to the wise is 'enough'!

The newspaper *Le Carrefour des Idées* (The Crossroads of Ideas) similarly called for my assassination on its front pages. Fortunately, our security officer, in reporting the headlines to the State Department, indicated that he did not believe that I was under any immediate threat: murderers seldom advertise their targets in advance. Nevertheless, Burundians live not only by murder but even more by intimidation and threat, and Ould-Abdallah and I were receiving treatment no different from that of many Burundians in public life. However, I would no more yield to their desire for my silence than I would yield to the same desire among some in the State Department.

I had drawn a line in the sand. Since the army had been unresponsive to my private approaches, I would go public with their atrocities. This chain of events was inevitable. First, no person of conscience could witness cruelty, injustice, and genocidal massacres and say, "It's none of my business." But after the television coverage of the bodies of dead American servicemen being dragged through the streets of Mogadishu, Somalia, I knew there would not be presidential, congressional, or popular support for unilateral

American military intervention. And without U.S. leadership, the United Nations would do nothing. My strongest card was therefore public disclosure of the daily slaughter in Burundi, largely unreported otherwise. I was convinced that only if the world knew of the killing and injustice would the people of Burundi be set free. Most importantly, a U.S. ambassador is the personal representative of the president of the United States, the leader of the most powerful nation in the world, and therefore is less at risk than any other person in the country. If he is unwilling to speak the truth, who will? It was not a complicated issue. There really was no choice.

I carried then in my wallet, and still do today, a statement that Winston Churchill made in his famous "Iron Curtain" speech in Fulton, Missouri, in 1947: "From what I have seen of our Russian friends and allies during the war, I am convinced that there is nothing they admire so much as strength and nothing for which they have less respect than weakness."

Bikomagu and the Burundi Army could not compete, in grand totals, with Stalin's seven million executions. But if one factored in that Stalin's slaughter drew from populations thirty times as large, and that he required over a decade to achieve those numbers, the killing rate of the Burundi Army could be seen to be far higher and far swifter than Stalin's troops and secret police had ever achieved. I reckoned that, like Stalin, Bikomagu respected strength more than weakness, and feared candor more than silence.

Fortunately, if I had offended some in the State Department and all in the Burundi Army, I had not offended the White House. The president himself, National Security Advisor Tony Lake, and African Affairs Director Susan Rice all enthusiastically supported my statements. Of more importance, to those threatened souls in Burundi who had been honestly elected to office and were working to keep democracy alive, the simple visit of an ambassador to the countryside brought encouragement. Just two months after my arrival, the "Frodebu Parliamentarian Group," which constituted 80 percent of the freely elected members of Parliament, passed the following resolution:

The majority Group is Parliamentarian expressing their gratitude to the American people for their effort to help the Burundian people put an end to the on-going crises.

His new Excellency Ambassador of U.S.A. at Bujumbura is perceived as a God sent savior by the Burundians in disaster. His visits to the displaced people and refugees in the interior, his personal interventions towards the diverse victims of violence, his public declarations in favour of peace are many concrete gestures which reinforce political and humanitarian contribution of the international community.

The Parliamentarian Group is proud of the attention preserved by the American people to the Burundian people, the two peoples being neighbors because of the development of modern communication technology. This witnesses the intensity and efficiency of the latest state visits of the American Government and Congress officials and even the personal delegation of President Clinton to Burundi.

In my judgment, had I remained silent, having seen what I had seen, the American people would have had every right to be ashamed of their ambassador.

TEN

DEMOCRACY EATEN AWAY

The Crocodile Is Never Satisfied

BURUNDI'S PRESS, PRESIDENT, AND PARLIAMENT

The brutal, wholesale, and indiscriminate slaughter of peasants in the Buta-ganzwa hills, unreported by the press, unacknowledged by the government, and unknown to a seemingly uncaring world, served as a watershed experience for me in Burundi, prompting me to reflect on my time there, especially given the varied responses that my press interview had evoked among the political groups in Bujumbura. From the Hutus in Frodebu who had been democratically elected came warm letters of appreciation for bringing the truth of their experience to the fore. From the extremist Tutsi press came not only threats of assassination, but writing that showed neither an understanding of democracy nor a desire for it. Although my press interview had made no mention of political parties or ethnic groups, almost all actions were seen through ethnic lenses in Burundi, which meant that to show sympathy for a slaughtered Hutu child was, in the minds of Tutsi extremists, to show hostility toward all Tutsis. Regrettably, as I reviewed my seven months in Burundi, I found neither advances in reconciliation nor forward movement toward an effective government.

Part of the problem was that Burundi's president was a frightened man. And while fear in the presidency would handicap any country, it poses a particular problem in Africa. There, the tradition has been that tribes are organized around a chief who wields broad powers over his people. Most tribes have never had anything comparable to a legislature to place limits on his authority. Therefore, a tribal leader, or the president of a newly independent country, is expected to be strong and authoritative.

Sylvestre Ntibantunganya, however, was neither. He never directly sought the presidency. A journalist and an intellectual, he came to his position through his editorship of Frodebu's newspaper, his appointment as foreign minister, and his being next in line of authority after both Ndadaye and

Ntaryamira were killed. Within his own party he was accused of prolixity, hesitation, and indecisiveness. He lacked experience in either business or government, in making quick, firm decisions. And his readiness to allow Uprona and the opposition parties to spend six months negotiating the Convention of Government weakened Frodebu's electoral mandate by a kind of Chinese water torture, steadily eroding popular hopes and confidence. At one point during those negotiations, he told a small group of us diplomats, "Without seeing where I am going, when I am going, or with whom I am going, it is difficult to navigate." But, he assured us, "This prolongation is not eternal; I understand Burundi." At the same meeting, he pleaded, "Don't rush me, or we will have October 21 all over again."

That last plea could have meant many things: a new coup by the army, massive and unrestrained killings across the entire countryside, or another round of beginning a new government—but one thing it surely meant: don't rush me, for if you do, I will be assassinated. One could not blame him for having that fear. His two predecessors had been killed within the first year after free elections. Moreover, on October 21, after Ntibantunganya had left his family and walked barefoot and disguised in gardener's clothes to hide out in Kamenge, his wife was shot dead by soldiers from the same army now assigned to protect him. He had legitimate reason to fear for his life, but as his fears persisted and grew, so did the control exercised by the army and their extremist Tutsi allies.

Meanwhile, the intimidation and assassination of legislative leaders that began on October 21, 1993, was continuing. Many Hutu parliamentarians lived in Zaire and commuted daily to Burundi, afraid to live in their own country. By autumn 1995, 21 of 83 members of Parliament—all Hutu Frodebists—had been assassinated one by one, a result comparable to 113 of the 435 members of the U.S. House of Representatives being assassinated in two years. Unimaginable in America; factual in Burundi.

Member of Parliament Shot Five Times—And Survives

One member of Parliament who survived an attempted assassination was Norbert Ndihokubwayo, representative from Ngozi. When I visited him in the Prince Rwagasore Hospital in Bujumbura on September 18, 1994, he was lying in bed, his right leg bandaged and raised, in a private room with no screens over its open windows, which fortunately lessened the smells of sickness that permeated the hallways. This powerfully built, bull-like man, who four days earlier had taken five bullets, was sitting up in bed, waiting to tell me about his experience.

Norbert had been driving back from Kigobe Palace, where Frodebu members of Parliament had been discussing the Convention of Government. Suddenly, a car turned directly in front of him, forcing him to stop, while a second car pulled up behind. From the back seat of the car before him, two men opened fire. Even as he was speaking to me, Norbert still had one bullet in his back; a collarbone broken from a second shot; a wound where a third bullet had passed through his neck, partly cutting his tongue; a bullet hole where a fourth shot had passed through his right leg, leaving him without feeling below the knee; and a shattered tibia in his left leg from a fifth bullet. The attack, in downtown Bujumbura, was swift and brutal, and the assailants escaped immediately afterwards. Two gendarmes, only fifty meters away, had watched impassively, neither apprehending the assailants nor helping Norbert, who was taken to the hospital by a passing motorist.

Astonishingly, Norbert had been warned three weeks earlier. A youth attending a meeting at the Uprona Party print shop had overheard plans being made to kill four Frodebu parliamentarians: two each from Ngozi and Gitega. Attending the meeting were four prominent members of the Uprona Party: François Ngeze and Alphonse Kadege, both known to have been involved in President Ndadaye's assassination; Amariel Nkundamazina, former ambassador to Tanzania; and Gervais Nzeyimana, a member of the Brothers of St. Joseph, a Catholic religious community in Giheta, who came from the same colline as Norbert. According to Norbert's informant, youths at the meeting were paid 200,000 Burundi francs, or $800, in advance, with the promise of further payment upon successful execution of the plan. By the time the youth warned Norbert, Parliamentarian Mpfayokurera of Gitega had already been killed.

Upon receiving the report, Norbert contacted Colonel Bikomagu, the chief of staff of the army, who immediately called in Sebastian Birahebura, the chief of police (or, the gendarmerie). The two offered neither to investigate nor to arrest anyone but, at Norbert's request, promised to warn the youths against such plans. However, investigators who visited Norbert after the attack denied knowing anything of such plans. When Birahebura himself visited Norbert in the hospital, his words were, "I see you're still alive. Let's not talk now. I'll be back later." He never returned.

After attacks of this kind, I occasionally heard of promises to investigate, but never once of a prosecution, trial, or conviction for any attack against a Hutu, whether peasant or parliamentarian.

The doughty, durable Norbert survived and, helped by friends, received medical care in Switzerland, after which he moved to Nairobi, Kenya, where, like numerous Burundians committed to democracy, he survived on very meager means. The monetary, physical, and psychological costs of a commitment to free government in Burundi often proved to be very high.

CIVIL AUTHORITY IMPOTENT BEFORE THE MILITARY

Like the majority of the population, I thought that the Convention of Government and the agreement of the political parties on the legitimacy of the president might allow effective democratic governance to proceed. But it didn't. The convention placed politicians in positions with governmental titles, but the flow of power continuously ebbed away from democracy toward tyranny and terror; despite occasional relative calm, the tide never turned toward elective government, peace, and reconciliation. The propaganda used by the Burundi Army and its extremist Tutsi political allies to justify their slaughter and subjugation of Hutus surprisingly and effectively minimized criticism from the international community. First, they greatly exaggerated the size and capability of the Hutu rebel forces. Second, they convinced the outside world that they were a legitimate governmental force acting to impose order during a civil insurrection, whereas in reality they were a monoethnic military maintaining its supremacy over the majority of the population.

Particularly adept at identifying this misrepresentation was Daniel Phillipin, who called on me in December 1994 before leaving as chief of the International Committee of the Red Cross (ICRC) in Burundi to take a position at ICRC headquarters in Geneva. He observed that many of the people whom the ICRC brought to hospitals and treated had suffered injuries from machetes, knives, clubs, or bayonets—not bullets. And most victims were women and children. His explanation for the preponderance of lacerations rather than bullet wounds was that the army was regularly bringing Tutsi déplacés from their camps in army trucks to act as their surrogate killers. "It's always the same scenario," he said: the army claims that Hutu bandes armées or peasants have attacked Tutsis, and then responds against Hutu villagers with army forces and déplacés, who, after their rampage, fill the army trucks with booty to be divided at their army camps. The army asserts that it is seeking arms hidden by and for the Hutu bandes armées. The problem with that claim, as Phillipin and all Western embassies had observed, was that the army never demonstrated that it actually found any arms.

A similar observation was made by the United Nations Commission on Human Rights, in its *Report of the Special Rapporteur on his Mission to Burundi from 19 to 29 April 1995:* "Operations to disarm citizens are carried out mainly against Hutus, although arms are rarely found during such operations. In the incidents at Kamenge [during April 1995] where at least 24 persons were killed, only one weapon was found" (12). In reality, the army raids into homes were but excuses for pillage and slaughter.

Seeking to verify my perceptions, I questioned an American missionary who had served for a number of years in Gitega: "Although I would guess that it was different in October 1993, my estimate would be that at this time 90 percent of the killing is Tutsis killing Hutus and the vast majority of that killing is perpetrated or encouraged by the army. Do you think that is more or less right?"

"No, it is 99 percent," he responded.

This violence was in no way thwarted by the elected civilian authorities, who, threatened by the army, ignored by the Tutsi bureaucracy, and shut out by the judicial authorities, never discovered an effective means of exercising the power granted them by the constitution and the electorate. Recognizing that fact, the extremists in Uprona became ever bolder in their attacks upon the elected government. In spite of agreeing to the Convention of Government, which offered them vastly more power than they could ever have won at the polls in honest elections, the Upronists continued their attacks on the Frodebu majority. By December 1994 they were insisting that Dr. Jean Minani, the elected Frodebu speaker of the National Assembly and therefore next in line for the presidency, be replaced. Uprona's charges were always the same: any Hutu leader whom they wished to see replaced was accused of having participated in genocide against Tutsis after the October 21 assassination. Facts and substantiations were never required; statements were enough to become myths, and myths to become reality.

When Uprona's leaders broke their promises, they justified their actions by saying that circumstances had changed. When President Ntibantunganya yielded to continuing pressure from Upronists and replaced Minani as head of Parliament, he only strengthened the public perception of his own weakness. Although Uprona's leaders had promised during the Convention of Government negotiations to allow all of Frodebu's leaders to stay in place, and next had promised publicly and privately to cease their insistence on changing leaders if Minani stepped down, his resignation only whetted their appetite. As Churchill once said of Hitler, the crocodile always says that with one more bite he will be satisfied, but the crocodile is never satisfied.

Upon Minani's resignation, Upronist leaders immediately focused their hostility on one of their own members—Prime Minister Kanyenkiko—a moderate, intelligent, and capable Upronist whose sin was to try to make the coalition government of Hutu and Tutsi, Frodebu and Uprona, work.

As Upronists began working to remove him, diplomats from the Western countries, the Group of 5, made every effort to keep him in office, but to no avail.

Leonidas Ndoricimpa and Antoine Nduwayo sought the position, which had been promised to the Uprona Party. When, on February 18, neither candidate was able to get a majority vote within their own Uprona Party, the Uprona Party headquarters were surrounded by 300 Brownshirt-style youths from the Tutsi gang Sojedem, led by a defrocked Catholic priest called Brother Déo. They insisted that Nduwayo be named prime minister, threatening to burn down Uprona headquarters and to hold all those present hostage until Uprona agreed. A terrified Charles Mukasi, Uprona's often drunk and penniless president, had earlier that day sought refuge from the Sojedem thugs at Ambassador Ould-Abdallah's house, and he managed to hold out against the mob until 4:30 a.m. At that time, however, according to Upronist and former minister of planning Salvator Nzigamasabo, Mukasi was phoned by Army Chief of Staff Bikomagu and instructed to accept Nduwayo. With that, the combined pressure was too much. Mukasi yielded, and Antoine Nduwayo, another Tutsi from Bururi, the region that had produced Micombero, Bagaza, Buyoya, and many of their troops, became prime minister.

In our G-5 meeting after these events, Ambassador Ould-Abdallah sought to put the best face possible on the change, saying that a form of democracy still existed because three important features remained: 1) the president was of the majority party; 2) he was assured of finishing his term; and 3) Parliament continued to exist.[1] But as he spoke with a stronger sense of realpolitik, he described Chapter 7 of UN policy, which authorizes the United Nations to send in armed international troops capable of using firepower to enforce UN directives. Then he acknowledged, "Burundians believe that Chapter 7 is a joke. They know the U.S. and Russia will not support it." He added that since the West was not willing to send in troops and was therefore not prepared to take any risks to impose real justice on this nation, the best we could do was to try to keep the lid on. His implication was that doing so would often mean compromise at the expense of democratic principles.

We in the diplomatic community, and the people of Burundi even more so, were willing to hope once more that somehow the latest governmental change would lead to improvement rather than to further deterioration of governance. But it was undoubtedly another defeat for democracy and another victory for terror and fear. And fear was the overarching dark angel that held Burundi in its grip.

ELEVEN

THE STANDOFF

Anyone living in Bujumbura learns to ride the ups and downs of violence in the city. Staying informed through the regional security officer at the embassy, other expatriates, and household employees was my best way of anticipating difficulty. Even so, I was surprised at how quickly the environment could change. January 23, 1995, brought just such a sudden and dramatic shift.

Before coming to Burundi, I had assumed that we might have U.S. marines or armed guards to protect the ambassador's residence. We didn't. One guard, or gatekeeper, was assigned to the residence twenty-four hours a day. The three guards who divided this twenty-four-hour rotation were all locally hired Burundians who spoke no English and were armed only with nightsticks. During my first week in Bujumbura, we returned from a dinner after dark to find our guard deep into a drunken sleep. We honked repeatedly, and finally Bob had to get out of the car and shout for several minutes before the inebriated guard awoke, stumbled up from his pallet, and unlocked the gate to let us in.

The only time an intruder broke into our garden, by climbing the wall, the guard radioed the marine on duty at the chancery and then fled into the banana grove at the edge of the garden to hide. We were on vacation, and the marine, unable to leave his post, called Gordon Duguid, the chargé. He hurried to the residence from the home of the friends he was visiting nearby. Gordon then had to climb over the wall, and brandishing a club-like device for locking a steering wheel, he apprehended the demented intruder. Bob, when traveling, was sometimes accompanied by Chris Reilly, the regional security officer, but the residence itself had no firearms, no competent guard, and no real protection against possible intruders. Fortunately, the extremists whom Bob offended probably had no idea of our vulnerability.

Picking up the girls from L'École Française at noon, I brought them home for lunch, as usual. Mariana and Sarah were competing with each other at the table to tell us about school when suddenly an explosion shook the windows of the house—the loudest and closest blast since our arrival in Burundi. Our household employee Jean-Marie Ntahondereye reported that the gatekeeper had seen injured and bleeding men and women running down the street in front of our house. A Tutsi youth had tossed a hand grenade into a group of Hutus gathered at the corner two houses away, creating pandemonium.

Because of the unrest, I did not take the girls back to school for afternoon classes. The German ambassador's wife, whose home was even closer to the explosion, kept her children home as well. For everyone else I knew, school went on as usual. The pockets of violence could be so isolated that most people were left unaffected.

Surprisingly perhaps, the children and I passed the afternoon ordinarily. We played games and read stories, although I made certain we did not go outside. I believe that because Bob and I did not feel fear or panic, the children felt calm as well. A year later, when we were back in Texas, Sarah and her kindergarten classmates were asked to describe a bad day they had each experienced. The teacher, Patti Beach, told me afterward that Sarah had thought and thought, then had looked up at her and said, "I've never had a bad day."

How grateful I was that we seemed to have protected her childhood joy and innocence even while grenades were exploding a block from our house.

On this occasion, the grenades exploding on Boulevard du Vingt-Huit Novembre proved to be a prelude to violence in other parts of the city. Ethnic cleansing was continuing, sometimes as the police and soldiers looked the other way, sometimes as they themselves participated. The army was driving Hutus from their homes. From our front porch, I could see columns of smoke rising from the burning houses as the unrest continued that night and through the week. As expatriates, we were not directly affected by it, but for one of our household employees it was a different story.

January 25 marked the second day that Jean-Marie had not come to work, and I began to worry for his safety. Our employees were reliable and hard-working. If they missed work, it meant they had problems. Through the morning haze, I could see smoke rising from burning homes in Kamenge, near where Jean-Marie lived. I decided to look for him.

I drove down Boulevard du Vingt-Huit Novembre, past the university, where clusters of students gathered along the street, and then made a right turn into a residential area. Like most "affluent" sections of Bujumbura, this was predominantly a Tutsi enclave. At the end of the paved street was the home of an army colonel who, for sport, regularly stood on his second-floor balcony to shoot an automatic weapon into the air, and also into the Hutu village of Mugoboka below him.

Once past his house, the paved street abruptly turned to red dirt and rocks. Deep ruts lined the steep incline as my Pajero crept down the narrow one-lane road into Jean-Marie's village and suddenly into another world. Twenty yards from the modern homes of Mutanga Sud, Mugoboka was a cluster of red mud-brick huts arranged haphazardly next to a deep gorge. None had running water or electricity.

Normally, the village was teeming. Smiling, barefoot children would gather around my car and run behind me; old men and women sitting on their front steps would look curiously as my white Pajero passed by. A one-room crumbling brick building, the local bar, sported a hand-painted sign that beckoned customers in for a beer. A woman sitting on the ground outside it sold small bags of peanuts that she had carefully arranged on a straw mat before her.

But on this day things were eerily different. The village was completely vacant, and a strange and foreboding silence hung over the scene. My heart sank as I viewed the once lively village, now a ghost town. Only the Burundi military had the power to frighten away an entire village full of men, women, and children. What had happened to them? Where were they now?

As I sat in my vehicle, pondering what lay before me, a solitary figure appeared from behind one of the huts. I recognized the man, very thin and with a weathered face, from the many times I had driven Jean-Marie home from work. Amid the desolation, he managed a smile and approached my window.

"Amahoro," I called, the Kirundi greeting of "Peace, hello."

"Amahoro," he responded, with a grin that revealed several missing teeth.

In broken French I explained that I was looking for Jean-Marie, not because I wanted him to work, but because I was worried about him and his family.

"I know where he is," the man replied. "I will get a message to him."

"Please tell him I will come back tomorrow morning at 10:00 and that I will help him."

I backed out of the village and headed home, relieved that Jean-Marie was at least still alive.

The next day dawned sunny and beautiful, like most days in Burundi. Sensing that there could be some risk in returning to Mugoboka, I asked Bernardin, Bob's official driver, who spoke Kirundi, to accompany me, and an off-duty marine, who brought along his girlfriend, but no weapon.

As we drove down the hill into the midst of the still vacant village, I saw Jean-Marie standing next to one of the huts, somber and exhausted. We stood together outside the car as he related his family's ordeal.

In early morning of the previous day, as the sun was breaking from behind the mountains surrounding Bujumbura, most villagers were still asleep in their huts, wrapped in blankets against the chill night air. Suddenly, echoing through the stillness came the desperate cry *"Nimuvyuke! Abasoda baraje!"* (Kirundi for "Wake up! The army is coming!").

Burundians living in Hutu areas of Bujumbura had long ago developed ways of coping with army raids. From a distance, they could distinguish between the sounds of approaching military trucks and those of civilian vehicles. Some villages organized patrols. If a shouted warning seemed too risky, the branch of a tree would be thrown onto the roof of a house to warn of approaching soldiers. In more isolated, mountainous, or rural areas, blowing a whistle or beating a drum signaled imminent danger. Adults as well as children often slept in their clothes to make running away easier. Even the youngest children sometimes lay awake at night, listening for the approach of military tanks or blindés. On the morning of January 24, 1995, they came to Mugoboka.

Awakening his three young children, Jean-Marie and his wife burst from the house as their neighbors scattered in every direction. Even the children knew by heart the all-too-familiar escape route down the steep hillside, across the gorge and its shallow stream, and into the mountains beyond. Edgar, who was only four, slipped on the uneven ground. His mother scooped him up as she continued running.

After their escape, they slept in the mountains, huddling under trees in the cold darkness with only the clothes on their backs. Fearing that taking shelter in homes of other Hutus nearby might put his family in more peril, Jean-Marie chose to stay in the forest, where he found a vantage point from which to look into his village below. He watched helplessly as the soldiers once again systematically ransacked his village, now empty of people. He saw them digging futilely in a banana grove, looking for weapons supposedly buried for the Hutu rebels. They found nothing. But this did not prevent their breaking into homes and pillaging the contents, as they did to Jean-Marie's simple house. From his mountaintop perch, once again, he watched the sanctity of his home and community being violated by a military consisting of his own countrymen. And it was from that same lookout point that Jean-Marie had seen my familiar white Pajero pull into the then-deserted village the previous day. I had always told him that if he were in trouble, I would come looking for him. He had known why I was there.

"They broke my door," he said resignedly. "I must fix my door."

"May I see your house?" I asked.

"Yes, please follow me," he replied.

To protect our Hutu workers from Tutsi youth gangs, I had often driven them home. Never before, though, had I gotten out of my car to see the inside of any of their houses. Most homes were too far up the mountains, accessible only by miles of footpaths, for me to walk safely. I could only drop the employees off at the nearest point on the road.

Now, as I followed Jean-Marie along the narrow winding path between the mud-and-brick houses and across a grassy field, I realized I had crossed a line into a Burundi unknown to me. As I stepped through the doorway into Jean-Marie's home, the wooden door hanging loose from its hinges, I confronted my own ignorance and prejudice.

Although I respected and felt affection for most Burundians I knew, I somehow hadn't visualized their lives as being parallel to mine. The extreme poverty, the warfare, and the lack of modern conveniences in so much of the country—how could their family life echo the emotions and traditions of my own home life?

A glimpse into the darkened rooms before me changed all that. Amidst the wreckage, I could see what had been a simple but comfortable home. On the wall above the couch hung a framed wedding photo of a proud Jean-Marie in a dark suit and tie, standing next to his wife, adorned in an elaborate white wedding dress and veil. His small house had three rooms, but no bathroom or kitchen. Cooking was done outside over a charcoal fire. While all the rooms were furnished, on this morning, lying before us and littered across the floor were the ransacked remnants of children's toys, clothes, dishes—everything that the soldiers had wantonly pulled out of drawers and cupboards lay in chaotic and ugly heaps. We stood quietly in the half-darkness as Jean-Marie stared at his life's belongings, now in total disarray. He seemed embarrassed, and ushered us quickly back out into the bright sunlight. I was disgusted and angered by what I had witnessed.

My arms folded, I silently followed Jean-Marie back down the worn footpath, my mind lost in thought at the destruction I had seen. As we entered a clearing into the field, I looked up to see four Burundian soldiers, AK-47s slung over their shoulders. They sauntered toward us. Halfway across the field we faced one another.

"Is there a problem?" one soldier asked in French.

"There is no problem," Jean-Marie responded calmly.

Trying not to show my revulsion toward them, but wanting to do what I could to offer some protection, I began speaking in a firm voice in simple

French: "I am the wife of the American ambassador. This man is my friend." Then realizing that one or two other villagers had suddenly come out of hiding and were standing nearby, I added, with a sweep of my arm, "They are *all* my friends."

"Does he work at your house?" asked one of the soldiers in French as he gestured toward Jean-Marie.

"Yes," I replied.

I looked over at the off-duty marine, with his signature military hair cut and a large walkie-talkie hanging prominently from his belt. His demeanor was casual but alert. After one of the soldiers made a few remarks about the marine's attractive American girlfriend, we all turned and continued walking down the narrow path, back between the closely spaced huts and into the dirt clearing where our car was parked.

I was startled by what I saw. Parked behind my vehicle was a large military truck filled with fifteen to twenty armed Burundian soldiers. Their commander stood thirty feet away, near the edge of the gorge. None of my group said a word, but we all seemed to understand what we would do. We would not leave that village until the soldiers were gone. If we were to go now, Jean-Marie and the two other Hutu men who had joined him would be left defenseless, and we knew what their fates would likely be: capture, torture, or death.

Oddly, I felt absolutely no fear—only a strong determination to wait the situation out. I leaned over to Bernardin, a Tutsi, and whispered, "Do you think I'm crazy?"

He looked me straight in the eye and firmly said, "No."

The next fifteen minutes were surreal. It was as though we were part of a slow-motion movie. The village around us was vacant and silent; the soldiers stood nearly motionless, automatic weapons in hand. Their commander turned his back on us and stared solemnly across the gorge to the towering green mountains and dense forests beyond. We remained outside our car. Jean-Marie and his two neighbors stood next to us. No one said a word. No one moved. There was not a sound as the minutes passed.

I watched the commander as he continued to stand with his back to us, his arms folded. His gaze seemed transfixed on the river below. I didn't know if he spoke English, but I had an overwhelming desire during those silent moments to walk up to him and simply ask, "Why do you kill innocent men, women, and children? Don't you know that a nation's army is supposed to protect its citizens, not slaughter them?"

Of course, I didn't ask such questions. But I wonder what his answer could have been. I looked gratefully at the U.S. marine, Sergeant Kevin Stackpole, accompanying us: a strong and visible contrast in morality and discipline.

Finally, the heavy silence was broken as the commander turned around and began walking toward us. "*Turagaruka,*" he sneered in Kirundi as he brushed past.

When the truck was out of sight, I asked Jean-Marie what the word meant. "He said, 'We'll be back,'" Jean-Marie uttered softly.

A sickening lump formed in my stomach.

My friends and I drove home as Jean-Marie returned to his mountaintop hiding place.

Later that day I picked him up, along with his wife and children, at a prearranged meeting point. They would come to live in quarters at our house for a while.

TWELVE

A LIFE OF CONTRAST

The last week in January was a period of unrest and displacement in Bujumbura. An insurgency by Hutu rebels in a small section of the city made for another night of grenades and gunfire. In an effort to retaliate, the military swept through the hillsides around the capital, burning, looting and killing. Word spread that over a thousand people—Hutu families driven from their homes—were camping out at the Monument to National Unity overlooking Bujumbura, less than a mile from our house. A British friend, Sarah White, who had lived in Burundi for over seventeen years and spoke Kirundi, drove with me to verify the report.

Rounding the hilltop, we found masses of people congregated on the broad concrete platform and in the amphitheater surrounding the tall monument. Driven from their homes, which had been recently pillaged by the army, this group of mostly women, children, and the elderly had spent two nights and days without food or shelter, exposed on a bare hilltop high above Bujumbura. Many saw below them the smoke and embers from their burned homes. They had brought whatever they could hastily gather and carry in their arms or on their heads. Most had only a thin cotton cloth to protect themselves from the heavy dew and chill night air.

Something needed to be done quickly. Sarah and I asked two friends to join us in the task. Lea Peters, an American whose husband pastored a large multiethnic church in one of the poorest sections of town, volunteered workers who would bring large black kettles for porridge we would cook over open wood fires at the monument. Sarah and I went to the Greek-owned bakery downtown and bought six hundred loaves of French bread at ten cents each. A British friend, Chrissie Chapman, who cared for a number of Burundian children in her home, assisted by gathering blankets, baby food, cookies, and sealed plastic packets of fresh water donated by Christ Church in Hungary.

The next morning we arrived early to set up our feeding program. Sergeant Stackpole, who had accompanied me on my quest for Jean-Marie, came along later to see if he could be helpful. I had never done anything like this before, but the other women had. I followed their lead as they skillfully and swiftly organized our efforts, assigning each of us specific jobs. We took our positions as Chrissie, playing the role of benevolent drill sergeant, shouted and nudged people into line. Soon we were standing face-to-face with 1,200 people who hadn't had a decent meal in three days.

Lea was mixing and cooking porridge in the large wrought-iron kettles as her church workers stoked the fires; Sarah and I ladled the lukewarm gruel out of large buckets into whatever bowls, cups, or cans the people had brought with them in the flight from their homes. Sergeant Stackpole led some of the children in a rousing set of calisthenics as they waited to get in line. During this time, four-year-old Andrew White sat patiently at his mother's feet. As lunchtime approached, she served him some porridge, which he eagerly ate. The fair-skinned, platinum-haired boy seemed perfectly at home as he quietly watched his mother, who had given nearly a lifetime of service in Africa.

Once the feeding program was underway, Chrissie formed a new line. Having noticed the day before that many of the children were coughing, we had brought along a Russian physician, Dr. Eleanor Boulaev, to examine the children. Once again, Chrissie organized the throngs, grouping the apparently sick children into a separate area. With a few simple instruments, Dr. Boulaev, whose physician husband, Uri, also treated many expatriates in Bujumbura, began examining the children.

While the two lines were moving forward, the sky grew dark and threatening. A strong wind blew in powerful gusts from across Lake Tanganyika below, and the temperature plummeted. I looked before me at what seemed an endless line of children, their clothes dirty, their feet bare, their bodies shivering in the cool air. Rain began falling as they thrust their containers forward to be filled by the only meal they would have that day. Although we tried to keep orderly lines, the desperation and hunger of the people caused them to begin pushing and shoving each other as they surged toward us. The tension became noticeably stronger and the crowd grew more agitated. Just then, the embassy walkie-talkie that I had thrust in my jeans pocket began screeching in tones that signaled an urgent message from the American embassy was to follow. The marine on duty spoke in even and measured tones as he announced that a grenade had been thrown in the market downtown and that people were fleeing from that area. We were warned to avoid the downtown region until further notice. Only moments before that announcement from the embassy, a sudden change, both striking and eerie, had come over the crowd. Although we were high above Bujumbura, and I, at least, had not heard the grenade, it was as if the vibrations of fear had mysteriously been telegraphed up the hills.

We continued our work as the rain fell in sheets from the dark gray sky. At some point, word reached us that Burundi government representatives were erecting tents for the people in their home areas. This was all the encouragement they needed to load their things back onto their heads and begin trudging down the mountain paths to find shelter. Sarah and I, soaking wet and half covered in spilled porridge, watched with Lea, Chrissie, and Mrs. Boulaev as the stark mountaintop soon became empty again and the towering Monument to National Unity stood alone against the dark sky.

Less than an hour later, after showering and dressing, I was sitting at a beautifully arranged table, surrounded by freshly cut flowers and lovely furnishings. My husband's personal secretary, Frances Wickes, had invited us to join her and friends for lunch at her home. As I reflected on the despair and hunger we had seen on the hilltop, I was struck by the life of contrast I was leading. Often, it seemed, I would witness the most abject poverty in one moment and enjoy refined elegance the next. Reviewing my daily calendar, I find that we held dinners for Americans, including National Security Advisor Tony Lake; Assistant Secretaries of State George Moose, Frances Cook, and Phyllis Oakley as well as their accompanying groups; and a presidential delegation that included various congressmen. Our Burundian guests included two prime ministers, former president Buyoya, and plenty of cabinet members and parliamentarians. Bob also hosted Burundi military leaders in our home many times. After my first few months in Burundi, as I saw firsthand the activities of the Burundi military, I refused for moral reasons to attend purely military gatherings, but I understood that Bob's job required him to keep an open door to participants on both sides of the conflict. Business lunches at our residence became nearly an everyday event once a 7:00 p.m. curfew in the city made hosting dinners difficult.

Our Burundian household employees, who walked many miles every day from their simple hillside homes to come to work, ensured the elegance of our entertaining at the American ambassador's residence. For a salary of $200 a month (which was the maximum that the U.S. State Department allowed us to pay), Marcien Rusuriye, who had cooked for six previous American ambassadors, prepared meals as delicious and sophisticated as might be served at the White House. Former ambassador Frances Cook had described Marcien as "the finest cook in Central Africa" when she urged our rehiring him as a chef upon our arrival. She was absolutely right. Whatever his main course, whether veal cordon bleu, beef Wellington, or breast of chicken Kiev, it was served on silver trays garnished with colorful green parsley and with tomatoes carved into perfect floral shapes. Guests responded with awe at the presentation of the meals even before they had tasted them. A dessert would follow, perhaps fresh mango mousse, strawberry charlotte, or cream puffs baked in the shape of little swans. Whether Marcien prepared French, Chinese, or American food, our guests loved it and long remembered their meals at the American ambassador's residence.

Yet, while life in the residence could seem elegant and calm, the world beyond our walls caused continuing concern. Tensions rose in early February. Sarah White and I cancelled a return visit to the displaced persons from the Monument to National Unity, who, it was reported, were living in a tent city on a nearly inaccessible nearby mountainside. We decided it would be too dangerous to venture out that far alone.

The rest of my regular routine remained the same, however. The girls went happily to school. I drove across town to a hair salon in the home of a Belgian woman, which was located on a back road near the Jane Goodall Institute's "halfway house" for chimpanzees. I was always amused when I compared that drive—through herds of cattle and goats, around potholes, and down dusty dirt roads—with my usual dash along the Loop 410 expressway in San Antonio to the hairdresser. Frankly, I preferred the drive in Bujumbura.

On Saturday, February 4, Uprona staged a demonstration in downtown Bujumbura. The route deliberately passed the American embassy. The six-man marine detachment assigned to Bujumbura took up defensive positions on the roof and elsewhere in the building. While my daughters and I stayed home and played in the pool, one mile away 3,000–5,000 people were marching through the center of town.

While passing the American embassy, some shouted, "Go Home, Yankees," and others held placards reading "Kayanza, Kamenge, Krueger." Angered that Bob had denounced military atrocities in Butaganzwa (Kayanza Province) and the Hutu quartier of Kamenge in Bujumbura, and had reported them to the international media, these Tutsi extremists linked his name to known areas of Hutu habitation—and annihilation. If this was supposed to be an insult, we didn't take it as such. It can be a compliment to be hated by murderers. Feeling intimidated, however, by the growing anti-American sentiments among some Tutsis, I removed the large U.S. flag decals that I had so openly displayed on my car windows. It was a futile attempt at anonymity. In such a small community of expatriates, most people could recognize my vehicle, with its diplomatic license plates, whether I displayed American flags or not.

After a rainy and quiet Sunday, Monday brought blue skies and bright sunshine to the hillsides of Bujumbura. My diary for that day reads, "I took the girls to school without incident." In a country as volatile as Burundi, even that simple act merited mention. The streets were busy and crowded as usual. All seemed well, but by Tuesday the mood had once again changed. Rumors were flying that a ville morte, or "dead city," was planned for the next day. If so, even expatriates could be targeted and harmed. Anticipating the "dead city," everyone hurriedly stocked up on food items, especially meat and vegetables. One never knew when these goods would be available again. Business boomed along with the anxiety level as we all prepared for the next day.

Coming from school, my daughters were in their own happy world, chattering excitedly in the back seat about their class carnival next Saturday, meant to be a Mardi Gras–style celebration. Sarah would parade around the school grounds as a pink flamingo; Mariana would be a strawberry. Her teacher told me she would need to wear green overalls, an item we had not thought of bringing with us from America. In a city as poor as Bujumbura, with no department stores or shopping malls, where would I find green overalls? The girls' voices seemed to get louder and more distracting as heavy traffic pressed in all around us. People appeared to be in a near panic as fear of the impending ville morte grew. And it looked as if everyone who could be was driving in the small city center, anxiously looking for vendors selling fresh produce along the streets and in the marketplace. To make matters worse, rumors of a full-fledged coup planned for the next day began flying.

After all the anticipation, the ville morte everyone expected was called off, and there was no coup. It prompted a moment of optimism in the country because the opposition had apparently backed down. However, since tensions were mounting in the country, Bob called a town-hall meeting for all American citizens, and about twenty people showed up at the Marine House at 4 p.m. on February 9. Such meetings were designed to keep Americans informed about U.S. policy in the region and to review security information. It was also a time for Americans not connected to the embassy to share observations and concerns. Those present expressed agreement with Bob's statements and actions in support of democracy and human rights, and none felt threatened by virtue of being American. In private, the missionaries who had been in Burundi for years repeatedly urged Bob to continue his outspokenness. He certainly had my full and enthusiastic support in all that he did.

The next morning, I drove the girls to school through a pounding rainstorm. The rainy season is a special time in Burundi. I loved watching the dark clouds rolling over the mountains and across Lake Tanganyika. The rain, cold and refreshing, never lasted long. Afterwards, the lush tropical landscape glistened in the sun and seemed even greener than usual. Returning home, I passed people walking and jogging in the streets, some even for sport. The marketplace was teeming with vendors selling fresh wildflowers and vegetables were on the street corners, eagerly hawking their wares. There was an aura of calm and security surrounding the city that day. I was almost startled to discover the existence of such an environment, which seemed to envelop everyone, Burundian and expatriate alike. Driving down the sun-dappled streets lined with avocado and mango trees, I rolled down my windows and breathed in deeply the warmth and peace of that day. It was Burundi at its best. I could only hope that it would last.

THIRTEEN

THE CONVENT AND THE CAMP

The school Mardi Gras carnival so eagerly anticipated by my children was a great success. A local American missionary, Ruth Johnson, lent me her son's outgrown pair of kelly green overalls for Mariana, solving one minor challenge. With a huge wooden strawberry fitted around her face, she joined her class of fruits and vegetables in a parade around the dirt school yard. Sarah was dressed in pink jeans, a pink T-shirt, and an elaborately decorated flamingo headdress made from cardboard and tissue paper. She smiled broadly as she held the hand of her American friend, Amanda Peters. All the students, from nursery school to high school, were dressed in bright, colorful costumes. I was amazed by the resourcefulness and imagination of teachers and students able to craft such detailed costumes in such an isolated and poor location. The bright splashes of color and the radiant faces of the three hundred or more students circling the school grounds stood out against the backdrop of lush green mountains surrounding us. Just outside the walls of the compound, Burundi soldiers ringed the school, ostensibly to provide protection.

After enjoying the frivolity of the school's celebration, we prepared for a more serious pursuit. An American delegation of high-level State Department officials was coming from Washington, after a stopover in Rwanda. We were to meet them at the Rwandan border and accompany them on an inspection of refugee camps in Burundi's interior.

The whole family drove up together in the Pajero, followed by Bernardin and Chris. By now, Highway 1 north toward Rubura was familiar: the vibrant stop at Bugarama for flowers and vegetables, the army checkpoints along the way. We usually flew the American flag on our right front fender to let people in the countryside know that the United States was interested in them. And now that Bob had spoken out publicly about the killings in Butaganzwa and other places, we found that our car and flag were frequently recognized. When we slowed down to pass through small towns and vil-

Mariana joining in a parade around the schoolyard, 1995.

lages, local people often ran toward the car, cheering, waving, and sometimes shouting "America" in Kirundi. It was reassuring to know that if Tutsi extremists in Bujumbura resented his public statements, people in the countryside appreciated them. At our residence, Marcien laughingly told Bob that Hutus in his village wanted Bob to be president of Burundi.

We spent the night with the Hansens, then drove seven miles in rainy gray weather to the border post near Rubura. The smoothly paved road with a painted center stripe seemed a strange luxury in a country where almost none of the native population owns a car.

At the border, Mariana, Sarah, and I sat in the Pajero with Bernardin as Bob and Graham White, Sarah's husband, who was working with the United States Agency for International Development, presented the proper documents to the Burundi border officials. Driving the few hundred yards into Rwanda to the border offices there, we passed a turbulent river, swollen and muddy from the heavy downpours. A woman standing alone in the rain hoed the ground near the water's edge. The Rwandan hills on either side enveloped us in a mantle of lush greenery. Known as the "Switzerland of Africa," Rwanda was a continuation of Burundi's mountainous terrain and dense tropical forests.

We sat in our car for over an hour as we waited for the American delegation to arrive. As rain fell intermittently from the dark gray skies, Bernardin stepped out to talk with Rwandans standing nearby. With only two or three people in sight, the border crossing was nearly deserted. It was hard to imagine a more obscure spot in the world, except that widespread media coverage of the country's genocidal violence temporarily had made Rwanda almost a household word.

While Bernardin was away, a soldier walked up to the Pajero, where the girls and I waited alone, opened the driver's door, and climbed in. Although armed with a machine gun, he appeared to be no more than fourteen years old. His uniform and weaponry couldn't camouflage his almost innocent, child-like demeanor. Smiling good-naturedly, he seemed curious about our car and perhaps also wanted a moment out of the rain. Within seconds, Bernardin strode over and ordered him out.

Later, a barefoot boy of about ten walked past and asked for something to eat. We gave him all that we had—American popcorn. He sat on the curb next to us. After his first bite, his face took on a pained expression. Apparently, he had never eaten popcorn before. He fingered the kernels suspiciously and slowly chewed on a few of them. We opened our windows, and the girls and I showed him that we were eating the same thing, but he nevertheless looked unhappy and perplexed. We wished that we had a bag of M&Ms or other chocolate candy to offer. Rare and expensive in that part of the world, chocolate was the food item we most often requested be included in care packages from friends in the United States. Sometimes we would share these treats with the children who inevitably surrounded our vehicle on trips into the countryside. On this occasion, we could have shared them with a fourteen-year old soldier as well.

Through the rain, we soon saw the small convoy of American embassy cars arrive at the border post. After exchanging greetings, we turned around and headed back into Burundi. My brief foray into Rwandan territory was over.

Over a winding mountain road, we made the short drive to the small town of Kayanza. Included in the American delegation were Phyllis Oakley, assistant secretary of state for population, refugees, and migration; Townsend Friedman, special coordinator for Rwanda; Margaret McKelvey, director of refugee assistance; and Ed Brown, Central African affairs officer. They would join us in an overnight stay at a Catholic convent near the edge of the city.

Located about fifty yards off the main road, the two-story yellow-brick convent was set among tall eucalyptus trees and native grasses. Its architecture was simple and austere. As we pulled into the small gravel parking lot, an older Burundian nun in full traditional habit emerged to greet us. She spoke very little, but had a peaceful and pleasant expression. Leading us down a long narrow hallway flanked by doors on either side, she assigned us rooms. Each had two single iron beds, a small sink in the corner, bare walls, and a cement floor. Toilet facilities were down the darkened hallway. Not wanting the girls to sleep alone, I put my few things into a room I would share with them.

The nuns announced that supper was ready, so we all gathered in the dining room with two other nuns, but no other guests. A framed painting of the Virgin Mary was all that decorated the simple room. Long wooden tables and benches lined the walls. They had prepared a tasty and abundant home-cooked meal of meat, potatoes, beans, and fresh vegetables. After wide-ranging political discussions with our visitors, we all retired to our individual rooms. Bob and I sat up with the girls until they fell asleep, and then he left for his room next door. Trying to make myself as thin as possible, I squeezed in next to Sarah in the narrow iron bed.

Before long, it seemed, dim rays of sunlight began creeping in through the small window of our bedroom, signaling the start of another day. Up all night with an upset stomach, I sipped hot tea while the others had a hearty breakfast. Our journey would take us deep into the northern and eastern Burundi countryside. Having never been there before, I was filled with excitement and curiosity at what lay ahead. To stay well, I drank Pepto-Bismol out of the bottle all day long.

Our first stop was in the town of Ngozi, where we met with John Bullard, who worked for the United Nations High Commissioner for Refugees. Pointing to a large map of Burundi in his office, he showed us the location of refugee camps throughout the country. His was a daunting task, since the influx of refugees from Rwanda was rising by hundreds, sometimes thousands, each day. To better illustrate his challenges, he led us by car into the largest settlement under his supervision.

Traveling along dirt roads that widened, then narrowed, through forests and past fields of manioc, potatoes, and cabbages, we convoyed into remote areas that offered some of the most beautiful landscapes I had seen. As we rounded a bend, I saw a broad, sweeping valley with what appeared to be small blue dots set in orderly rows on the green hillsides. As we drew nearer, the dots revealed themselves to be low rounded tents of blue plastic sheeting. Their sheer number was overwhelming. The UN camp known as Magara, with over 45,000 Rwandan Hutus, was, by population, the second-largest city in Burundi. Eight thousand of the occupants were orphans.

We parked our cars inside a fenced compound. My immediate impression was that this was an extremely well-organized and orderly community. During the two hours that we remained, that impression strengthened. In a

The UN camp of Magara, housing over 45,000 Rwandan Hutus under blue plastic UN sheeting, 1995.

Bob at the Magara camp, 1995.

remote central African valley, nowhere near sources of electricity or running water, forty-five thousand people who had lost their country, their homes, and possibly their families were being sheltered and fed. It was a no-frills operation, but one that provided lifesaving refuge for people caught in a tragedy of worldwide proportions. Stretching before me as far as the eye could see was one group among many lost and forgotten souls of the Rwandan civil war. It was a sobering sight.

Our walking tour of the refugee camp began in the hospital—a large canvas tent, clean and bare except for rows of fifteen to twenty iron beds and basic medical equipment. Maintained by the courageous and generous organization Doctors Without Borders, most of its beds were blessedly empty that day. One young boy lay with his bandaged leg straight in the air, seemingly in traction. Two older patients, sick and solemn, looked at us with wondering eyes as we passed by and out through the open door of the tent.

Beyond the fenced compound, we entered the crowded, teeming world of a refugee camp. We made our way down narrow dirt passageways between row after row of blue plastic hovels, squeezing through hordes of people and stepping over their meager belongings as we went. Smoke hung in the air around what seemed to be community kitchens, where black kettles sat on embers from wood fires. In many ways, the Magara camp was organized like any other city. There was an orphanage, a bar, even a barbershop. Family and friends clustered in small groups, talking as children ran and played nearby. Stepping into a larger opening, we found a marketplace of sorts. Several women were busily weaving ornate baskets with the distinctive cone-shaped lids traditional in that region. Rather than using just grass and straw, however, these resourceful refugee women used the blue and white plastic of UN sheeting to create bright decorative patterns. The results were striking and unique. Borrowing some Burundi francs from Graham White, I bought one, which I treasure.

There were no streets, per se, in the camp, only dirt paths dividing one tent from another and a broad dirt road surrounding the perimeter of the settlement. The sun beat down as we walked among the people. No grass or trees grew anywhere within the camp. I could only imagine the mud and muck that the refugees lived in during the rainy season. Another fenced area, perhaps two acres in size, held towering, two-story stacks of neatly cut firewood. Trees from area forests were the only source of fuel for cooking and warmth in the camp. The presence of such large communities in the mountains of the Great Lakes region of Burundi, Rwanda, Zaire, and Tanzania presents a real threat to the local environment. The United Nations initiated controlled deforestation to try to lessen the impact on surrounding vegeta-

*Resourceful refugee women at Magara weave scraps of
UN plastic sheeting into baskets, 1995.*

tion. The camps in Burundi alone, however, used several tons of firewood a day. It was a grave challenge with no easy solution.

As I fell behind my group, stopping to take pictures and to absorb what I was seeing, I looked ahead at Bob, who was walking around the edge of the camp, holding each of our daughters' hands. He looked like the Pied Piper. Growing lines of barefoot and curious children streamed alongside and behind him as more joined in with each step. Gently poking Mariana's and Sarah's clothes and long straight hair, the children seemed fascinated by the blonde Americans in their midst. Laughing and running, these refugee children appeared not to have lost their sense of joy and playfulness. In a hastily constructed city of plastic hovels, they had made their homes and, no doubt, new friends. As only children can, they seemed to have adapted well to the place where life had brought them.

Some of Bob's coworkers at the embassy suggested that we were putting our daughters at some risk of disease by taking them to refugee camps, and they were probably right. However, we thought it important for them to grow up aware that in Burundi far more people lived in blue-plastic-roofed hovels than behind high white walls on Boulevard du Vingt-Huit Novembre.

A few months later I heard a report that Burundian soldiers had fired automatic weapons into the camp and that the entire population had panicked and tried to flee into Tanzania. I could hardly imagine the thriving, well-ordered community in a state of chaos and fear, resulting in abandonment, which the Tutsi military attack must have created.

Reorganizing our convoy, we headed out of the camp and into the hills. I turned to see the thousands of shelters blur once again into tiny, indistinguishable blue dots as we climbed higher into the Burundian mountains.

Among those living in squalor were the Tutsi families in the next camp we visited. Fifty miles from Magara was a displaced-person camp housing Burundian Tutsis who had fled the vengeful rampage of their Hutu neighbors after the assassination of President Ndadaye. The United Nations is mandated to care only for international refugees—not those, like these Tutsis, displaced within their own country. Although the UN facilitated some donations of medicine, food, and water, the camp lacked the organization, equipment, and expertise of UN refugee camps. Before me I saw a hodgepodge of poorly constructed single-room tents made from sheets of torn plastic, cloth, and branches: crowded and dirty, it was a breeding ground for disease, poverty, discouragement, and resentment. As I looked to the edge of the camp, I saw an armed Burundian soldier leaning lazily against a tree nearby.

Since the hour was late and we needed to return to Bujumbura before curfew, we could do little more than drive briefly into the center of this tented compound. I stayed in the car with Mariana and Sarah as the usual crowd of onlookers surrounded us. Raspy, hacking coughs reverberated through the crowd—sounds always present in large groups of poor Burundians. Although the young showed the same exuberance I had seen in the refugee children, the eyes of the adults reflected lives that had lost hope and purpose. Swept up in fear and violence that fed one from the other, they were in a permanent state of suspension; too afraid to go home and unable to live happily where they were.

Preoccupied with a sense of sadness as we convoyed back through the forests toward Bujumbura, I suddenly noticed that something was amiss. The forests and fields to our left and right were totally vacant. No one was walking along the roads, no women were tending their crops; partially destroyed red-mud huts with crumbling walls stood like empty shells across the landscape. It was eerie and highly unusual in a country of six million people jammed into an area the size of Maryland. It seemed as if a plague had swept the land. The forests were silent. Not a single person was in sight. Suddenly, the cars ahead of ours stopped. The Burundi Army had set up a roadblock and would not let us pass. Then I understood what had happened to the people. Only the Burundi military could scare away or kill entire families of Hutus.

My heart pounded as it always did at army checkpoints. We were on a very remote rural road, and I hadn't expected this kind of encounter. Soon we learned there was a problem. An American from the U.S. Embassy in Rwanda had brought the Washington delegation down from Kigali, and he was driving the lead car. His Rwandan license plates caused the soldiers' concern. As a soldier walked back to my Pajero, his machine gun dangling from his hand, Bernardin rolled down the window and explained to him in Kirundi that the American ambassador was accompanying the convoy. Bob had been riding in the Toyota Land Cruiser ahead of me, with the group from Washington. I was so glad that we had brought Bernardin along, and felt that his being a Tutsi was an advantage to us. After several minutes of discussion, the roadblock was lifted and we continued on our journey.

We arrived back in Bujumbura before curfew—I with two sleeping girls in the back seat and an empty bottle of Pepto-Bismol in my hand.

FOURTEEN

BURUNDI AT WAR AND AT PEACE,
AND FROM THE SKY

Upon returning from the camps, we learned that a ville morte was expected the next day. It seemed like an ill-timed assault, since an international conference on refugee issues was also beginning in Bujumbura then. Numerous high-level officials from many foreign countries, as well as the United Nations High Commissioner for Refugees, Madame Sadako Ogata, would be attending. Their impression of Burundi could not be positive in such chaos. But that may have been the intent of the organizers: to embarrass the democratic government.

This time the terrorists did not back down. I wonder how well Mrs. Ogata and the other foreign dignitaries slept at the Source du Nil Hotel downtown. Their first night was "a noisy one," as we used to say, not jokingly. Grenade explosions and gunfire were heard throughout the city. Large-artillery fire interrupted the smaller rat-tat-tat of the machine guns and the deep boom of the grenades. Standing on our veranda, I saw tracers streak across the sky. More than usual, this seemed like serious warfare. I phoned my friend, Lea Peters, the young missionary wife who lived with her husband, Jamie, and their three children near the French School in the center of town. Sponsored by an Assembly of God church in Florida, they had hearts of gold that fortunately were matched with nerves of steel.

As was often the case when I talked to Lea during troublesome nights, the explosions around her house were close enough for me to hear them clearly over the phone. Living near Hutu sections often targeted by the army, she repeatedly interrupted our conversation with exclamations such as "Boy, that was a loud one!" Yet, she was calm. I was calm. Knowing that we were not the targets of the warfare made all the difference.

But, of course, that knowledge didn't provide complete protection. Baptist missionaries from Texas, Steve Smith and his wife, living just a few blocks from Lea, were startled when the roof of their porch was hit by debris from large-artillery fire. Yet they showed only mild concern when I phoned them. It is surprising how accustomed we all were becoming to being witnesses to a war.

The ville morte continued for several days. Supplies of perishable foods dwindled in everyone's kitchens as the Hutu farmers were prevented from bringing their fruits, vegetables, and live chickens into Bujumbura. Nervous tension filled the air, although the city was quiet during the day. As always, work at the embassy continued uninterrupted. The refugee conference went on as scheduled, luncheons were held, Sarah White even had several children over to join her five sons in rousing outdoor games. Perplexing as it may seem, normal life for expatriates often existed parallel to the ravages of war that others experienced.

By the fifth day of the ville morte, food supplies were so low that Sarah suggested some of us convoy into the countryside, where vegetables could be bought along the mountain roads. Several American families joined us, and Graham White led the caravan of cars. Once out of range of the marine post at the embassy, we all switched on our walkie-talkies to communicate with one another. Soon Graham pulled over to the side of the road, where boys held large baskets overflowing with ripe red strawberries. "Who wants strawberries?" Graham radioed back to the rest of us. "They're only 300 francs, including the basket!" At approximately $1.25, this was a bargain by anyone's standards.

As the convoy of four or five cars continued winding up the mountain, Graham lurched to the left or right side of the road when he saw produce he thought looked appetizing. His lively radio transmissions kept us all laughing as he negotiated with the vendors in his flawless Kirundi and then reported the prices back to us. At a crossroads, boys were selling large bunches of deep green broccoli. We loaded up, buying for friends back in Bujumbura who hadn't come along. We also filled our cars with fresh cabbages, cauliflower, carrots, leeks, and potatoes as we stopped over and over again.

Our mood on this strangest of shopping trips became sillier and sillier. At one point my children, who sat in the back seat with their friend Kate Duguid, decided to serenade the others over the walkie-talkie. With loud little-girl voices they sang "John Jacob Jingleheimer Schmidt." Later I learned that many miles away, in the middle of Lake Tanganyika, U.S. marines out for a day of waterskiing paused as they thought they heard children singing over their military radios. Shaking their heads in disbelief, they continued their recreation, believing that surely it was their imaginations!

Contrary to the tensions felt in Bujumbura, the mood amid the lush mountainsides was serene and peaceful. No fear was reflected on the faces of the peasant farmers we encountered, no rush in the strides of the bare-foot families along the highway or through mountain paths. Turning onto a narrow dirt back road, the Whites led us deep into the tropical forest, to a vacant stone house known to them for years. Nestled amid green hills and surrounded by trees, the overgrown grounds failed to camouflage what must have been an idyllic mountain retreat. Although the quaint rock cottage with its pitched tile roof and brick chimneys had been deserted for years, one could still feel its charm and comfort. I peeked through the windows and saw large bare high-ceilinged rooms. Now owned by a Belgian shopkeeper, it once had been a religious haven. Amid the native grasses and plants shrouding the perimeter of the home stood an ancient, towering avocado tree. Its large twisted branches and broad leaves reached almost to the ground, providing a cool, shady enclosure beneath. A small waterfall gurgled within yards of the abandoned site. Overhanging the clear-running stream was a simple wooden platform, constructed amid branches, used by the former inhabitant for his morning prayers.

We sat on rocks along the bank and ate our picnic lunches. The older children threw pebbles into the stream while Melli Johnson, of the legendary Johnson missionary family in Burundi, held her newly adopted Burundian baby, Sarah, in her arms. The infant, named after Sarah White, slept peacefully as we sat talking and enjoying the magic of the day. Standing silently on the rims of the hills around us were groups of villagers who had come to observe us. The Burundian people among whom we lived were never intrusive or rude on such occasions. They simply watched with polite curiosity. When we called to our children that it was time to go, they emerged, trailing in a row, laughing and singing, from amidst the dense undergrowth. I savored the joy and innocence of that moment. Fortunately, I didn't know how little time I had left in Burundi.

The next two and half weeks were perfect for our family. The ville morte ended. The girls went back to school. We spent weekends at Ruzizi National Park watching the hippos and crocodiles in their lazy poses next to Lake Tanganyika, and enjoyed Sunday afternoons by the pool with our good friends the Belgian ambassador and his wife. Our children were thriving as they spent long happy hours playing outdoors. Television held no interest for them. Their self-confidence and joy grew stronger as they mastered French and made new friends. The equatorial sunshine and fresh mountain air were healthy for them emotionally and physically. Life for the children and me took on a simplicity and fullness seemingly impossible to duplicate in the fast-paced world of the United States. I knew that having the opportunity to live in central Africa was a unique privilege, and never ceased feeling grateful, as well as astonished, that I was there. I told Bob I wanted to stay in Burundi for twenty years.

My happiness was intensified on Sunday, February 26, when a home pregnancy test showed that I was pregnant. As with our daughters, this baby was planned and deeply wanted. Bob and I were overcome with joy and felt profoundly blessed by the news.

It was this pregnancy and my intense maternal instincts toward Mariana and Sarah that almost caused me to miss one of my greatest experiences in Burundi. During a visit from Dallas friends Kathryn and Craig Hall, we were offered a chance to tour Burundi by helicopter with UN officials. I tossed and turned all night as I debated the risks of such a flight. I felt it was irresponsible and dangerous. I exhausted myself with concern. Finally, realizing that the chances of crashing were slim, I decided to go. As I boarded the large UN helicopter at Bujumbura Airport, I told the two pilots of my concern. "We don't want to crash either," they said amiably. And, they assured me, they had good mechanics in Kigali, Rwanda, where they were based.

I strapped on a seatbelt and affixed the large earphones that would allow me to communicate with the pilots, and then we gradually rose above the shores of Lake Tanganyika and into the mountains to the north. While I had witnessed firsthand Burundi's dense population during our many drives throughout the country, seeing it from the air gave me an even fuller perspective. I pressed my face against the window. Few roads crisscrossed the landscape. The footpaths that linked neighbors could be seen as tiny lines running up and down the hills. Below us, rust-colored thatched-roof huts and carefully tilled fields covered every single hillside and valley in view. I simply saw no expanses of uninhabited land.

The purpose of our trip was to visit Tutsi displaced-person camps in the interior of Burundi. Nearing the first camp, the pilots made a pass-by over the school compound where we were to land. As we flew in ever-smaller circles, I saw a large group of people gathered below. The propellers caused a gust so forceful that the tall grasses and small trees beneath us bent double. Two villagers standing closest to us covered their faces from the dust and wind. As we landed, it seemed the people would be blown over as they strained against the dirt and debris kicking up all around. The pilots turned off the engine and we jumped to the ground.

A small group of Burundian men dressed in Western-style suits approached us, among them the governor of the region. With them were uniformed soldiers. Three thousand displaced Tutsis lived in two camps in this area; hundreds had gathered to meet us. After fleeing their homes two years earlier, many had been given refuge in the single-story brick school buildings behind where they now stood. We walked toward the sea of faces that were attentively and silently watching our every move. Grouped together in rows, they were far too numerous to count.

After a brief welcome in Kirundi and English, we were led to four-wheel-drive vehicles and driven a short distance down narrow red-dirt roads. As I gazed out of the window, my eyes met those of a solitary woman in native dress peacefully walking by. Even in the midst of civil war, Burundi seemed so nonthreatening at times.

A scene of poverty and sickness greeted us at the next camp. Set among tall trees and crowded with barefoot men, women, and children dressed in dirty and ragged clothes, this settlement of displaced Tutsis revealed the turmoil and suffering brought on from years of conflict. Their despair saddened me as I thought of how little we could realistically do for them. A few in the group politely showed us their primitive shelters, which were constructed from corrugated tin, plastic, and branches and set on ground now barren of grass. Wide-eyed children, frail old men, and women in faded traditional dress gathered around us everywhere we walked. Many of the children were coughing. Their bodies, weakened by the cold nights, poor nutrition, and scarcity of medical supplies, heaved with the raspy sound. Yet there was a dignity about the people we met, even in those bleak circumstances. We paused in a dirt clearing as the midmorning African sun shone down through the thin branches of the trees around us. A middle-aged man stepped forward as spokesman for the group. Head and shoulders erect, and with a voice that projected to the crowd clustered in circles around us, he spoke as one who was used to addressing audiences. His personal pride and graciousness shone forth despite his dirty tattered clothes, his bare feet, and the desperate conditions around him.

The UN translator standing with Bob and me whispered into our ears in English as he tried his best to interpret what the man was saying. "We people are in a very bad condition," he began. Then, after thanking us for coming, he described the needs of those in the camp. When he finished, the crowd applauded.

Stepping forward, Bob responded movingly as tears came to our eyes. Kathryn and Craig Hall stood next to me. They could not have felt farther removed from Dallas, Texas, than at that moment. It was impossible not to be affected by the weary faces before us. I felt small and helpless against their overwhelming suffering. With sorrow, we said goodbye and drove away. As we left, a large UN truck arrived, bringing water and supplies from aid orga-

Bob addressing hundreds of displaced Tutsi families near a school building, 1995.

nizations. I silently gave thanks as we passed. Not everyone had forgotten the needy souls I was leaving behind. I turned my head to see them laughing and shouting as they crowded around the relief vehicle—at least there would be one bright spot in their day.

Back at the school compound, the large throngs of people who had first greeted us were still standing in the sun, shoulder to shoulder in rows near our helicopter. Bob briefly addressed the crowd, using simple words and short phrases, and pausing after each sentence so that the UN representative could more easily translate his words into Kirundi. I turned on my video camera to record the event.

"I want to thank all of you for being here today to greet us," Bob began. "I have visited just up the way with some of your relatives and friends and brothers and sisters to hear about their concerns and their problems and to see with my own eyes what you are living."

The people listened attentively as he continued: "They have spoken to me about the problems you have—needing additional medicine. I know, too, by my own eyes and by what they have said, that many of you need clothing for your bodies, food for your stomachs, and soap and water in order to keep clean. I can only promise you my best efforts. But I can tell you that I am here representing the people of the United States because the people of the United States believe that all people are tied together in the same fabric of humanity. And because we are all tied together in the common bonds of humanity, we the American people are brothers and sisters with the people in Burundi and the people right here in this camp. We believe that the same God has made us and loves us all the same. And, therefore, when I report to my government, I will be reporting that our brothers and sisters in Burundi have needs of medicine and food and clothing and soap and water. And I will ask that your brothers and sisters in the United States respond with opening their hearts in assisting with your needs. So I am their eyes and ears here to take back the message of what I have seen, and we will not forget you. Good-bye for now and God bless you."

We returned to the helicopter sitting in the grass nearby. As we rose, I could see, beneath the whirlwind of dirt and grass, lines of people, faces turned upward, arms outstretched, waving goodbye.

By the time we reached the next displaced-person camp, where 2,600 Tutsis lived in near squalor, I was beginning to feel the effects of morning sickness. The pilots set the helicopter down on a dirt road near a large compound of buildings that seemed to combine a school and convent. Remotely located, it was a place of refuge from feared Hutu reprisals. Nuns were obviously in charge, and one young sister guided us across a broad field and into the center of a settlement teeming with people and activity. Barefoot children ran to and fro through the grass and dirt. Long-horned cattle meandered through a primitive communal kitchen, open-sided and covered by a thatched roof. Seemingly unnoticed, the cows deftly stepped around the blackened iron cooking pots and open fires beneath. A woman sat on a straw mat, her legs stretched before her as she wove a basket. She impatiently slapped the curious children who hovered around her when we stopped to greet her. The nun showed us a room where many of the children slept. It was dark, filthy, and crowded. Blankets that appeared never to have been washed lay haphazardly on the cement floor.

"We need beds," the nun implored in French.

I was beginning to feel ill, and told Bob I thought we should leave. Morning sickness and human filth didn't mix well. I regretted cutting our visit short and hoped that I didn't seem unsympathetic to the suffering there. As we boarded the helicopter, I waved and spoke a few sentences in Kirundi to the large group that gathered to say farewell. They enthusiastically responded to my simple phrases, seemingly pleased and surprised that an American could speak their language, however badly. They shouted and waved as we ascended, again burying everyone in a swirl of wind and dust.

We flew north over UN refugee camps, their signature blue tents in neat rows below us, but didn't land. Banking to the right, the pilots gracefully guided the helicopter south toward Bujumbura. It had been a smooth trip, but I was relieved when we were back on firm ground.

Less than an hour after returning, we were seated with the Halls at a large and airy restaurant near our home, a stark contrast to the scene we had visited that morning. There were few restaurants in Bujumbura. This one had an ambience so tropical and African that Bob always said he expected to see Humphrey Bogart walk in the door. Or maybe Katharine Hepburn. After all, the final scene of their old movie classic *The African Queen* was set on Lake Tanganyika, upon whose shores Bujumbura was built.

Before leaving Burundi, the Halls left a significant financial donation to be used for school supplies in the camps we visited. Arrangements for purchasing these goods were well underway when increasing violence in the countryside prevented the project's completion. With the Halls' permission, therefore, the funds were divided equally between two American missionaries in Bujumbura, who used them for humanitarian aid in the city.

FIFTEEN

THE DARK CURTAIN

A Family Divided

By mid-March, the idyllic peace we were enjoying was interrupted once again. After taking the girls to school for Saturday classes, I returned home and lay down in my bedroom. The early months of pregnancy always left me feeling exhausted. Before I could fall asleep, Bob called to tell me that the Burundi minister of energy had just been assassinated on a major street downtown. Within seconds my walkie-talkie erupted in the screeching tones that signaled an emergency message. The marine on duty, Sergeant Charles Vasser, delivered a warning that was brief and to the point: "Attention all personnel, attention all personnel. We have been informed that the minister of energy was killed downtown this morning. We also have a report of brief gunfire in town by the post office. We advise you to refrain from going into the city unless absolutely necessary. We will keep you advised if there is anything further to report. Thank you and have a good day."

Bob had sat next to Energy Minister Kabushemeye at dinner only a week ago at the German ambassador's residence, and had found him to be a very intelligent, confident, and conscientious public official. His assassination meant that Tutsi extremists were continuing to target the strongest Hutu leaders in order to weaken Burundi's frail democracy. His killing downtown in broad daylight was especially unsettling.

I returned to the French School at noon to retrieve Mariana and Sarah. Everything appeared normal along the route. Sarah's teacher told me that they had rushed the children off the playground when they heard the shooting, but my daughters didn't mention anything unusual happening and seemed unaware of the assassination. I greatly admired the French School staff members, who, amid trying circumstances, both maintained high academic standards and saw to the emotional well-being of their students.

That night a few grenades went off, and we could hear the popping sound of automatic-weapon fire as we fell asleep. Though not as bad as some nights, it marked the beginning of another period of unrest. The next day Jean-Marie didn't appear for work, as often happened after particularly noisy nights. Since he lived in a very vulnerable area, we were always concerned when he failed to appear. Bob and I drove to look for him. We found him stranded in his village, the streets and paths around him full of roaming Tutsi youth gangs. He had listened to the fighting all night, poised to run with his family if necessary.

Yet life for us, as for most expatriates, went on as usual. That afternoon we hosted a small luncheon outdoors to say farewell to Christa Griffin, the administrative officer at the embassy, whose tour of duty was complete. Suddenly, a grenade exploded just two blocks away. We immediately reported it to the marine on duty, then went on with our lunch.

As we dined amidst cool greenery and tropical flowers, we watched our children's two pet crested cranes, a gift from the Egyptian ambassador, nesting near the edge of the pool. Elegant birds, almost four feet tall, with long legs and golden crests atop their heads, they pranced through our carefully manicured gardens with a regal air that added to the idyllic setting we enjoyed each day. I never ceased being near breathless at the view from our spacious white veranda set high above Bujumbura. Beyond the striking silhouette of the fan-shaped traveler's palms against the changing sky were the vastness of Lake Tanganyika and the mountains of Zaire in the distance. From sunrise to moonlight it offered as beautiful a view as I had ever known.

But on March 19 my world changed dramatically. At 11:00 p.m. we received a call from Ambassador Ould-Abdallah that three Belgians, among them a woman and her four-year-old daughter, had been killed by Hutu rebels on the highway from Ijenda. Through the night, from both Ambassador Ould-Abdallah and Ambassador Van Craen, we learned the tragic details. Two Belgian families, in separate cars, had been returning to Bujumbura from the countryside after curfew, having been delayed earlier in the afternoon by a flat tire. Rounding a bend on the mountainous road that we had often driven to the alleged "Source of the Nile," which is marked with a stone monument, the cars were caught in an ambush meant for a minivan of Burundian soldiers who were expected to be traveling down the same highway. Logs with spikes had been laid across the road, and when these punctured their tires, the Belgian cars careened into a ravine, and two Burundians in a third car were reportedly killed in the crash. Some among the Belgian group successfully ran into the banana groves to escape. However, one mother with her four-year-old daughter stood in the ditch and pleaded with the rebels in Kirundi, "Don't shoot, we are Belgians."

Since expatriates had not been targeted before, she thought they would be safe if she identified herself clearly to the assailants. Nevertheless, a Hutu rebel shot both the woman and her daughter in the head at close range. A family friend lying injured in the car warned the woman's other young daughter, lying next to her, to pretend that she was dead. Amazingly, the child had the composure to comply, saving their lives.

The killing devastated me. I called Mrs. Van Craen at midnight, and we both grieved over the tragedy. Whatever nonchalance I may have had about living in Burundi drained from my psyche. A mother and a child the same age as my Sarah had been brutally murdered at close range along a road we had traveled just weeks before. It was as though a dark curtain had fallen around me. Yes, Burundian children every week had been murdered in equally gruesome ways by the military. Yet I can't deny that I had not been as affected by those deaths. Despite the horrendous massacres and suffering that surrounded us, I had always felt that our family was safe, since we were obviously neither Hutu nor Tutsi. These murders ended that sense of security.

I had not respected the Hutu rebels before. Now I detested them, especially after the flippant statement made by the rebel leader after the Belgians were killed: "In warfare, lives are lost, both innocent and guilty." Small in number and inefficient, they made futile raids against the Burundi Army and then fled. In their wake, the Tutsi military swept the hillsides surrounding the area of the attack, killing innocent Hutu men, women, and children who had had no part in the rebel incursions. These bandes armées brought more pain and heartache to their ethnic kinsmen than they ever prevented.

The next day I was too stunned to take the children to school. I wanted them close to me. When we returned to L'École Française, I discovered that a sense of grief had fallen over the entire expatriate community. The victims had been well-liked, and were deeply mourned. Many of the mothers gathered in the school parking lot were bitter and angry. Everyone felt Burundi had entered a new realm, in which no one was safe.

On March 24, Ambassador Arlene Render, director of the State Department's Office of Central African Affairs, arrived from Washington. Bob, Sarah, and I met her at the airport. Knowing that Washington had been nervous all along about dependents living in Burundi, I hoped that the week would be quiet and peaceful.

My hopes were totally dashed. By four in the afternoon, widespread shooting had erupted all over the city. Nothing like it had happened in all my time in Burundi. Ambassador Render was in our living room, meeting with two Burundian government officials. I hurried in, carrying my walkie-talkie, which was exploding with anxious messages from Americans across the city: "I've got people stranded in the Asiatic Quartier." "There's shooting next to the USAID building."

Ambassador Render jumped from her seat. "They're shooting the USAID building?" she asked anxiously.

"No," I reassured her, "he said *near* the USAID building."

Urgent reports of gunfire were transmitted nonstop. We could clearly hear the machine-gun fire and grenades outside. Warfare was exploding all over the city at once. It was nearly deafening.

I cannot forget the expression on the faces of the Burundian officials, who had remained seated on our couch. Both were Hutus who had lived with violence most of their lives. Apparently unperturbed, they looked at us as if to say, "So, can we continue the meeting?"

Standing with me on our front veranda overlooking the city, Ambassador Render took my hand, asking, "Do you understand why I'm concerned about you all?"

I did understand. I understood that being responsible for the lives of Americans overseas is a tremendous burden for anyone, but I wanted to stay. To wait out the violence. To pull in when necessary, and in between to absorb and thrive on the Burundian culture, language, and people I had grown to love. I felt that my entire life's spiritual journey had led me to this place, where I felt my efforts were imbued with a meaning and purpose I had never known before. I didn't want to be taken away from a place where I felt so completely fulfilled.

As machine guns continued firing and grenades exploded, I looked past the palm trees and flowers to Lake Tanganyika and the mountains in Zaire. I could feel Burundi slipping away from me, and my heart filled with sorrow.

Stepping inside, Ambassador Render took Mariana's and Sarah's hands and began to teach them a dance and rhyme she herself had enjoyed as a child:

Little Sally Walker, sitting in a saucer, rise, Sally, rise.
Wipe your weeping eyes and put your hands on your hips and let your
   backbone slip.
Shake it to the east, shake it to the west, shake it to the one that you love
   the best.

As usual, the children were not afraid of the explosions in the neighborhoods below us. I appreciated her efforts to distract them.

Ambassador Render was staying at our house overnight, and she spent most of that time on the phone, since calls to and from Washington were numerous. She was open with us about the concerns that were being expressed at the State Department. She hadn't used the words "evacuation," "ordered departure," or "voluntary departure," but I knew they were coming.

The next day I began wrapping framed family photos in newspaper. They were among the few personal items we had brought other than clothing and some books. Holding out hope that we wouldn't have to leave, Bob asked me to stop. But by the next evening, March 25, the decision was final. Families of American-embassy employees would have to return to the United States. It was called a "voluntary departure," but there was nothing voluntary about it. Our government had sent us to Burundi, and now was asking (ordering) us to leave. The girls and I would be flown out on a Belgian airliner in two days. We could take only two suitcases apiece. I felt as though someone were tearing my arm off.

Ironically, the Saturday and Sunday before the children and I left were peaceful and beautiful. We were told that a couple of grenades had exploded during the night, but we hadn't heard them. Sunday afternoon, as we sat on our veranda, I was struck by how utterly tranquil our surroundings were. And yet we were leaving. Bob phoned my parents in Bandera, Texas, to let them know we were coming back. "We're being evacuated, Grandma," Mariana said innocently.

That morning I had attended church services led by Graham White. Because of the unrest, the small congregation had gathered at the Whites' house, just two blocks away. Like most meetings that I attended in Africa, it was an international group. Word was out that American embassy families were leaving. That decision affected the emotions and plans of others living in Bujumbura, as well as the theme of the worship that morning.

The service was beautiful, the music uplifting, the message positive and inspirational. American missionaries, a few employees of the American embassy, Germans, British, Indians, Africans, and others crowded into Sarah White's living room for the simple ceremony.

Outside the sun was shining, flowers were blooming, birds sang in the trees. A soft breeze blew through the open doors from the balcony. I stepped outside to be alone. Below me in the lush back garden was a swing set and next to it a rabbit hutch. Beyond, the green trees, the tropical flowers, the blue lake, and the purple mountains fading into the distance all seemed so peaceful and familiar. I lingered in that moment, wanting to become one with the vision before me. Like a hand in a soft glove, I felt this was my right place, a place where I was comfortable, where I was happy, where I was at home. When I rejoined the group and tried to sing the hymns, my throat clenched. It took all my strength to hold back the torrent of grief welling up inside me.

Back at home I had work to do. Decisions had to be made about what each of our two suitcases would contain. Other things had to be organized for possible shipment back to Texas in the future. Ambassador Render kindly cautioned me not to overexert, since I was two months pregnant, but I felt strong, and focused on what needed to be done. With the growing crisis, added to by the departure of Americans, Bob worked at the embassy up until curfew, and then remained on the phone most of the night. The telephone lines to and from Paris, Bonn, and Brussels were burning as hotly as those to Washington, D.C., as the international media began arriving in anticipation of a major conflict.

Sabena Airlines in Belgium agreed to send an additional plane to accommodate all the Europeans who were also leaving. Many French citizens had been urged to return to Paris for the upcoming Easter holidays and to wait and see how things developed in Burundi. I decided to use most of my luggage space for the children's clothes and special toys. Pregnant for the third time, I found that most of my clothes were already too tight, and I hoped to return to Burundi after our baby was born, when the clothes I was leaving behind would fit again.

Because of the violence, the French School was closed for an extended Easter break, but Mariana's teacher asked that I come down at 9:30 in the morning for a meeting and to pick up her schoolwork. It was a sad trip. I walked across the empty schoolyard where, on the first day, Mariana, not knowing French, had made friends by writing her name in the dirt and inviting others to do the same. I gazed at the row of plain classrooms that had been filled with the beautiful voices of children singing French and Swahili folk songs at the end of the school day. I walked the sidewalk where I had so often stood with German, Indian, African, Iranian, English, French, and Belgian mothers and fathers who, I quickly learned, were so like us. I stood alone in the middle of the bare grounds and looked at the lush green mountains around me. What a wonderful experience it had been for my children to be students in a French school in the heart of Africa, surrounded by people of different cultures, languages, and religions. I would never forget it. I hoped they wouldn't either.

As she handed my daughter's schoolwork to me, her teacher begged me not to let Mariana lose her knowledge of French, which she had learned to speak in such a beautiful accent. "She was one of my top students," she said to me wistfully, as we said good-bye.

"When will you be back?" she asked.

When would we be back? Oh, how I wished to know the answer.

"I will return after my baby is born," I responded, only half believing my own words.

Back at the house, I finished straightening and packing for the children. Bob, of course, would be staying behind. He seemed the saddest I had ever seen him.

On March 28, Bob called a town-hall meeting for Americans, at the U.S. cultural center downtown. The children and I came along. About twenty people attended, including several aid workers whom I had never seen before. Bob was somber, but at ease, as he explained that embassy families were departing because of generally increased violence and deteriorating security. We both had come to accept what lay before us, and tried to take a positive attitude about it all. But it wasn't easy.

He concluded by offering to help any aid workers and missionaries who wanted to leave the country. I looked down at my two little girls sitting quietly next to me. I was sure they didn't realize the full import of his words.

The meeting was adjourned, and we returned home through drizzle and rain. Low gray clouds and fog blocked any view of the mountains. We would spend one last night together in Bujumbura.

On March 29, Bernardin drove Bob, the girls, and me to the airport in the bullet-proof car. It was early morning, but the terminal was already filled with passengers, families, reporters, and international television crews. After speaking briefly to CNN International, we joined Americans and others in a private lounge area. One might have thought we were all leaving on a long-anticipated cruise. The mood had a veneer of happiness. Some lucky enough to be staying, such as the Graham White family, who as British citizens were not affected by the voluntary-departure order, were present to say good-bye. Pictures were snapped and video was taken of what we all fervently hoped would be only a temporary farewell. Mariana and Sarah were excited because Kate Duguid, with her mother and siblings, would be on the same flight as we were.

Suddenly, it was painfully time to go. Bob walked us out onto the tarmac, and was allowed to escort us up the stairs to the door of the plane. A Reuters photographer captured our good-bye kiss, which was printed in the *New York Times* and other publications. As the flight attendant closed the door behind us, my two little girls and I found our seats in the midsection of the plane. The flight was entirely full of what appeared to be almost exclusively Europeans and Americans. Many were truly just going home for the Easter break. The fifteen Americans on board had a more serious status. As we taxied down the runway, I strained to see, once more, the fertile tropical

Dependents and families returning to the United States: Bob walked Kathleen, Sarah, and Mariana onto the tarmac and escorted them to the door of the plane, Bujumbura Airport, March 29, 1995.

landscape of my adopted homeland. I remembered the anticipation I had felt when we arrived five months earlier. Although we had flown all night from Brussels to Bujumbura, I had felt no weariness, since my excitement at the new life ahead of us had filled me with energy and joy. Now, as the plane gradually ascended, I could scarcely believe that it was all to be over so soon.

That morning I had written a final letter to my friends back home. At five, as the early-morning light illuminated the flowering gardens outside my bedroom window, the words tumbled from my heart:

> With regret, this will be my last letter from Africa for awhile. In four hours the children and I will board a plane, bound for Europe and then the United States. The State Department, National Security Council of the President, Defense Department and others feel the security situation has become too dangerous for us to stay.
>
> I don't want Africa to be my past. I want it to be my present. But, it seems that it is time to go for now, so we will. Back to wonderful Texas and to familiar friends and family. But, my heart will live in Burundi for a long time. This has been a happy time for us and I am so very grateful for the

chance to experience this fascinating land. . . . I will count the days until our return.

If the violent episodes are extracted, and fortunately none of those were ever directed at us, the experience of Burundi has been heartwarming, inspiring and magnificent.

This is not, as Bob has often said, a white gloves and chandeliers assignment, but when diplomacy by the world community is successful, is a post where thousands of lives can be saved. No position that Bob has ever held has been more meaningful or satisfying.

As the pilot turned to cross Lake Tanganyika, I caught one more glimpse of this breathtakingly scenic land before closing my eyes in sorrow.

Twenty-four hours later our plane touched down at the San Antonio International Airport. Since we would be arriving late at night, I had asked Bob's sister, Arlene, if she could meet us. When we entered the terminal, however, I was overwhelmed to find most of my very large family and several close friends there, as well as members of the press. I had never expected such a welcome, and was overcome with emotion. I fell into my mother's arms, exhausted and heartbroken, haunted by the images and people I had left behind.

Burundi, a land whose natural beauty is marred only by the pain and suffering of its people, would remain a part of me forever.

SIXTEEN

GASORWE

Hundreds Massacred and a Reporter Murdered

TO MAGARA AND MUYINGA

It was Friday morning, March 31, just forty-eight hours since I had said good-bye to my family at the airport, when Chris Reilly, the embassy security officer, came to my office and asked to see me. Chris had a fairly calm manner; if he was asking for immediate time, something important was up.

He had received word that at least seven men, three women, and two children had been killed, and twenty-two or more wounded, in a grenade attack against Rwandan Hutu refugees in the UN camp of Majuri, in northern Burundi. The Burundi Army was thought to be complicit in or directly responsible for the killings, which had sent panic among the more than 30,000 refugees at Majuri. When news of the attack reached the nearby UN refugee camp at Magara, the largest in Burundi, the terror had spread like wildfire through the blue plastic-covered tents housing the camp's almost 50,000 inhabitants. At morning's first light, they had hastily gathered their paltry yet precious possessions, loaded each family member big enough to walk with something to carry, broken camp, and set off eastward. Already refugees in one strange land, the Rwandans from these two camps were now headed for another—Tanzania, roughly eighty miles away.

Ominous as the report sounded, so accustomed had I become to the army's slaughter that I felt a touch of relief that "only" twelve had been killed for sure. But that relief paled at the prospect of perhaps 50,000 Hutu refugees passing through isolated villages and small towns on a several-day trek to the border, for the violence would inevitably increase and might easily explode into a major massacre.

Knowing that Magara was several hours from Bujumbura by car and that the refugees were already on the road, Chris and I decided to leave without delay. We hoped to find influential refugee leaders who, together with government officials, could persuade the Rwandans to return to Magara; we also needed military officials who could ensure their safety there. Before departing, though, we knew we would have to find a Kirundi speaker to accompany us, since almost none of the refugees would know English and only a few would speak French. Fortunately, Cosmas Vrampas was available. Since there would be few restaurants en route where one could expect to eat and be free of dysentery, my secretary, Frances, called our cook, Marcien, to prepare an ice chest of food. My Pajero was fuelled; a high-tech battery-operated Inmarsat satellite telephone was made ready so that we could be in touch with Washington or Bujumbura, and we were ready to walk out the door.

Just then, the visiting U.S. defense intelligence officer entered to tell me that he thought my trip a mistake—that I would be putting the United States unnecessarily at risk and that little, if anything, could be accomplished.

I had long thought this officer should have remained a paratrooper rather than become an intelligence officer. He flew into Burundi from another African assignment for two or three days each month, and spent much of his time on the golf course with expatriates or Tutsi bourgeoisie, or having drinks with Burundi Army officers. Although I understood the need to meet and know the Burundi military in comfortable surroundings, I figured that if occasionally he had gone into the countryside, he might have gotten a better sense of the Burundi Army's philosophy and actions than he was getting on the fairways and putting greens. Moreover, being already in a hurry, I was not inclined to be dissuaded by someone contradicting the assessment of the embassy's regional security officer, who thought the situation was potentially critical.

I was nevertheless brusquer than I should have been. Shutting the door, I asked him to sit down, and pointed to a commission, framed and hanging on the wall, stating that William J. Clinton, president of the United States, "reposing special trust and confidence in [my] Integrity, Prudence, and Ability . . . [had appointed me] Ambassador Extraordinary and Plenipotentiary of the United States . . . authorizing [me] to do and perform all such matters . . . as to the Office appertain." "Do you understand what that statement means?" I asked.

"Yes sir," he replied.

"Then you understand that the commander in chief has named me as his personal representative, with his powers, in this country?"

"Yes sir."

"All right, Colonel," I said, "Keep that in mind. I will ask your advice when I wish it and heed it when I find it convincing, but I don't ever want to have to pull rank on you again. Do you understand?"

"Yes sir."

Smoke rising from the small campfires of weary refugees, whose numbers stretched as far as the eye could see, Gasorwe, March 31, 1995.

And with that matter settled, I got behind the wheel, picked up food and clothes for our trip, and headed north with Chris and Cosmas.

North of a line extending from Kayanza and Ngozi to Muyinga were located most of the approximately 300,000 Rwandan Hutu refugees then living in Burundi. They constituted 5 percent of the total Burundi population, roughly comparable to 3 million refugees in the United Kingdom or 14 million in the United States. Homeless, hapless, dependent, and sometimes desperate, 50,000 or more of these refugees were now moving from misery to almost certain persecution, violence, and conflict.

Shortly after passing the turnoff for the Magara camp, I could see smoke rising over the highway from the small campfires of weary refugees who had paused for some hot cassava or manioc. Then came into view the long pulsating line of weary and frightened refugees, stretching along the winding road as far as I could see, until they and the treetops were lost in the vast African sky. As I dropped the car into a lower gear and we slowly threaded our way through the tired travelers, I saw no tears and heard no cries, but all about me I saw and felt yearning eyes and looks of fear, discouragement, and puzzlement. Probably few, if any, of the refugees had ever been along this road, or to Tanzania. Perhaps many, especially the children who composed the majority of the group, knew not where they were going, but only that they were going somewhere else. Like battered shuttlecocks in a deadly badminton contest, they were bounced from one location to another, seldom knowing or controlling where they went, but longing for the end of the game.

Ahead of me, wrapped in brightly colored cotton garments, were barefoot women carrying bottles, blankets, beans, and bundles of clothing, all tied together and carefully balanced on their heads. No children, except those strapped to their mothers' backs, were too small to carry something. Even sticks of firewood were considered necessary enough to carry from Magara and Majuri to their unknown destination. How they survived without despair was beyond me, but the stoic resignation and fortitude that characterizes people in this region somehow sustained them.

As we neared the front of the long column, we came upon a group comprising regional administrative officials, three members of Parliament, and several high-ranking military officers. The agreement that they reported having reached had convinced the refugees to return to their camps without fear of reprisal or attack. How valid the agreement would prove, especially if some of the soldiers got high on banana beer or marijuana—a common occurrence—was by no means certain. Yet all in all, most of the refugees while in camp had faced dysentery, malaria, and diseases as their principal enemies, not their army guards. They would be safer from armed attack and better able to receive enough calories to stay alive if they were in the UN camp rather than on the road to Tanzania. Thus, if the shuttlecock was flying back to Magara rather than to the Tanzanian border, it could expect a safer landing.

By this time it was already late afternoon, and we were unable to return to Bujumbura before the evening curfew. In any case, for several weeks I had wanted to come to Kirundo province, having received numerous reports of widespread and unchecked violence by the army. The bishop of Muyinga, who had been the object of attack while performing a mass last August, had earlier invited me to visit the region. And as we were packing the car in Bujumbura, Frances had arranged for us to have dinner with him and to stay in the dormitory-style rooms available for rent on the church grounds. They offered both hot and cold running water and sheets on the mattresses, and so were easily superior to the only hotel in town, where I had stayed before, and which could provide neither.

The dinner was for me a unique experience. Gathered together at the simple but tidy table befitting a monastery were the bishop, his assistant, and five missionary priests from the Catholic Missionaries of Africa order, popularly known as the "White Fathers." This group of five came originally from

Passing carefully through tens of thousands of refugees from Gasorwe headed toward Tanzania, March 31, 1995.

France, Italy, and Switzerland, and had served in Africa for periods of ten to fifty years apiece. All had been in Rwanda when that nation exploded in 1994. Then, when the congregations to whom they had ministered had fled as refugees to Burundi, the priests came with them. They would not abandon their flocks until they found safety—which had been provided by the UN camps in the region. Yet they spoke not of themselves or the hardships they had encountered, but of what had transpired during the past few weeks in the villages of this region, where they now served. My notes began:

> Province Karuzi—Commune Gitaramuka—25 March—Massacres with over 100 killed: Hutus are afraid to go to Church.

When I asked a priest if he could be certain of the numbers, he replied, "Of course. They were members of my parish, and we have buried them." My notes continued:

> Giteranyi: *bandes armées* killing one and leaving five wounded who later died. Many small bands attack this area—in small guerilla groups. The *Sans Échec* then take the opportunity for revenge against the guerilla groups and all Hutus. In the process, they take the opportunity to steal.
>
> Buhinyuza: 70 killed this month, since 1 March (69 Hutus plus 1 Tutsi wife killed by *déplacés*. Twas [pygmies] brought there by Army.)

The list went on:

> 29 March, 9 killed at Bihago and Rukongwe: 20 seriously wounded (head wounds) caused by bayonets, machetes.
> 31 March, 8 killed on Nashuhu.
> 20 March, 8 killed at Commune Gitaramuka
> 25 March, 12 killed at Colline Gashanga, sector Bugwana
> 7 dead at Colline Bugwana
> 60 killed in the sector
> 10 killed at Mugende

The catalogue of destruction continued in my notebook for several more pages, reporting tens and scores of killings in regional locations with names painstakingly spelled for me by the priests. To me, the collines, villages, and communities were strange and unknown. To the priests, the names identified places where they served and people whom they had loved, and buried.

In Kizi two days earlier, over one hundred Hutus had been killed. A communal administrator, himself a Hutu, had been rewarded or coerced by the army into selecting those most deserving to die. Invited by the more experienced army members to join them in the killing had been members of the local chapter of the Tutsi youth group Sans Échec, some of whom, like young lion cubs, were allowed the thrill of drawing their first blood. Though disguised in army uniforms, the youths were recognized by survivors. After the attack, the village itself had been abandoned.

Worst of all was the village of Gasorwe, where the priests were certain that over 150 people had been killed in the past four days. Of those, approximately 60 had been buried, and even more were not yet buried; of the survivors, 10 had been taken to the hospital, and most had fled into the forest. The priest there, a White Father, had reported by messenger that ten people had been killed that very morning, and the murder was continuing.

I asked the bishop whether he or someone else would accompany me to Gasorwe the next morning. He declined, fearing that his priests might suffer revenge upon my departure. Even so, he said that I was free to contact Père Mauro, the local priest, since I would arouse less suspicion by arriving on my own. I concurred, put my nine pages of notes on the floor, took a sip from the glass of red wine before me, and began to bathe in the ambience of this extraordinary group.

How many years of service in Africa, in total, did they represent? Somewhere between 100–200 years, I reckoned. What were the backgrounds and shaping influences in devotion and faith that had brought men so far in time and space from their homes, that had prompted them to leave the families in which they had been reared, and to take vows requiring them to abandon all hope of having biological families of their own? I wondered how many possessions and memories they had left behind. And yet I felt myself in the presence not of poverty but of spiritual riches. They had followed their faith; they had followed their flocks—these modern shepherds who lived not on open hillsides, but certainly in simplicity. None of their faces showed regret. Balanced, poised, taciturn, yet caring, they were as devout and dedicated a group, and as self-sacrificing without being self-pitying, as any that I was likely to dine with again. And while the food served at my residence in Bujumbura was more sumptuous, the guests whom I could invite did not compare. The priests' vocations required vows of poverty, but they had the advantage of ministering to the wounded and suffering. My vocation, I reflected, required me to invite people like former President Buyoya and Colonel Bikomagu to dinner—the perpetrators of such suffering, those who delivered death.

ETHNIC CLEANSING IN GASORWE

After an early breakfast with the missionary priests the next morning, Chris, Cosmas, and I drove ten miles west, to the village of Gasorwe. On arrival, we needed no search for evidence of death and destruction; it was everywhere. Houses burned, buildings shattered, and scarcely any evidence of life. Unable to find anyone to give directions, we made our way to the village church, visible on the hill. There, we concluded that a simple gray stone residence attached to the church must lodge the priest. We knocked. No answer. Seeing a parked car, which we assumed was his, we knocked again, persistently. Finally, after calling loudly in French and English that the bishop had sent us to talk with Father Mauro, the door opened.

A slightly bent, balding, but wiry and bright-eyed priest admitted us and, learning our mission, offered a cup of tea while apologizing for his delay in opening the door. Less than an hour ago, however, he had been roughed up by youths from Sans Échec, who had stopped his car as he was driving an injured Hutu to the hospital. The thugs had reached into his car, stealing his identity papers and some personal documents that included lists of the dead and wounded. They attempted to steal his keys so that they might take his car as well, but he successfully fought them off and escaped with his car, his passenger, and his life. He credited his safety from attack during the past three days of butchery in the village to the intervention of the recently retired Ganwa bishop living nearby, Roger Mpungu, who had convinced the leader of the military operations to leave the church and priest's residence free from pillage.

Communicating mostly in French, with occasional bits of English and Italian, he recounted that on the previous Monday the army had called for a town meeting and instructed the people not to run if the army came. Those who fled would be considered members or supporters of the bandes armées and would be fired upon. Nonetheless, only yesterday Father Mauro watched as the army, a short distance from his residence, had surrounded a group of ten unresisting villagers, largely women and children, and attacked them with rifle butts and clubs, bludgeoning them all to death. Helpless to stop the brutality, the priest took photographs of the carnage. Then, looking furtively around the room and imploringly into our faces, he said, "During the genocide in 1972, a soldier put a bayonet to my throat because I called him an assassin. If my identity is revealed, not only will I be killed, but so will many of the people who live here."

During each of the past five days, his parishioners had been ruthlessly slaughtered. Precisely how many in the village and nearby hills had been killed he did not know, but he knew the number was well into the hundreds, and many of the wounded who had escaped their hunters had, like crippled animals, gone into the forests to die. Only a few had dared to go to hospitals, where doctors and nurses were almost all Tutsis, and where Hutu peasants generally feared that they would be killed, refused care, or reported to the army as collaborators with the bandes armées.

The army's excuse for its attacks, as always, was that it was looking for arms and supporters of the Hutu bandes armées, but Father Mauro added scathingly, "*Ça ce n'est pas le désarmament. C'est du génocide exécuté par les forces de l'ordre*" (It is not disarmament. It is genocide carried out by the military). Then he added, "*Plus de 50 percent sont des enfants et des femmes*" (More than half are women and children).

He had photographed a number of victims. If we promised to have his film privately developed, we could keep the pictures. Were the photos to be commercially developed, and his own face to appear on them, his identity as the photographer could be revealed, bringing military retribution, he said. So, I took the film, had the pictures developed by an Associated Press reporter in his Bujumbura hotel room, and a few weeks later showed them to the president of the United States in the Oval Office.

Departing from the church and driving through the village square, we saw no dogs, no goats, no people, no life. Doors on most houses were open, but it did not matter, for neither inhabitants nor possessions were left within. The name of the village was Gasorwe, but it might well have been Guernica. One was in Burundi, the other in Spain, but both communities and their populations had been destroyed by vicious militaries. Guernica, however, had light-skinned people, and Picasso to capture its horror, and so the world remembers. In Gasorwe, the people were black, they had no artist to capture their pain, and hence few people to know or care.

As we returned to Muyinga around noon, I realized that it was not just the town of Gasorwe but the surrounding hillsides for miles around that were vacant. With the melody and words of the folk song, "Where have all the flowers gone?" echoing in the chambers of my mind, I wondered, "Where have all the Hutus gone?" And the answer was that they had fled. To observe fertile hills at midday without workers tilling them, in one of the two most densely populated countries in Africa, is to know that terror was covering the hillsides like morning mist. Fear of the army was keeping the peasant farming families from their fields. The next question was where could they go. Tanzania might not be accessible to them: it had put up roadblocks and barriers at some border crossings, since, as one of the world's poorest countries, it felt unable to absorb and care for any more Burundians and Rwandans. Finally, I asked myself, how many lives had been lost not only to the soldier's bayonet and the Sans Échec machete, but to hunger and exposure on the hillsides? We would never know.

We returned to Muyinga, a town large enough to have a variety of stores, a marketplace, and a bishop, but a community that was, like the countryside, captured by fear. The priests had informed us that no Hutu businesses remained in Muyinga, having been subjected during the past month to repeated looting and sometimes to arson. Hutu women, they added, came to town to shop only in groups so that they could offer one another a modicum of protection.

ONE HOSPITAL AND ONE DOCTOR FOR 80,000 PEOPLE?

The town had one hospital, a small one-story brick-and-cement structure set back from the road, sheltered beneath the quivering leaves of tall eucalyptus trees. Inside I met Cyprien Ntamagara, a moderate, compassionate, and humane Tutsi physician, and his assistant, Sister Christine, who were caring for the wounded in a simple, unadorned, and minimally equipped community hospital with fewer facilities than are found in a physician's office in a developed Western nation today. According to the parents, relatives, and victims themselves, all the patients were victims of military attacks, and almost all the victims were women and children, most from Gasorwe. The first patient to whom Dr. Ntamagara introduced me was an eleven-year-old boy who had been shot in the cheek and blinded in the left eye by soldiers in Gasorwe on Wednesday. The doctor said that he had lain in the forest for twenty-four hours before being brought to the hospital, and considered it miraculous that he had survived the operation. White bandages covered half his face, but his gleaming black skin and bright right eye shone forth, and he somehow managed to smile for his elders in spite of his pain.

Lying next to him was a thirteen-year-old boy, Clavier Sibomana. His entire skull was bandaged because, if we understood Dr. Ntamagara correctly, his brain was protruding, his skull having been sliced by a *couteau* (knife). In the adjoining room was a fifteen-year-old boy who had been hospitalized for four weeks, ever since someone had tossed a hand grenade into his classroom at the Rugari School, killing two and wounding approximately forty. His presence was evidence that the tactics of Micombero and Bagaza—i.e., keep the Hutus from going to school so that they will remain subjugated—had continued beyond the end of their repressive dictatorships.

Déogratias, a twenty-year-old kitchen worker from the village of Naha-biri, in Bihago, explained how, while he was baking bread in the kitchen of a bistro there, several members of the military had entered to buy beer. Although some customers had fled on their entry, the soldiers offered to buy beer for all who had stayed. But when it came time to pay, instead of stepping up to the bar and putting down their money, they ran to the door, tossed in a grenade, and, after the explosion, strafed the room with automatic-weapon fire. Five lay dead, four had been shot and wounded, and others, like Déogratias, had been injured by the grenade.

As I moved from bed to bed, trying to comprehend the stories related by the physician, the victims' relatives, or the victims themselves, I was proceeding from horror to horror, knowing that the fifteen to twenty patients whom the hospital held were but a minute fraction of those requiring medical attention. On several occasions after my arrival in Burundi, I had inquired into how many trained physicians treated its six million people. Unfortunately, official statistics on such matters were unreliable. One Western development officer had said there were thirty-six physicians in Bujumbura and perhaps an equal number spread across the remainder of the country. That would have meant one physician for approximately 80,000 people, a staggeringly small estimate that I believed to be too low, but that one missionary of many years experience in Burundi thought too high. And judging from my travels, I would have been even more surprised if in all Burundi there were even 200 physicians, or one for every 30,000 people. Further, most physicians were Tutsi, and treated mostly Tutsis. As a result, then, of ethnic bias and fears, and the paucity of physicians, many Hutus rarely or never received medical care.

Finally, however, it was not the uncertain statistics on medical care, but the last patient I saw in the Muyinga hospital, that most poignantly conveyed the suffering of the Burundian people. Dr. Ntamagara took me to the bed of a tiny, lovely, eighteen-month-old girl who lay fast asleep, the upper half of her body visible and unharmed. Then he pulled back the white covers that lay over her lower torso and explained the attack she had suffered: little Felicité had been bayoneted deeply in the vagina. Some crazed Tutsi soldier had been determined to assure that this Hutu would never bear children.

That was enough barbarism for one day. A long drive lay ahead, and we needed to return home before curfew. I had enough to reflect on. After less than a week of army activity, the known dead and buried exceeded 400, and the estimated dead and wounded as well as those who would die for lack of treatment moved the number into thousands—all from rural villages and hillside settlements within a radius of ten miles of Muyinga.

These were deaths I had discovered by accident. Had it not been for the temporary camp closing at Magara, I might not have come to Muyinga for several more weeks. And if the Rwandan refugees had not turned back, but had continued on their way to Muyinga and the Tanzanian border, the soldiers and the thugs in Sans Échec who had frolicked with their machetes, clubs, and automatic weapons in the villages would have enjoyed a festival of killing as the helpless refugees with their few possessions on their heads offered the troops long lines of desperate, frightened people for target practice. They could hardly miss. I concluded my notes describing the plight of Hutus in the region, altering one word, with one of the cruelest lines in Shakespeare:

As flies to wanton boys, are we to the (Army);
They kill us for their sport.

THE PRESS RESPONSE TO RETURNING REFUGEES

As we headed back toward Bujumbura, within an hour we came upon the vast crowd of Rwandan refugees, now trudging westward to UN camps. The agreement reached the previous afternoon, flimsy because it depended upon the army's willingness to restrain itself from killing, was nevertheless these unfortunates' best hope. Joining them by now were thirty or more members of the international news media. The British Broadcasting Company, Agence France Presse, the Associated Press, Reuters, and a variety of international television camera crews had come to cover the massive exodus. After their arrival, some of the media had remained in Bujumbura to cover the departure of American and European families three days earlier, whereas others had flown in to cover the march of the refugees. Their presence provided me a rare opportunity to discuss with international journalists the plight of Burundian citizens. Knowing that my private remonstrances to the military authorities regarding their malfeasance had brought only occasional changes in their behavior, I hoped that worldwide attention might encourage them to sheathe their *couteaux* and silence their guns for a while. And while speaking on the record to the BBC and French television from the roadway, I at the same time urged the reporters to visit Gasorwe and the Muyinga region, where I could certify that at least 430 people had been killed during the past week, and was confident the real total was far higher.

The response of the international media to the massacres in Muyinga varied considerably. Two reporters decided to travel eastward rather than return immediately to Bujumbura. Peter Smerdon, Nairobi bureau chief for Reuters News Service, and his wife Katherine Arms, a reporter with CBS News, went together to Muyinga. At the hospital they at first received a different story from that given to me. A hospital administrator, obviously afraid to tell the truth, stated that the injured boys (whose wounds the physician had carefully described to me as coming from bayonets, bullets, and grenades) had been injured in falls from bicycles. The nurse, similarly fearful, would not respond to their questions where she could be overheard. However, she asked to borrow Katherine Arms's notebook. There she wrote, "*plus de 400 tués*" (more than 400 killed) in the area surrounding Gasorwe. The scale of the killing was further confirmed for Smerdon and Arms by a UN representative working in the region and by their own investigations. They reported the massacres to the world the following day.

Almost all the other international reporters, having returned to Bujumbura, decided to stay there a few more days to see how events developed. And Radio France Internationale on April 4 concluded a report on the refugees and massacres in Burundi with the following bit of Gallic irony:

[Announcer:] An interesting detail: the U.S. ambassador, who has confirmed the massacres, has been described by Tutsi extremists as a target [for assassination]. Furthermore, a seminar on human rights is currently taking place in Burundi with the participation of army officers, no less. This is one of the many paradoxes in the country.

Ambassador Ould-Abdallah was unhappy with my revealing the massacres to the media because he maintained that to reveal such horrors only encouraged more killing. My assessment was the opposite: I thought revealing the truth was the only way to slow the slaughter.

In order to give the appearance that something was being done, the minister of defense on April 4 issued a formal statement in which he referred to the "supposed massacres of the population perpetrated by the army in Gasorwe as revealed by American Ambassador, Robert Krueger." The defense minister's statement maintained that it was Hutu armed bands, disguised in army uniforms, who had been responsible for any violence in the region. Although, upon Ambassador Ould-Abdallah's advice, the defense minister established a commission of inquiry to investigate the matter, he concluded his statement with the comment, "Meanwhile, those who put oil in the fire and who [predict] the Apocalypse need to be convinced that they do not serve the interest of the people of Burundi." His commission then took weeks to respond. Its report stated that the army had concluded that twenty-one people had been killed, although it acknowledged that the people living in the area stated that at least 430 had died. While the report of the commission led to neither disciplinary action nor prosecution, its establishment brought a change of military commanders, stopped the massacres, and slowed the uninhibited killing in the region for a while.

Meanwhile, the international coverage of Gasorwe gave the Hutu parliamentarians in Bujumbura new hope that since people outside the country were taking notice of their plight, some action might be taken to help them. Parliamentarians came to the embassy asking that we visit their home constituencies to view the violence there, and international journalists phoned to ask if they could accompany us into the countryside. At the same time, the defense minister complained in a cabinet meeting of such visits and asked why the American ambassador should be allowed to travel at will about the countryside. The foreign minister replied that customs of diplomatic reciprocity and the Vienna Convention guaranteed foreign diplomats that right. When Defense Minister Sinzoyiheba was adamant that such visits should stop, Foreign Minister Ngendahayo agreed only that his office should be informed in advance of any ambassadorial visits, but indicated that there was no way that the visits themselves could be prevented.

In response to an invitation from two members of Parliament from the Butaganzwa region, I agreed to travel with them to inspect violence in their area; and together we agreed to be joined by an Associated Press reporter and an ABC News cameraman who wanted to cover our findings. We met at my residence at seven in the morning, and just before I got behind the wheel of the Land Cruiser, I dutifully telephoned the foreign minister to inform him, "I will be going into the countryside somewhere in the north." Although I am certain that he did not pass on that information, once we had arrived at our first stop, we were nevertheless soon joined by an army officer and a truckload of Burundian soldiers.

To my surprise, neither the soldiers nor the cameras seemed to intimidate the villagers, who had lost relatives and neighbors. We visited burnt-out houses, which the cameraman filmed; we found fresh graves and heard people tell of army killings; and we went from one location to another to interview villagers desperate for help and hopeful of change. Even so, we would have felt more confident of receiving accurate accounts if the army were not present. Therefore, as the day wore on, we became increasingly eager to get away from our chaperones. The opportunity to do so came unexpectedly.

Most roads in Butaganzwa, as in much of Burundi, were twisted, hilly, and unpaved. Our Toyota Land Cruiser was well built for such rough roads and for the log bridges that covered many of the streams. Similarly, the Mercedes military truck persistently following us was even better suited to rough terrain, though not as fast as our Land Cruiser. Early in the afternoon, I was driving toward the village of Nikishi, being directed by Parliamentarian Emmanuel Mpfayokurera, when I saw that directly ahead our one-lane road was entirely covered by water. The previous day's rains had obviously flooded the road, and although my vehicle had four-wheel drive, I had no idea how deep the water might be, and no desire to be stranded and dependent upon the Burundi Army while sixty miles from Bujumbura. So, seeing only one spot wide enough to turn around without getting stuck, I turned around there, and, narrowly managing to pass the army truck without either of us sliding into a wet ditch, I headed back in the direction from which we had come. Then, my rearview mirror revealed that the big Mercedes truck was taking much longer than we to negotiate the turnaround. And at that point, the American ambassador suddenly reverted to being a Texas teenager.

I remembered how as a teenager, years ago before radar had become the norm for catching speeding cars on U.S. highways, I was driving through Louisiana at sunset when, atop a small hill, I passed a highway patrolman headed in the opposite direction, and in my rearview mirror I glimpsed his brake lights go on. I knew he was turning around to ticket me for speeding. But instead of slowing, I sped up, turned quickly down a side road, turned off my lights, and watched him go racing by. Then I got safely back on the road behind him, knowing that he would be driving at a high speed in pursuit, and I could comfortably follow at the same speed as before. I reckoned the same technique should work now. So I put the accelerator pedal to the floor, flew out of sight, turned at the first crossroads, and hid the car behind a clump of trees. As expected, seconds later the army truck went roaring past on the main road. Once it had passed, we emerged, took a different road, and proceeded to a small hospital, where, with no soldiers listening, we were able to interview the patients freely and to receive full accounts of the army's butchery. It took our pursuers forty-five minutes to find us again, and by that time our work was complete.

SOLDIERS AMBUSH PRESS REPORTERS

We were home before sunset and curfew, and after saying good-bye to the parliamentarians and reporters, I stood on the long columned porch and gazed wistfully past the traveler's palms to the lake beyond. No doubt it was as beautiful as before, but without my family to share the scene, the sound of our crested cranes sounded more like a squawk than a mating call, and the orange ripples of sunset on Lake Tanganyika had lost much of their luster. As when I had first arrived in Bujumbura, I would be dining alone. But now, instead of anticipating the arrival of my family, I could think only of their recent departure.

After a shower and a meal, I didn't have much time for sentimentality before the phone rang. It was 9:30 p.m. Robin Lubbock, a producer with Worldwide Television News (WTN) of South Africa was calling with a strange and ominous story.

He was deeply concerned about the safety and whereabouts of two South Africans working with him in Burundi: Vincent Francis, the Johannesburg bureau chief, and Victor Dhlamini, a freelance cameraman. That morning the three of them had learned from other journalists at their hotel about my trip with the parliamentarians into the Butaganzwa countryside. Concluding that they might find a better story there than in Bujumbura, Francis and Dhlamini decided to rent a car, hire a driver and an interpreter, and set out to join our expedition.

"Did you see them?" Lubbock asked. "No," I responded, "I neither saw them nor knew of their mission." Perhaps unable to return before the Bujumbura curfew, they had decided to spend the night at Ngozi, I suggested. "No," he replied, "They must have run into trouble." Within the past half hour, the owner of the car had come to the hotel, found Lubbock, and related that the car had been seen about ten miles north of Bujumbura by someone driving past. That passerby reported seeing the occupants standing behind the car, legs spread apart, hands on the trunk, apparently being searched and robbed by bandits. The owner "feared the worst." Lubbock therefore urgently needed to find his crew and learn their fate. "Can you help us?" he asked.

In response, I called Chris Reilly, our security officer, who after several phone calls learned that the car had been attacked with gunfire; one South African had survived and was hospitalized; the other had perished along with both Burundians. Since Chris had a permit to drive after curfew, we picked up Lubbock from his hotel and shortly before eleven arrived at the Roi Kahled Hospital. Set near the base of the mountains, its design was modern, simple, and efficient, but without waiting rooms. Visitors waited outside on simple benches or sat on low retaining walls.

We approached the hospital clerk, knowing only that one South African had survived. Who had lived and who died, we did not know. And they would not say. While we were pleading for admission, the "forces of order" stepped in, in the form of a six-foot officer dressed in a grey jogging suit.

Staring coldly at us through metal-frame glasses, he introduced himself as Lieutenant Colonel Marc Nahimana, head of this sector of the gendarmerie in Bujumbura, and without explanation refused us entry to the hospital. "Sit down, rest a few minutes," he insisted mockingly.

As we stood outside, uncertain whether displaying our displeasure or hiding it would gain us quicker entry, a physician emerged, offering to let us in. But as we hurried toward the glass door, the commandant shouted to two soldiers to keep us out.

We were at an impasse. And I knew my recent reports on army massacres in Muyinga would not win me favors from higher-ranking officers. So I phoned Ambassador Ould-Abdallah. He arrived with a cell phone, his pocket notebook of important telephone numbers, and a determination to assist. But he too struck out. Thus we were left to pace the concrete walks, stare at the equatorial moon, and wonder about the madness of a society in which strangers were gunned down for seeking to report the truth.

Meanwhile, Peter Smerdon, a friend of Lubbock, arrived to join us. He had encountered difficulty in leaving the hotel because an army officer able to provide transportation after the curfew had delayed him by insisting Smerdon should not go alone. The officer had taunted him, saying, "Burundi is an open country. We want you to see that. We do not want to take just one journalist in a single car. We need to take an entire busload of journalists to the hospital so that you know we do not restrict your freedom."

After almost an hour of arrogant intransigence from Nahimana, our group was finally admitted just before midnight. The glass door was opened, the iron-bar gate unlocked, and we were taken to a large room with perhaps a dozen patients lying on hospital gurneys. There we found Victor Dhlamini, terrified but not hysterical. He immediately pleaded, "Please, get me out of here before they kill me. Get me home to South Africa." He continued, "Otherwise, Mr. Ambassador, please take me to your house, where I'll be safe. They'll kill me if you leave me here." Unfortunately, either putting him on a plane at that moment or taking him to my home was impossible. He had bullet wounds to his left finger, left leg, and his skull, which had been grazed. Attached to tubes for intravenous transfusion, he would require intensive care throughout the night. In his desperation, though, he scribbled on a piece of paper a telephone number, saying it was that of his uncle, President Nelson Mandela of South Africa. Standing nearby, Nahimana laughed scornfully, ridiculing that claim as preposterous. Nevertheless, he then walked away and left us alone.

Next began a kind of verbal tug-of-war between Lubbock and me. Knowing that Dhlamini needed to rest and recover, Lubbock wanted him to save his energy. I, however, knew that if I did not get an account immediately in Burundi, I usually did not get it at all. So I wanted to question him right away. Promising to be brief, I took notes on his harrowing tale.

He related that as their car was returning from the hills of Butaganzwa along the major north-south route, Highway 1, at 6:30 p.m. they encountered a roadblock of heavy branches placed across the darkened road. Forced to stop, they were immediately engulfed by gunfire from both sides. Within seconds, Dhlamini's three companions were dead. Fortunately, the eight assailants thought Dhlamini was dead too. They approached the car, removed a few items, then walked north and disappeared into the darkness. (Unbeknown to him, an army outpost was located only a short distance in that direction.) Once the attackers were gone, he crawled—about two kilometers (about one and a quarter miles), he estimated—to a point where he was able to flag down a passing Coca-Cola truck, which then took him to a gendarmerie checkpoint, from which he was taken to the hospital.

Dhlamini was afraid that the hospital doctors would either allow him to die or attempt to kill him; therefore, Lubbock stayed with him through the night. At their request, I telephoned Dr. Uri Boulaev, the Russian physician for whom we at the embassy had immense respect, to request his help. Though it was midnight, he came, treated Dhlamini's wounds, and stabilized him enough to be transported the next day in a medically equipped, chartered aircraft to South Africa, where he later recovered.

As Ould-Abdallah and I emerged from the hospital in the moonlit midnight air, we speculated on the identity of the assailants and their motives. Our investigations over the next few days were to convince us who was responsible.

When Chris and I examined the bullet-ridden car the next day, the bloodstains on the seats confirmed that the three who died had all been shot and killed within the car. Moreover, Dhlamini had related unequivocally that there had been no direct encounter with the assailants. He too had been shot while in the car, and had later crawled to safety. The entire story of a passerby viewing a robbery had therefore been a fabrication. Ambassador Ould-Abdallah and I had no doubt of the identity of the assailants or their motives. The ambush was by the Burundi Army. Its purpose was not robbery but intimidation through murder. During that night at the hospital, Lubbock and I had each been allowed to see the body of the slain Victor Francis. Still on his body at that time were his wristwatch, his moneybag, and other personal possessions. As Ould-Abdallah pointed out, had the attackers been Hutu bandes armées, they would have taken money and left the photographic equipment. Instead, the assailants left the money and watches and took only the TV camera and film that might have documented army atrocities. And as usual, they took innocent lives.

It was the Burundi Army's way of sending a simple message to international journalists: if you come to Burundi and have the temerity to try to report the truth, it may cost you your life.

The presence of a large number of international reporters, who came to cover the story of the more than 50,000 refugees on their way to Tanzania, was unique in my Burundi experience: the only occasion on which more than two or three reporters at the same time came to the country during my tour of duty. The BBC kept William Wallis there for a month or so after this event. Otherwise, however, reporters—experienced, intelligent, well intentioned, and hardworking, but also almost always entirely unfamiliar with Burundi—were flown in to cover a story, and then immediately flown out again. Those who came rarely had enough time to get broad and varied viewpoints. The world was therefore restricted in what it could learn of one of the most insidious genocides underway on the planet.

On one occasion I telephoned the head of a major cable-news organization to say that I had received reports of over one hundred civilians being massacred, and could take a reporter to the site. But the reporter in Nairobi to whom he referred me replied, "Oh, you know, people are tired of these stories, after all the killing they saw in Rwanda. There really is no interest." And he did not come. But had a hundred or more *white* people been massacred in Israel, Ireland, Bosnia, or Oklahoma, I think the international news organizations would have sent their reporters. The news networks were reflecting the cultural and racial biases of their viewers. Yet my experience suggested that, given the reluctance of international governments to send troops to defend against the slaughter of civilians, international reporters were the best defenders these people had.

If the international press was largely uninterested, the local Burundi press was largely intimidated—or else, so partial and partisan as to be unreliable. Unfortunately, except for 102 days under Ndadaye, Burundi had known only despots in government and, for the most part, sycophants and hatemongers in journalism. The society, government, and media had never enjoyed a well-established tradition of dispassionate analysis. Burundi's journalists received no training in objectivity. With a few exceptions, the media was viewed purely as an instrument of war, a device for fomenting ethnic strife. The only radio and television station with national coverage was operated by the government, which also printed the fullest newspaper, a daily with a circulation of 2,000–4,000. None of these three sources could be counted on for objectivity or accuracy.

Even worse, however, were the slanderous political screeds, most of them only four to eight pages long and distributed free, which were issued by political parties or extremists to espouse their prejudices. Smaller towns outside Bujumbura were largely without newspapers, and the entire country had only a few small, sporadically printed publications that might sometimes be reliable. Moreover, international newspapers and television were unavailable. Shortwave broadcasts from the BBC, Voice of America, and French National Radio provided international news, but even these excellent networks had no permanent reporters in Burundi, and therefore frequently were victims of misrepresentation when they sought to report on the country. The networks would telephone from their home offices in London, Paris, or Washington and speak briefly with an "official" government spokesman or Burundi Army information officer. The callers rarely knew anyone to call for opposing views or alternative perspectives, and, therefore, they often became the unwitting agents of Tutsi extremist political propaganda. The insularity of Burundi thereby accentuated the dangers to the population.

My experience in Burundi was to etch quickly but indelibly into my consciousness the immense importance of a free, accurate, and responsible press in defending democracy and assuring justice. Reporters like Vincent Francis and Victor Dhlamini went into the countryside and opened a rare peephole into the cavern of terror in which Burundians lived, and of which the outside world was largely unaware. And for opening that peephole even briefly, Vincent Francis made the ultimate sacrifice.

SEVENTEEN

VORTEX OF VIOLENCE

ETHNIC CLEANSING

Burundi's grip on democracy in early 1995 seemed to be slipping, since Dr. Minani had been forced to resign as speaker of the National Assembly and Nduwayo had been installed as prime minister through mob action. Yet both these acts could be viewed as primarily affecting political parties. In the last ten days of March, however, began a process that moved far beyond struggles between political factions and toward a plan of massive ethnic cleansing in the nation's capital.

Bujumbura is administratively divided into over a dozen quartiers, or neighborhoods, most of which had historically been multiethnic. And although life in Bujumbura had become increasingly difficult for those who were not Tutsi, two neighborhoods were known as locations where mixed ethnicities lived peacefully together. In Bwiza and Buyenzi, not only Tutsi and Hutu but also Zairois and the families of Asian businessmen lived side by side.

Until March 22. From that date, the harmony and civility that had been built up day by day over decades was destroyed in a week as the army, gendarmerie, and Tutsi youth groups swept through the two quartiers in a program of systematic destruction, intimidation, and killing, creating a vortex of violence from which Burundi seemed unable to escape. From the white-columned veranda of the embassy residence I could see the night sky illuminated with tracer bullets and bursts of orange flames as incendiary shells set fire to the straw roofs of countless homes. The scent of smoke was perceptible on our hill, two miles distant, and the entire crescent of Bujumbura that reaches around the northeast portion of Lake Tanganyika wore a pall of smoke in the early morning.

Previously, the soldiers and their Sojedem and Sans Échec accomplices looted and killed mostly at night, but during this week they brazenly pillaged in daylight, driving people from their homes. Their excuse was that they were searching for weapons hidden by the bandes armées, and their mode of operation was predictable. The blindés went in first, firing at random and hoping to draw return fire from the houses. If a Hutu fired a weapon to defend himself, he then drew cannon fire or machine-gun response from the blindés. During the first two days, the number of known civilian dead exceeded six hundred, and topped eleven hundred later in the week.

Those figures excluded the 50,000 residents who fled the two quartiers, one-fifth of the population of the nation's capital, and some of whom were killed by gunfire, disease, or exposure. The stream of refugees heading for nearby Zaire extended for miles as they filed down the narrow highway with clothes, bedding, food, or whatever few possessions they could pile upon their heads or grasp beneath their arms. While a few were wealthy enough to own cars or bicycles, most had to rely on their bare feet to take them to their next location. The report that the wheel was unknown to many Burundians until the arrival of missionaries seemed strangely confirmed in this sad exodus. One rarely saw wagons or anything wheeled being used to ease the move. Instead, one witnessed frightened, vacant faces and bodies clutching and carrying what they could save from their meager possessions; the backdrop provided by the extraordinary beauty of the clear sapphire-colored waters of Lake Tanganyika and its diverse and elegant palm trees only magnified the sorrowful plight of the people.

To an observer, the events of late March and the month of April seemed to be a strange combination of systematic destruction and absolute randomness. Orderly destruction was evident not only in the coordinated efforts of the Tutsi youth militias and the army, but also in the swift and overwhelming way in which two major neighborhoods were ethnically cleansed of 50,000 inhabitants in one week. Prime Minister Nduwayo was quoted in a Reuters news report on March 27 as saying that he was prepared to create ethnically pure Tutsi villages where Tutsis displaced in 1993 or frightened by living as a minority in ethnic ghettos could return to normal life. He promised to find new houses for them, but said nothing about the 50,000 Hutu, Zairois, and Asians who had just been displaced by Tutsi groups in Bwiza and Buyenzi. The same news report quoted an observation by President Ntibantunganya: "I really see a genocide, because these things [i.e., killings and looting] were well prepared and carried out fairly systematically."

Some of the systematic killing was of targeted individuals. Ernest Kabushemeye, the minister of energy, was shot dead in his car before many witnesses. President of the RPB political party, which was closely aligned with Frodebu, this prominent Hutu intellectual, holder of a doctorate in engineering from a Belgian university, was gunned down by assailants waiting in a cream-colored Mercedes as he was leaving a pharmacy downtown. His wounded bodyguard returned fire, killing one assailant, and two suspects were detained. Our Group of Five ambassadors and Ambassador Ould-Abdallah met immediately afterward with the prime minister to voice concern over such lawlessness and to urge capture of the assailants. Very likely there was only one cream-colored Mercedes in all of Burundi, which had but one passenger car per one hundred people. The arrest of suspects would have been easy if the gendarmerie had not been cohorts of the murderers. Yet, although the prime minister promised that "justice must really be justice this time," there were no prosecutions, trials, or convictions. Instead, a retired army colonel was killed, probably by Hutu armed bands, as he traveled his regular route to his farm in the countryside. He had no known or suspected connection with the Kabushemeye assassination; he was simply a somewhat prominent Tutsi whose life was taken in exchange for the loss of a prominent Hutu. In Burundi, "justice" often meant only ethnic retribution.

Equally common through these chaotic weeks was the kind of random killing described to me by Lea Peters, a Bujumbura missionary wife. One of her Hutu parishioners, while returning to his house in Bwiza, was stopped, searched, and robbed at a military checkpoint by a Burundi soldier wielding an AK-47, who then told him to run. After covering only a short distance, he slipped, but providentially fell just as the soldier released a burst of gunfire that passed over his head. Looking back as he lay on the ground, he saw the soldier turn his weapon and blow away the next person waiting to pass the checkpoint. In genocide, killing one Hutu is just as good as killing another.

On March 27, France 2, a public-television network, carried a story in which the reporter, M. Manier, described having seen dozens of corpses in Buyenzi and Bwiza. He interviewed on camera the director of a secondary school, Buyenzi College.

> College director: The soldiers came. They came here. They broke the door down. This is what is left of the door. There were only young boys here, whom you can see over there. They are all there boys in the penultimate year of secondary school.
>
> Manier: They are dead?
>
> College director: They are dead. [Video shows bodies of young boys laid out in row] This one [he points to boy's body] was also at the school. He was murdered. That one there, the little one, was still in primary school.
>
> Manier: A few meters away from the college, other eyewitness accounts implicate the police and the army, entirely controlled by the Tutsis. They

sealed the area off on the evening of 24 March. The official reason given was that they were searching for Hutu extremists, and they entered the houses.

The same program contained the following interview:

> Unidentified woman: We saw three gendarmes. They said, "Either you open the door, or we will enter by force." Then they entered the house suddenly. They said, "Either you give us money, or we will kill all of you." There were only women here. Then they started to fire on everyone. [Video shows shot of women's bodies lying on the floor] I happened to have 40 dollars, which I gave them. I said, "You take it and leave me alone." I gave them 40 dollars, and they left me alone.
>
> Manier: This district of Bujumbura was one of the last in which Hutus and Tutsis lived side by side after a fashion. Now that is over.

FOREIGN OFFICIALS' RESPONSE TO ETHNIC CLEANSING

On the same day that this report appeared on French television, a cabinet member from France, Mr. Bernard Debré, was completing his brief visit in Bujumbura. His perspective on events in Burundi, quoted in *Le Figaro* on March 27, 1995, included the following comments by Debré, as translated by the U.S. State Department FBIS (Foreign Broadcast Information Service) news report:

> I had long talks with the defense minister and the army chief of staff. The latter, Colonel Bikomagu, is an extraordinarily decent man. So I am convinced of three things: First, they [the Burundi Army] oppose extremists. Second, they have decided to preserve order while respecting political authorities. Third, they have been waiting for orders which are not forthcoming. . . . In short, while the army is loyal and has no intention of grabbing power for its own ends, it will not remain idle should the political power base collapse. The high command will remain loyal to the authorities as long as there are authorities.

Regarding the ethnic cleansing in Bwiza and Buyenzi, Debré said:

> It all started with Hutu and Tutsi extremists conducting harassment actions against the army. So the latter responded to those actions. The army's

goal seems clear to me: to put an end to mixed districts, and only tolerate monoethnic districts in the capital.

Asked by the interviewer why he opposed sending in an international military force to interpose between the warring factions, Debré replied:

We need to support those elements in the army who remain loyal. Sending to Burundi a UN or OAU intervention force, or U.S., Belgian, or French troops, would amount to expressing our distrust of Burundi's army and government. . . . As I said earlier, the army recognizes the rule of law. . . . I would add that out in the hills, the situation is way quieter than in the capital.

This was the most extraordinarily misinformed statement by any high-level visitor to Burundi during my entire time there. To those who knew the situation, the statement was as plausible as if a French government official in 1940 had called Adolf Hitler "an extraordinarily decent man" and had maintained that "the Gestapo recognizes the rule of law." But there is an explanation: a national election was imminent in France, and Debré's comments were intended to reassure French voters that the French government had a firm grip on violence in francophone Africa.

France's long relationship with Africa had often been ambivalent, and that with the Great Lakes region of Zaire, Rwanda, and Burundi had recently been particularly vexing. In Zaire—the ungainly giant of the region, much of which was anarchic and really under no one's firm control—France and the United States had both maintained a long-standing relationship with the embarrassingly corrupt and long-enduring dictatorship of President Mobutu. Mobutu had been helped into position by the West, and despite being recognized as wicked and self-serving, was accepted because of his anticommunist alignment throughout the Cold War. There had been regular flows of financial aid from the governments of France and the United States to Mobutu (whose personal fortune was immense), and considerable evidence of counterflows of funds from Mobutu to French politicians at election time. It was a cozy, sleazy relationship that had satisfied both parties for many years. And although Mobutu's health and hold on power were both weakening, he remained the only figure in Zaire with whom any government could deal. The main population of eastern Zaire was ethnically nearer to the Hutus than the Tutsis, and for various reasons, Mobutu generally favored Hutu over Tutsi interests. France was attempting, especially during the weeks leading up to its elections, to maintain a comfortable relationship with Zaire. Yet it wanted to avoid alienating the Tutsi army and political leadership in Burundi as it had angered Tutsi leaders in Rwanda.

France's recent role in Rwanda had proven especially painful and nettlesome. It had supported the Hutu government of President Habyarimana for many years, training and arming his troops, the FAR. Then, during Opération Turquoise in 1994, French troops sent into southwest Rwanda had protected both the retreating remnants of the defeated Rwandan government forces and more than a million Hutu refugees fleeing the retribution or vengeance of the victorious Tutsi RPF. Some critics of Opération Turquoise asserted that French president François Mitterand and Rwandan president Juvénal Habyarimana had for years had a joint operation to grow marijuana in the Nyungu Forest in southwest Rwanda, and that the French motivation for protecting that region and its inhabitants from the RPF was not humanitarian but corruptly commercial and political. Whatever its motivation, France in this process saved the lives of far more innocent Hutu women and children than of guilty génocidaires. Moreover, France was the only nation with the guts, decisiveness, and capacity to move in forces quickly enough to prevent a counterslaughter by the RPF that would have otherwise been even larger than it was.

By March 1995, the French knew that they had supported a losing cause in Rwanda, had an enfeebled ally in Mobutu's Zaire, and were perceived by the increasingly powerful Tutsi community in Burundi as having favored Hutus over Tutsis in Rwanda. They therefore sought two things from Debré's visit: (1) to make amends with the likely winner, Burundi's Tutsi army, which France had trained for many years; (2) to prevent, if possible, a major conflagration before the upcoming French elections. While events in Africa have negligible impact on national elections in most developed countries, their impact is larger on the French psyche and its sense of national destiny—and therefore on French elections—than is the case in other Western countries. For centuries the French have taken great pride in their language. Now that all former French colonies have achieved independence, France takes comfort in the belief that it retains special influence in francophone Africa, including Burundi. Hence, Debré visited Burundi to fashion a piece of paper that might give the appearance of meaningful accord between the warring parties in Burundi.

By promising small amounts of financial aid for cooperative development, Debré persuaded Tutsi and Hutu political parties to sign a document that promised a three-year delay for any international inquiry into the October

1993 assassinations (which pleased the Tutsi putschists), and that promised, without specifying a date, to establish a multiethnic military (a sop to the Hutu parties). As we diplomats sat for five hours awaiting the signing we had been asked to witness, one experienced Western ambassador whispered that the document would achieve nothing except to postpone accountability and encourage impunity.

Minister Debré's meeting with the Euro-African Press Association upon his return to France should have reassured Tutsi extremists. The *Washington Times* of April 13, 1995, recounts that interview:

> France expressed doubts Tuesday about sending a multinational force into Burundi but sought to play down a rift with Washington after a high French official called the U.S. ambassador to Burundi a "warmonger."
>
> France contends that no foreign countries are willing to send troops to deter ethnic violence in the central African country.
>
> On Monday, Cooperation Minister Bernard Debré went a step further, criticizing the U.S. ambassador to Burundi, Robert Krueger. "I am a little wary of the American ambassador because he wants intervention, but he does not want to commit American troops," Mr. Debré told the Euro-African Press Association.
>
> "I have met him several times. He is a warmonger," Mr. Debré told a press luncheon when asked about reports last week by Mr. Krueger about ethnic bloodletting in Burundi.

Debré was right about the U.S. position, but wrong about me: he and I had met only once and had never discussed any country's sending troops. It is not, however, unusual for French politicians to attack the United States during periods leading up to their elections. And Debré was relying on an old trick used in electoral politics everywhere: blame a foreigner for your problems, since his friends will not vote in your domestic election. While it is unlikely that Debré's comments significantly affected French elections, they probably brought a smile of amused agreement from the putschists at Camp Muha. After all, they now learned that the highest-ranking French official to visit Burundi in the past year thought that their leader, Colonel Bikomagu, was "an extraordinarily decent man," that the army tried to "recognize the rule of law," and that it was "loyal [with] . . . no intention of grabbing power for its own ends." At the same time, Debré found an ambassador to be a "warmonger" for reporting "ethnic bloodletting in Burundi," thereby creating instability requiring suppression by the "*forces de l'ordre.*"

As Bwiza and Buyenzi were being ethnically cleansed, and as weekly killings moved from the hundreds to over a thousand, Washington became concerned that a major new genocide, Rwanda-style, might erupt. A friend in the State Department telephoned to say that apprehensions were high, papers were being written, and meetings were being held. In the end, the U.S. position that emerged was, in a nutshell, that France and Belgium should supply the fighting forces necessary to prevent a major conflagration, and the United States would be willing to fly them there. The "we fly and you fight" policy was understandably unpopular in Belgium, France, and elsewhere. Although the person who informed me of the first draft of the U.S. proposal said that nineteen State Department recipients were listed for that copy, the views of the embassy and the U.S. ambassador in Burundi were never sought.

During this period, the UN Security Council met to consider appropriate international action. UN Secretary-General Boutros-Ghali proposed establishing a 500-man multinational force capable of swiftly entering Bujumbura, enforcing order there, and holding the line until a larger international force arrived. But all five permanent Security Council countries demurred. My guess is that even so small an international force, if given a mandate to act, might have somewhat stabilized the situation. The French used a small force to stop the advance of the RPF in Opération Turquoise, partly because African forces are extremely reluctant to engage Western troops with superior firepower and training. The Burundi Army, far less capable than the RPF, having spent its time largely in killing women, children, and other defenseless people, has never faced a foreign army. Simply the sight of the U.S. marines who arrived at Bujumbura Airport to evacuate expatriates fleeing the Rwandan genocide in 1994 reportedly sent tremors from the spines to the ankles of the onlooking Burundian troops. Thus, possibly even a small international force of 500 troops might have stemmed some of the violence in 1995. But at the Security Council the idea went nowhere.

The inaction of the UN Security Council was duplicated by the Organization for African Unity (OAU). A high-level delegation led by OAU Secretary-General Salim Salim came to Burundi, saw, talked, and did nothing. On his departure, Salim stated privately that he was unwilling to recommend enlarging from forty-seven to sixty members the small observer mission that the OAU currently had dispatched to Burundi. His reason? He believed such an expansion would be resented by the Burundi Army, which might then take vengeance against members of the mission, and Salim did not consider the risk worth taking for what he viewed as a hopeless effort.

MEETING WITH PRESIDENT CLINTON

During the second week of April, I received instructions to return to Washington for consultations. I inferred that the enlarging violence of the previous few weeks and the possibility of a major governmental upheaval meant that Washington wanted an on-scene assessment. One embassy officer with long-time Washington experience, however, thought it the State Department's way of calling me home for a few days of "cooling off," after receiving what it might have considered my excessively assertive statements on human rights, including a cable in which I had termed events in Burundi "genocide." The State Department fears the use of that term. One friend at State told me, "Bob, you could fill your cables with the 'F-word' and cause less consternation than by calling the Burundi killings 'genocide.'" The problem for the State Department is that according to the UN charter, the United Nations (and implicitly, the United States) is obliged to intervene, militarily if necessary, where genocide occurs. The United States in 1994 was so reluctant to send troops to Rwanda that it waited until Rwanda's population had been decimated before it used the term "genocide." By then, the main killing had ended, and what little could be done was too little, too late.

I had sent a long cable outlining my firm conviction that genocide was occurring in Burundi, and it was referred to the legal section of the State Department for analysis. Some weeks later I was told that a legal opinion had emerged: "acts of genocide" had taken place, but in the attorney's opinion there was insufficient evidence to say that "genocide" was occurring. It was a fine legal point that I did not understand. And I was convinced that the Hutu peasants being slaughtered would not have understood.

At that time, CNN reported that 3,000 people had been killed in Haiti during the previous four years. Yet more than 3,000 people had been killed in Burundi during the last three weeks. Haiti had received 20,000 foreign troops to stop the killing and foster stability. But Burundi had received only 47 military observers from the OAU, and the UN secretary-general was unable to get even 500 international troops for the country. The world did not consciously value the lives of Haitians more than Burundians. Haiti's violence, however, had sent refugees to the United States, thereby creating social problems and financial costs for a powerful nation: being on our doorstep, Haiti could not be ignored. But Burundi was isolated both from the United States and Europe; hence, people could overlook the lives lost there.

A bit of tension often exists between career State Department officers and "political appointee" ambassadors, and such tensions sometimes surface when an ambassador returns to visit the Washington offices. Political appointees, almost by definition, are likely to know political figures and to expect to see them. They are also accustomed to setting their own schedules. The State Department, however, being a large agency, loves structure and hierarchic organization. Its custom is to have "the desk," i.e., the midlevel desk officer responsible for interacting with a particular embassy, request and arrange appointments with all officials at State and other agencies. A junior officer then normally accompanies the ambassador to these appointments as a "note taker" who observes, records, and reports the essence of the conversations.

For this visit, the desk had arranged a meeting with Lieutenant General Wesley Clark, executive director of the Joint Chiefs of Staff in the Defense Department. Within the State Department, it set meetings with assistant secretaries of five bureaus: African Affairs, International Organizations, Diplomatic Security, Political-Military Affairs, and Democracy and Human Rights; the undersecretaries of three areas: Political Affairs, Global Affairs, and Management; and the deputy secretary. In short, almost all the top officials in the department except the secretary of state.

But the desk was nervous about appointments it did not arrange, especially appointments outside the State Department, where it might not have a note taker. Hence, my personal secretary received a cautionary phone call from a State Department official who learned that we had independently arranged meetings with several senators, White House Chief of Staff Mack McLarty, and National Security Advisor Tony Lake. She was told: "You should arrange all official meetings with executive-branch officers through the desk, and all meetings on the Hill [with congressmen or senators] through State's Congressional Relations Office; in fact, all appointments except those with personal friends."

"But, Madam Ambassador," my secretary replied, "The senators, White House chief of staff, and national security advisor *are* all his personal friends."

Silence.

The desk did not trouble us in the future about appointments.

My White House appointments came on the first day of my Washington visit. At about five thirty in the afternoon, during a meeting with National Security Advisor Lake, the Oval Office called: Would I care to see the President?

The answer was, "of course." The instructions were that I should come immediately. As I walked toward the Oval Office, I tried to focus on how to make Burundi stay in the mind of this exceptionally gifted but exceptionally busy man. Within three hours, President Clinton would present his annual budget message to a joint session of Congress, one of his most important annual addresses. Despite President Clinton's famous ability to focus without distraction on issues before him, I somehow had to make tiny Burundi, with its six million people and one-billion-dollar economy, remain on his mind after talking about a trillion-dollar U.S. budget.

The meeting included only the two of us. He greeted me with a firm handshake and warm smile. Guiding me to the chair beside his, he first asked about Kathleen and her pregnancy. But when he asked about Burundi, I followed the maxim "A picture is worth a thousand words" by handing him a photograph developed from the film given to me by Father Mauro in Gasorwe. It showed the upper torso of a man whose forehead had been bludgeoned into featureless pulp by the Burundi soldiers. "Here's what we are facing, Mr. President. A man who has lost his face because of his ethnicity."

"What can we do, Bob?" he asked.

"Mr. President, you recently sent me a very generous letter commending my work on human rights. If I might release that letter so that the killers in Burundi will know that I'm speaking not just for myself but for the president of the United States and the American people, it could be helpful," I said.

"We can do more than that, Bob. I'll do a radio statement indicating that the American people are unwavering supporters of democracy and human rights, and that you have the full backing of the United States government for your statements on this matter."

The next day his statement was released, and if any of the people with whom I had appointments had intended to caution me about outspokenness, they swallowed their words. If the president of the United States was for me, no assistant secretary could be openly against me. And I hoped, even more, that the president's words would be heard not just in the capital city on the Potomac, but in the one by the shores of Lake Tanganyika.

KILL A HUTU FOR THIRTY-FIVE CENTS

Upon my return to Burundi in late April, after less than two weeks away, I saw that the lawlessness had gotten undeniably worse. And sometimes the sheer effrontery of Tutsi extremists in government agencies was dazzling. I learned that at Kobero, a border crossing point with Tanzania, Tutsi déplacés had stolen eighteen World Food Program trucks, loaded with 465 tons of food intended for Rwandan Hutu refugees. After parking their trucks in the large open parking lot, the drivers, while walking toward the Burundian customs office, were stormed by forty to fifty déplacés, who put knives to

Bob with President Clinton at the entrance to the Oval Office, 1995.

Photo shown to President Clinton in the Oval Office, 1995.

their throats while their compatriots climbed into the rigs and drove away in a convoy. Witnessing the entire minidrama in this remote border station were members of the Burundi Army, gendarmerie, and customs office, who cheerfully looked on as food intended for Rwandan Hutus went instead to Burundian Tutsis.

Outraged, we Western ambassadors, representing donor countries that had paid for most of the $500,000 worth of food in that shipment, met with Prime Minister Nduwayo and Nicolas Mayugi, a former Uprona party president and currently minister for the displaced. We expressed contempt for the "security forces" that, though assigned to safeguard this humanitarian assistance, obviously had been complicit in the theft. Instead of apologizing, the two ministers insisted that the donor nations must now give more food than before to make up for the loss. Our response, almost in unison, was that they could not compound theft with blackmail.

Although the theft of food and trucks had brazenly defied the efforts of the international community to encourage a more humane and law-abiding society, the hijacking was a one-time event. For months, however, the Hutu community of Bujumbura had been progressively, continuously squeezed within the iron fist of the Burundi Army. Trying to escape, many of the victims of ethnic cleansing in various parts of the capital had fled to the quartier of Kamenge, the final remaining Hutu refuge. In late May, Kamenge sheltered 50,000 people. Two weeks later, it sheltered none.

Upon orders from Prime Minister Nduwayo, the army began its encirclement of Kamenge on May 31. It placed barricades across streets, required identity cards at checkpoints, and began house-to-house searches—ostensibly searching for arms and members of the Hutu bandes armées, but in reality seeking to terrify all residents into flight and submission. Accounts of the final days are conveyed by two Reuters news reports. On June 7, William Wallis wrote the following:

> Hundreds of Burundi government troops seized control of the last major stronghold of the Hutu majority in the capital Wednesday, smashing barricades with bulldozers. Gunfire rocked the city for much of the day after troops of the Tutsi-dominated army pushed into Kamenge suburb at dawn in armored vehicles mounted with cannon and machine guns. Despite their earlier defiance, Hutu militiamen seemed to have melted away to avoid a fight. There were few casualties, according to first reports. By late afternoon Kamenge was a ghost town except for troops holding all its entrances and bulldozers pushing down barricades abandoned by de-

fenders. Witnesses said sporadic shooting echoed around the surrounding hills as the army pursued retreating Hutu fighters.

Troops also moved into the neighboring suburbs of Kinama and Gasenyi. Houses were set ablaze, sending smoke over Kamenge, and grenade blasts could be heard during the operation. Red Cross officials said a number of people were evacuated but there were no confirmed casualty reports. "They've fired a few times but I don't think they (Hutu gunmen) can resist the army," army chief of staff Col. Jean Bikomagu told reporters. "Up until now all has gone well." The operation went ahead with international observers and journalists confined to a missionary center designated for them near Kamenge but too far away to see casualties or damage in the area. Aid officials said the latest in a series of army operations this year was a major step toward clearing Bujumbura of Hutus even if this was not a primary aim. "I have difficulty using the word 'Hutu-hunting' because I think it's too strong," said Francis Heon of the U.S.-based National Democratic Institute, which is monitoring developments. "But I think there was a lack of discipline in the way the military attacked innocent civilians over the last week. . . . There are reports of women, children and others who have been shot, stabbed. In my opinion, that is not a sign of discipline," Heon told reporters. Prime Minister Antoine Nduwayo, a Tutsi, Monday ordered troops in. Hutu gunmen had vowed to fight the army despite a week-long siege of Kamenge, normally home to some 50,000 people.

A story by Corinne Dufka on June 8 completes the journalistic picture:

Bodies of children, women and the elderly lay scattered in the last Hutu bastion of Burundi's capital on Thursday after an army offensive against militiamen besieged there. Journalists who entered the Kamenge area of Bujumbura a day after the attack by the Tutsi-dominated army saw at least 25 dead civilians, among them a boy and a girl. Most of the victims were elderly and many were female. Many were apparently killed on Wednesday during the army sweep because the bodies were still fresh. They were killed by bullets and blades. I saw one dead woman with big gashes across one breast made by a knife or bayonet. The bodies of a child, her mother and her grandmother lay huddled together. An old man lay dead next to his cane. He was too lame to escape. The army, backed by armored vehicles, cleared Hutu militiamen out of Kamenge on Wednesday after a week-long siege. But the militia melted away without putting up much of a fight against better-equipped troops. None of the dead I saw were young males. Troops manned one checkpoint at the entrance to Kamenge on Thursday but there were no foot patrols of the dangerous area where the residents are all from Burundi's Hutu majority. Civilians scattered as one armored car sped fast through the streets, past burned-out houses. At least half of Kamenge's estimated population of 40–50,000 fled the area before the army crackdown, taking refuge in hills overlooking the lakeside capital. But there were still plenty of civilians inside the suburb who emerged gingerly from their hideouts after a week of shelling and gunfire. Kamenge was calm on Thursday after an army operation praised by Burundi's government for its relative restraint.

The flight of 50,000 innocents from Kamenge to the hills was but one major stone in an avalanche of destruction that roared across Bujumbura in June. As the army lobbed cannon shells and mortar rounds for days and nights into Kamenge and the nearby forests, preparations were underway for a mass meeting of Tutsi extremists at the Odeon Palace.

The Odious Palace (as it was referred to at the American embassy) had, over the years, given birth to many of the most monstrous hatreds to afflict the people of Burundi. This large cement hall in downtown Bujumbura was the favored indoor meeting place for Tutsi extremists from Uprona, Parena, Sans Échec, Sans Défaite, Sojedem, and similar groups. Meetings in this dark, hot, ill-lit, virtually windowless building inevitably carried the bodily stench often found among crowds in tropical countries where most houses are without running water and baths. The meeting on June 11 was convened by Frère Déo Niyonzima, the same defrocked Catholic priest whose Sojedem followers, after threatening to burn Uprona headquarters, had succeeded in getting Antoine Nduwayo named prime minister. The following account derives from a four-page firsthand report prepared by a staff member of a high-level Burundian government official, and has been supplemented and confirmed by two other attendees.

Participating in the Sunday meeting were the heads of most of the minor extremist Tutsi political parties, which, all together, had failed to receive even 2 percent of the votes in the national elections in 1993. However, the passion of their enmities and their capacity for creating mayhem extended far beyond their numbers. Their purpose was to form the Alliance des Forces pour la Sauvegarde de la Nation, AFOSANA (Alliance of Forces to Safeguard the Nation). Early in the meeting, which lasted from 9:00 a.m. to 3:30 p.m., they selected as their leader one of the most detestable of Burundi's extremists, Mathias Hitimana, president of the PRP, a political party that received less than one-half of 1 percent of the vote in 1993. Hitimana maintained a residence in Brussels, but spent much of his time in Bujumbura, where his wealth and influence derived from his serving as the principal middleman for army arms purchases. On one occasion, Hitimana inadvertently provided Ambassador Ould-Abdallah with a list of those who financed the villes mortes and other political violence in Bujumbura. It showed Hitimana to be a principal contributor. In fact, he was known as someone who had helped finance numerous assassinations of Hutu political figures.

On this day Hitimana arrived at the Odeon Palace in his shiny white Mercedes, accompanied with a retinue of bodyguards. Tall, virile, a bit dashing, and dapper in his crocodile Gucci loafers and fashionable European clothes, a man without scruples or shame, he entered the Palace with a confidence and bearing befitting a Mafia leader. And while the extremism of his notions of ethnic superiority would seem laughable in many national capitals today, in a struggling country where the average income was less than fifty cents a day, this well-dressed, arrogant, racist arms dealer presented to the crowd an image of sophistication and success. According to three different observers, Hitimana in a rousing speech urged his followers *"tuer tous les Hutus"* (to kill all the Hutus).

When Ambassador Terence Nsanze, Burundi's representative to the United Nations and president of the Abasa political party, spoke after Hitimana and proposed a more moderate policy of killing only those Hutus whose names appeared on a lengthy list then being circulated at the meeting, he was booed and hissed into embarrassed silence. Meanwhile, swaggering through the assembly were teenagers with grenades and pistols suspended from their belts, acting as guards to watch over the activities. They, in turn, were supervised by Burundi Army officers and Tutsi civilian government officials.

The assembled group voiced its approval for four principles: determination, action, terror, and an unspoken principle that their leaders said should not be made public. The group agreed on a number of points:

- A classic coup d'état should not be attempted at this time because it might prompt an international intervention force.

- President Ntibantunganya must be cornered and forced to cede power to the Tutsis by whatever means possible.

- The group must accelerate the assassinations of Hutu intellectuals so that Ntibantunganya would be forced to abdicate more quickly.

- They must attack any Hutus still residing in Bujumbura and must not spare women and children.

• They must strive to abolish the evening curfew, thereby facilitating attacks at night.

• They must bring Tutsi youths from the interior of the country to undertake military training on the university campus.

• Immediately following this meeting they must build upon the four murders performed the day before at the Lycée du Saint Esprit. They must kill as many Hutu university students as possible; thirty were reported already to have been killed. The proponents assured the group that the army and police would not oppose the action, but would look the other way. Indeed, some attendees reported that members of the forces de l'ordre had accompanied the youths of Sojedem in some of the university killings.

• The actions should intensify during the week of 11–17 June, with the hope that the "destitution" of Ntibantunganya and Frodebu would be complete by the week's end.

According to the written report which I received on June 12, the meeting was not held in secret, and all recommendations listed above were openly agreed to. Five political parties formally accepted AFOSANA and its decisions: Parena, the PRP, Raddes, PIT, and Abasa. Only Uprona refused to sign—reportedly not because Uprona disagreed with AFOSANA's tenets, but because, as the oldest and largest Tutsi party, Uprona felt entitled to provide the leader of AFOSANA, and resented that Mathias Hitimana, the president of the PRP, had been elected to that position. Thus, several political parties that had presented candidates in the 1993 elections and had participated in the Convention of Government were publicly advocating murder, sedition, treason, and genocide.

As Chaucer's rural parson asked, "If gold does rust, what will iron do?" Or, if leaders who drive Mercedes and wear Gucci loafers urge youths who have no cars and only one pair of shoes to engage in mass murder, can one be surprised if killing follows?

Within three hours, it did. As I later learned from two written eyewitness accounts and by interviewing one student survivor, fifteen Hutu students were killed on the Burundi University campus during the evening and night of the Odeon Palace meeting.

On June 11, Alexis Ndayisaba and Gordien Rurimuziko were captured by a group of Tutsi students at six thirty and taken to a room on the university campus for torture and questioning before a Tutsi mob. Rurimuziko was lynched at nine thirty; then, at eleven thirty, Ndayisaba was questioned, tortured, and finally killed, according to an eyewitness, "in the presence of the military, the Rector [i.e., the President] of the University of Burundi, and the Director of University Administration." Aided by members of Sans Échec, many of whom had been smoking hemp, Willy Madirisha reportedly then set in motion a massacre of Hutu students living on campus. Another eyewitness report describes a mob killing two other Hutu students on campus "under the eyes of the military." Portions of that description follow:

> The throat of one was ripped open by using a jagged glass bottle, its top and neck having been broken off. . . . The bottle was then forced into the throat of the student. The other student was stoned to death. . . . One of the soldiers who was observing was heard to comment, "If the Minister [of Defense] comes to see the corpse, he will say that the student is taking a *siesta*."

The virulent bloodlust propagated at the Odeon Palace was coursing through all the arteries of Bujumbura. Not just Hutu intellectuals and university students, but common laborers were targeted. And not just for death, but for sport. Of course, sporting events sometimes charge admission for spectators and a premium for participants.

Early on the morning of June 26, a large group of armed Tutsi youths from Sans Défaite abducted thirteen Hutu day laborers working at a gravel pit for Services Techniques Municipal (SETEMU) just outside the city. The hostages were taken to a large open grassy area in Nyakabiga, the home quartier of their captors, and held there for three hours while other gang members spread through the neighborhood, selling admission for the upcoming spectacle. For sixty Burundi francs (roughly twenty cents) one could be a general onlooker; for one hundred francs (thirty-five cents), a participant. Stones were provided for those requiring them, but participants were given time to fetch their favorite weapon or device for torture.

Like most entertainment, the show could not be allowed to end too quickly. Therefore, six were selected for the initial killing at eleven o'clock. Most of these were stoned and bludgeoned to death, although various supplementary tortures were also practiced. During this activity, however, the remaining seven somehow briefly escaped, running to hide in the brush along the Ntahangwa River. Five were captured there and executed, their bodies laid out as trophies on the grass slopes of the riverbank. Two escaped entirely. Their story was confirmed by the director of SETEMU, by the president's director of intelligence, and by a one-page photocopied news release from Kamenge. The prime minister and the head of the gendarmerie, on being informed the next day, made no response. Perhaps their attitude was "boys will be boys." The president, attending an OAU meeting in Addis Ababa, Ethiopia, revealed his powerlessness through his silence.

Their style of death was different: pay-per-view killing, with the option of direct participation for fifteen cents more. But only the style was new. The fact of slaughter was all too well established.

For over a month I had been amassing the statistics of death by ethnic cleansing, learning of killings for sport, reading and hearing the murderous rhetoric of crazed extremists. But it was a single phone call that most poignantly conveyed the bizarre irrationality of the fires I had seen from my veranda and the explosions I had heard. Calling me was my friend the professor, Prosper Mpawenayo, who had been my guide and translator in the hills of Butaganzwa five months earlier. For over two weeks he and his family, driven from his simple but attractive home in Kamenge, where I had visited them, had been living in the forests on the hillsides surrounding Bujumbura, sheltered only by the trees and the few blankets they had taken with them.

He began with a report. And since he was a professor of physics, a scientist whose profession dealt with numbers and required accuracy, I always gave careful attention to his observations. Less than 1 percent of the population remained in Kamenge and Kinama, he believed; 100,000 had by then been driven from their homes, 30 percent of which had been burned or destroyed. In the forest, he personally had counted 67 dead bodies and encountered 9 grievously wounded, but knew this to be a small snapshot of a vast panorama of suffering. "The Nyabagira River ran red with blood," he said, adding with generous understatement, "The army is not willing to be democratic."

And then, in the indirect and unassuming manner of gentle Burundians, he gave utterance to his deepest pain. As he, his wife, and their five children had fled in the darkness, his twelve-year-old daughter, Grace, had disappeared. For all their searches and their inquiries of others hiding in the hills, they had not yet found her. Meanwhile, as they hoped to avoid the more than 1,000 soldiers moving through the hillsides and the mortar rounds being lobbed aimlessly into the hills, he wondered when they might return to their home. Was it still standing? (It was.) Would they find Grace? (They did.)

"In the meanwhile, could the government not even give us one hill to gather on and be assisted by humanitarian organizations?" he asked. Then he added, "Can you imagine a man like me [i.e., a well-educated university professor in a country in which most of the population could neither read nor write] being chased by a twenty-year-old with only primary-school education? What kind of country is this?"

To his last question, I could no more give a brief answer than he, but I was reminded of W. B. Yeats's lines in his poem "The Second Coming":

> Things fall apart; the centre cannot hold;
> Mere anarchy is loosed upon the world,
> The blood-dimmed tide is loosed, and everywhere
> The ceremony of innocence is drowned;
> The best lack all conviction, while the worst
> Are full of passionate intensity.

For all the maelstrom of unreported violence in the capital, the countryside was suffering, even less observed, from the unrelenting harassment of the Burundi Army and its partners. In June, an American missionary, who with his family had spent enough years in Burundi to speak Kirundi fluently and to know the populace intimately, came by my office. His observation was that the slow but steady elimination of Hutu leaders in the countryside was more effectively achieving Tutsi dominance than what could have been accomplished by a single bold military coup, which might have provoked armed resistance or international intervention. He cited the recent establishment, with the concurrence of a beaten-down Parliament, of the *laissez-passer*, newly required of all Burundian citizens. All Burundians were now required to have a laissez-passer, or pass, issued by the local military administration under the minister of the interior, in order to travel outside their own community or neighborhood. Such passes terrified Hutus, who saw them as a step backward to the massive genocide of 1972. Passes provided a way for the army and the Tutsi extremists to control all movement throughout the country, to isolate Hutus from one another (since those issuing the passes were all Tutsi), and to compound the fear and subjection of the Hutu masses.

The missionary himself required a laissez-passer to travel to Bujumbura, but for a white expatriate it was only an inconvenience, not a threat. For Hutus it was very different. The missionary maintained that every wealthy Hutu merchant in Gitega, the third-largest city in Burundi, had been killed. The *chef de zone,* communal administrator, and party chief of each colline, or hill, in the Gitega region—all members of Frodebu—were all currently in prison. Even Hutu soil conservationists and schoolteachers had been taken from their jobs and put behind bars. One of his parishioners, the teacher Meomile, was freed only because he had Tutsi friends to testify for him, but was nonetheless required to report to police headquarters weekly. The catalogue of suffering tumbled from his lips. After a narrative of tales of imprisonment, beating, torture, and killing, he concluded: "Every educated, active Hutu in the region has been either imprisoned, killed, or is in hiding. It is a deliberate, gradual thing so that it creates less notice. But those who live it are absolutely living in terror. Anything a Hutu does is an excuse for them to be killed. Why, last Sunday, everyone riding a bicycle to church was arrested, and the gendarmes asked for a 5,000-franc bribe [roughly fifteen dollars] to be allowed to proceed and to keep the bicycles. The persecution is so terrible that even some of the Tutsi military feel bad about it, but they feel powerless to stop it or to speak out against it."

MEETING WITH PRESIDENT NTIBANTUNGANYA

In a small country such as Burundi, where only a small fraction of the six million people have been provided education, power, or position, the ambassador of a major country is likely to see the head of state often. I probably spoke with President Ntibantunganya once a week, and the absence of middlemen to prevent such conversation was refreshing. Even so, I always found myself smiling when I phoned the presidential residence. When the phone was answered, I usually began: "*Bon soir. C'est l'ambassadeur des États-Unis. Je voudrais parler avec le Président, s'il vous plaît.* (Good evening. It's the American ambassador. I'd like to speak with the President, please.)"

"*C'est lui-même* (This is he)," came the unfailing reply. The president always answered his own phone, and it always surprised me, pleasantly.

Since everyone knew that many calls were intercepted by the army, foreign diplomats and civilian government leaders were reluctant to communicate anything confidential by telephone. Hence, we normally made appointments by phone and had serious conversations in person. But occasionally events were more secretive. Late in the afternoon on June 12, an emissary from President Ntibantunganya came to the embassy to invite me to join the president for a private conversation the next evening at six o'clock.

Accompanied by Gordon Duguid, public affairs officer of the embassy, who could take notes and assist when necessary in translation, I arrived at the gates of the presidential residence overlooking the city. Although in reality no Hutu, whether president or peasant, was secure in Burundi, the rituals of governmental protection remained, even when the reality was assassination and anarchy. Thus, Gordon and I were required to pass through two Burundi Army security checkpoints. There, from the same battalions that had assassinated Ntibantunganya's predecessor, Ndadaye, were tall Tutsi soldiers wearing berets and spiffy camouflage uniforms, their trousers tucked into brightly shined boots. They pointed their Kalashnikovs at our car as we drove up, placed the butts of their weapons on the ground as they peered into the car to verify our identities and make sure we bore no weapons, and then allowed our car to enter. Protocol is observed even when legality is not.

We were directed to the broad steps of a spacious house of modern design, with long, low horizontal lines and brightly painted white stucco walls. An aide dressed in a suit of iridescent black cloth opened our car door and invited us in. The broad terrazzo-floored passageway led into a reception room that could have seated twenty, although tonight there would be only four. I was to sit to the president's right in a large comfortable chair covered in the shiny gold-colored velvet found in many stately mansions in Africa. The carpets were long-tufted, loosely woven imitations of Persian rugs. As I waited, I was somehow comforted that the small resources of the country had not been squandered on genuine antiques in its effort to provide posh propriety for the head of state.

Accompanied by an aide, the president, entering slightly late, walked in briskly, shook hands, and explained that he had just completed a meeting with his security council. His habit in conversation was to offer extensive background before leading to his main concerns, and on this occasion he began with a general discussion of violence in Burundi, identifying three principal causes: (1) attacks by Hutu rebels; (2) attacks by Tutsi déplacés; (3) attacks by Rwandan Hutu refugees, who were also victims of attack. Then, turning to an analysis of the horrific violence of the previous week in Kamenge, the president, to my astonishment, embraced the position of the Burundi Army. He said Hutu armed bands had caused the problem. Here was a president who in the past two weeks had witnessed 50,000 citizens of his own ethnicity being driven by their own nation's army from their homes and forced to live in the forests instead. And he was blaming a group of 50–200 (at most) armed Hutus in Kamenge as the source of the conflict while publicly and privately praising the "restraint" of the Burundi Army in that operation.

He spoke next of Hitimana's call two days earlier at the Odeon Palace to "kill all Hutus," and considered it a prelude to an ethnic cleansing that constituted "genocide." The Tutsi opposition parties, he believed, wished to force his abdication from office by making the capital chaotic and ungovernable.

The president then spoke extensively of the murder of the fifteen university students, fearing that this horror might be prologue to the Tutsis converting the schools and university into military training academies for Tutsi youths (as AFOSANA had also suggested).

How the president could in the same monologue praise the army for "restraint" in Kamenge, yet discuss massacres, foresee further genocide against the Hutus, and express fear that educational institutions would become Tutsi military academies, I could not fathom.

But then I got a clue. He mentioned that on that very morning Colonel Bikomagu had tendered his resignation, insisting that Tutsis saw him as the tool of Frodebu, while Frodebists accused him of plotting another coup. Without explaining why, the president said he had refused the resignation and had persuaded Bikomagu to continue. With that remark, I was reminded of how prisoners sometimes become enamored of their captors. Since Hutu rebel groups had publicly stated that Ntibantunganya should be replaced, I also wondered whether he considered that to hold his position as president would be more difficult with a Hutu rebel victory than with the present Tutsi army in control. Did he care more about holding his office than protecting his people? I hoped that my unspoken question was too harsh.

His monologue continued by expressing the concern that Tutsis now wanted a "final solution" to the political struggle, and he prophesied, "We are very near a coup d'état by Bagaza." Even after that crescendo, however, he returned to his personal fear as he described his former rival within Frodebu, and current nemesis at CNDD (the National Council for the Defense of Democracy), Léonard Nyangoma, as a "real enemy who wants a Hutu autocracy rather than a genuine democracy."

Having listened for over an hour without interrupting, and sensing where I thought he was leading, I managed to shift the hour-long monologue to dialogue. I prefaced my remarks with a reminder that unilateral U.S. military intervention was not in the cards, but inquired how the international community might help save democracy.

He replied that he knew an international intervention force was impossible, but chose not to encourage Tutsi extremists by saying so publicly. He continued, "Minister Debré of France promised the Tutsi that there would be no foreign military intervention," and had thereby emboldened Tutsi extremists. Perhaps in desperation, he asked if the United States and other Western powers might assist in training the Burundi Army to fight armed bands without killing civilians. But he then acknowledged that unless the government recruited at least 4,000 Hutus, making the army into "a truly national force," it would continue to slaughter civilians. Finally, in a plea that must have saddened us both, he asked me to assist in getting the army to accept his civilian, presidential leadership, lamenting that the army had ignored his pleas to end their "scorched earth" policy in the province of Cibitoke. When I asked why the army had continued in spite of his directives, he replied that the military commander in the area was the brother-in-law of

Chief of Staff Bikomagu's wife. Somehow that seemed to him an adequate explanation. The explanation he never attempted was why he had begged Bikomagu to stay on as chief of staff when Bikomagu would not obey his presidential orders. Truly, the president had become a hostage enamored of his captors.

I returned home poignantly aware that the president, formerly one of the most intellectually capable people in the country, was like a corralled steer. In any direction he lunged, he butted his head against a different rail. Meanwhile, the lassos were falling, almost unnoticed, around his head and limbs. He could shake his head and bellow, but sound was almost the only expression left to him. He was trapped and tied and no longer able to lead. What would it take, I wondered, to break Burundi free?

EIGHTEEN

AMBUSHED ON A MOUNTAIN ROAD

JUNE 13: THE NIGHT BEFORE THE AMBUSH

I had returned home on the night of June 13 saddened by my visit with President Ntibantunganya, who, imprisoned by his fears, had allowed his soul to be captured by the army. Recent days had been racked with slaughter: university students tortured and murdered by their peers, day workers killed for sport, and who-knows-how-many slain peasants whose bodies lay bloated and unrecovered in the forest, food for vultures. A huge crescendo of violence was overwhelming the land. Some students and professors were fleeing the university, heading to the bush to join the rebel forces opposing the army, for reasons both of personal safety, and to take arms against a sea of troubles, and by opposing end them. Perhaps it was my sense that the times were out of joint that prompted me to call a good friend, Ann Kunath, in San Antonio, Texas. A minister in a church that I had never attended, she was nonetheless someone whose insight I valued. At six dollars a minute, my phone calls were infrequent, but that night I wanted her perspective. Although most of our discussion consisted of ordinary conversation, she concluded, as she frequently did, by voicing what her intuition led her to say and by expressing what she inwardly saw. It was not until twenty-four hours later, though, that I felt the full import of what she had said.

The next morning, I awoke with eager anticipation. Foreign Minister Jean-Marie Ngendahayo and I were to tour the northwest province of Cibitoke, which borders Zaire and Rwanda. Our planning had begun one evening two weeks earlier, when Jean-Marie, who lived next door, had telephoned to ask if he might stop by for conversation. Such informal visits had become more frequent recently, since we had both become bachelors: the State Department had ordered my family home, and Jean-Marie's family had moved temporarily to South Africa because of death threats against them in Burundi.

When he arrived that evening, I met him on the front porch with a glass of his favorite scotch, but I held loyal to Jack Daniel's bourbon. As we were walking inside, our conversation quickly fixed on Cibitoke. Having received reports that the army was following a scorched-earth policy there, we wanted to see for ourselves what was happening. Jean-Marie asked whether I might wish to travel there with him. "Of course, Jean-Marie, if you think it's safe," I recall saying.

He responded, "I'll discuss it with the minister of defense and ask him for a military escort to assure our safety."

"Let's do it then. When can we go?" I asked.

"As soon as possible," he promised.

We had agreed to go on June 14. On that day we were to meet at eleven in the morning at the office of Ambassador Leandre Bassole of Burkina Faso, who had been invited to join us. He represented the Organization for African Unity (OAU) in Burundi, and therefore oversaw the forces of the Mission International d'Observation pour le Burundi (MIOB; International Observation Mission for Burundi), whose members had been assigned by several African countries after the October 21 assassinations to monitor and report on the violence in Burundi. The MIOB forces had, however, in my judgment been useless—a fig leaf for inaction. Their forty-seven international military observers could travel only where the Burundi Army allowed them and only when accompanied by army troops. Thus, the observers saw only what the Burundi military chose for them to see. Their reports, which were never shared with the international community in Bujumbura, went to OAU headquarters in Addis Ababa, where nothing became of them. In sum, the MIOB forces were a sleight of hand to soothe international consciences, a pretense of effective international monitoring when in fact there was none. The pity of the sham was greater because the MIOB teams included several physicians who, in providing health care to the rural populace, were well positioned to report on violence in the countryside. Yet they had no visible effect on OAU or UN policy. I was therefore pleased that Jean-Marie had invited Ambassador Bassole. Traveling together, we three should be able to compile a credible report.

THE CONVOY BEGINS TO ASSEMBLE

Arriving in advance of Jean-Marie, I was taken up cement steps to Ambassador Bassole's simple but tidy office, with steel-framed desks and chairs. The ambassador, a small and friendly West African, greeted me warmly, but appeared somewhat nervous and uncomfortable. Having heard that Colonel Bikomagu opposed our trip because he believed the bandes armées in Cibitoke might endanger our security, Bassole suggested we might wish to delay our visit. I responded that we had already delayed a considerable period, that the situation was unknown but perhaps worsening, and that Jean-Marie had been assured by the minister of defense, who outranked Army Chief of Staff Bikomagu, that the trip was on. When Jean-Marie arrived, he telephoned both the minister of defense and Bikomagu, who confirmed that we could go, although we would be driving without an army escort for the forty miles from Bujumbura to the town of Cibitoke, where we would be met by a protective Burundi Army force.

Once outside, I asked Jean-Marie whether we might want to travel in my Chevrolet. "It has light armor-plating, if that's an advantage," I said. But, I added, "I've seldom driven it outside the city because it's heavy and low. Still, if the roads won't be too rough for this kind of sedan, I'd be glad to use it." And we did.

As we were about to leave, a French photographer and reporter with the Gamma photo agency, Ann Nosten, asked to join our convoy. "Do you think it's safe?" she inquired. "Well, I'm going," I replied. "Besides, the foreign minister has obtained an army escort, so we should be all right."

We set out from Ambassador Bassole's office in a four-car convoy. A white MIOB Land Cruiser led, and another followed at the rear, each bearing green MIOB emblems on its doors and flags on front fenders to identify the vehicles as those of neutral observers. Our Chevrolet came second, followed by our embassy's Toyota Land Cruiser. In our car, Jean-Marie sat in the left rear, Ambassador Bassole in the rear center, I in the right rear, and security officer Chris Reilly in the right front. Behind the wheel was Eddie Rukara, a new driver, replacing Bernardin, who, after many years of service to the American embassy, had recently immigrated to the United States. Chris had sought to enroll Eddie in a special driving course offered by the U.S. State Department's Bureau of Diplomatic Security: it gave instruction in evasive actions in case of attack. But the bureau refused, for budgetary reasons.

Following us in the embassy's Land Cruiser was Larry Salmon, an angular, six-foot-four-inch white-haired Diplomatic Security officer who looked like a Marlboro man. Washington had recently assigned him, after threats were made against me, to accompany me personally on all travel. Joining him in the front seat was Ann Nosten. In the rear was Jean-Marie's security guard, Corporal Bosco, wearing Burundi Army camouflage fatigues and carrying an AK-47. To Jean-Marie's puzzlement, just before we left, Bosco had pleaded with Jean-Marie to release him from going on this trip. He begged to be relieved, but would give no reason. And being a corporal, he of course had no choice except to do as the foreign minister instructed. But clearly he was afraid of something. Jean-Marie wondered what, and why.

As we set out northwest along the well-paved highway to Cibitoke, we crossed nearly level plains that sloped gently and drained into the upper rim of Lake Tanganyika. Long yellowing grasses bordered the roadway, but we scarcely saw animals in the fields, traffic on the road, or people in the villages. The homes came sometimes in clusters, sometimes singly. They were usually the simple three- or four-room houses of rural peasants, their bricks fashioned from the ochre-colored earth of the area. Few of them had ever had glass windows; most had received ventilation through rectangular openings. But now hundreds of houses had jagged holes that had been blasted through their sides by army cannon fire. Very few had been spared from attack; almost all appeared to be empty. Jean-Marie was therefore apprehensive. Cibitoke was the province in which he had been reared, the home of his parliamentary constituency. Where were the people he represented? What had happened to them? An aristocrat trained to control his emotions, he remained largely quiet and thoughtful as he witnessed the desolation. He broke his silence, however, shortly before we reached the town of Cibitoke. There he pointed out a plain white church with a large wooden cross near the road; several weeks earlier, he explained, sixty-nine people had been slain there by army troops while they were worshipping.

THE GOVERNOR VERSUS THE LIEUTENANT COLONEL

An hour after setting out, we arrived at a group of cinder-block buildings with metal roofs in the town of Cibitoke, expecting to meet our army escort. Instead, we were met by a small group of peasants and the governor of Cibitoke province, Sylvestre Mvutse. Attired in a gray double-breasted suit, this trim, virile man of perhaps forty greeted us with bright dark eyes and a broad smile with perfect white teeth. The governor shared with us a four-page letter he had recently sent to President Ntibantunganya—the most direct, visceral, and potent factual account of Burundi Army rapacity that I had seen from any high-level official. A Seventh-Day Adventist minister, Mvutse radiated both courage and compassion in his face and words.

Arriving an hour late was the army commander for this province, Lieutenant Colonel Ndayisaba, the brother-in-law of Colonel Bikomagu's wife.

A tall man in a combat uniform, with a pistol in the holster on his hip, he had the haughty manner of someone who had killed and was proud of it. After introductions, although Jean-Marie and I were eager to get our journey underway, the lieutenant colonel wished first to give us a briefing.

It was extensive. He defined the situation as "precarious." Armed Hutu bands, perhaps composed of Rwandans from the defeated FAR, or perhaps Burundian *maquisards* (partisans), were harassing the entire region. The only workable and effective response, he claimed, was *nettoyage* or *ratissage*. This policy of "cleansing" or "raking" meant that any buildings even suspected of sheltering Hutu armed bands should be destroyed, whether homes, businesses, schools, or churches. The only way to root out the evildoers, he said, was to give them no place to hide. To me it sounded desperately familiar and desperately wrong. Destroying homes and villages had not brought victory for U.S. troops over the Viet Cong in South Vietnam, and was unlikely to win the hearts of Burundian peasants. I listened, appalled, as the colonel spoke proudly of the army's having so successfully "disciplined" the populations of Buganda, Bukinanyana, and Murwi that they had entirely abandoned their villages. In contrast, he praised the people of Rugombo, who had collaborated by turning over to the troops alleged members of the bandes armées. As the colonel completed his comments, a broad smile of self-satisfaction crossed his face. But within two minutes it became a scowl, as the governor began openly and firmly rebutting everything the colonel had said.

Mvutse began with examples from his letter to the president:

All the commune of Murwi is scorched in the passage of the military through the villages. About 600 homes were set afire in this commune, which lost its administrator in unclear circumstances. 136 persons lost their lives between June 4–9. The reason that the population deserts the villages is that the military do not discern the differences between honest citizens and malefactors. When the civilian government leaders present a spirit of collaborating with the military, these leaders are the first to be killed by them. . . . In Mugina, in the evening of June 7, the military passing through on a truck in the locality of Gisoko fired into the air in order to frighten the population and see it take flight. . . . In Buganda, by June 9 at 2:00 p.m., 50 percent of the surface of the commune was in fire and blood. The people have fled their burning houses. The sky is blackened by the smoke of houses that are burning. The full accounting of dead is unknown at this time since no one can enter except the military, but an analysis of the dead bodies recovered proves that it is often the old, who have no weapons, who are killed.

Hearing that sentence, the colonel jumped up from his folding chair and furiously berated the governor, shouting that the guerillas were "in the midst" of the people. "That's not true," the Governor replied. "There are children being killed, and they are not guerillas." Thus, the governor stood his ground as he defended his people in a calm but intense voice. It was a bold, inspired performance. Awed by the bravery of his rebuttal, I tore a sheet from my notepad and privately handed him the following message, which I had quickly penned in simple though imperfect French:

> M. Gouverneur—14 juin 1995
> Vous avez courage. Je vous respecte. Si c'est possible que je vous aide, je voudrais faire ce chose.
> (Mr. Governor—14 June 1995
> You have courage. I respect you. If it is possible that I can help you, I would want to do that.)

I had no way of knowing then that more than a year later, when serving as ambassador to Botswana, I would receive by mail a photocopy of that very note. Mvutse's widow, enclosing photographs of herself and their three children, and of the governor's bullet-ridden body, wrote to provide me a three-page account of how Mvutse and his driver were gunned down by Burundi troops at an army checkpoint on June 13, 1996. And she asked for his family now to receive from me the help I had spontaneously offered after hearing his brave presentation on June 14, 1995, one year earlier.

It was two before the colonel's briefing and the governor's rebuttal were concluded, and Jean-Marie and I were anxious to get on with the purpose of our travel: an inspection of the countryside. Jean-Marie therefore presented our proposed route to Lieutenant Colonel Ndayisaba.

Once the colonel realized that our route differed from the one he was expecting, and that we planned to make a loop, returning by a different road, he seemed perplexed, and then insisted that he must leave to get additional reinforcements for security. Another hour then passed before he returned with two jeeps and a brown Mercedes army truck. Its open bed carried twelve to fourteen commandos in full battle uniform, armed with hand grenades and AK-47s.

THE ENTIRE CONVOY MOVES

The day therefore was already far gone when our complete convoy set out at three in the sequence directed by Ndayisaba:

1. The brown Mercedes army truck with twelve to fourteen commandos.

2. A brown army jeep with Burundian soldiers.

3. A brown jeep carrying Ndayisaba, his driver, and one or two soldiers.

4. A white MIOB Toyota Land Cruiser, green OAU flags flying.

5. Our white Chevrolet.

6. Our U.S. embassy's white Toyota Land Cruiser.

7. A white MIOB Toyota Land Cruiser, flags flying.

8. Governor Mvutse's small blue Toyota.

9. (After the first village en route, cars carrying several Frodebu members of Parliament, who joined the convoy.)

As we headed northwest, the farther we got from Bujumbura, the worse the damage became. I was reminded of Sherman's march to the sea during America's Civil War, and its epic portrayal of wholesale destruction in *Gone With The Wind*. Here, however, there had never been plantations and columned mansions, carefully trimmed trees, or neatly manicured lawns and gardens. This road was lined only with the orange-red mud-brick houses of countless peasant farmers, each surrounded by ground trodden hard by the bare feet of many children. Yet a farmer can treasure his hut as much as Scarlett O'Hara valued Tara. And lightning from the cannons on a modern blindé strikes faster and more fiercely than the mule-drawn cannons of Sherman's forces. Huge holes had wrecked the façades of almost every cottage we passed. A solid roof was a rarity. As the pitiless blasting and leveling of houses unfolded before me, I wondered whether slaves in the Old South, in one way, might have had better lives than these peasants. For all the soul-destroying infamy of servitude, the lives of slaves, being property, had some value to their masters. To the Burundi Army moving through Cibitoke, the lives taken had none.

We stopped in several villages, and there Jean-Marie, a descendant of Burundi's royal family, moved among his constituents with the common touch

The Burundi Army took delight in destroying homes. Photo by Judy Walgren, 1994. Courtesy of the Dallas Morning News ©.

of a skilled politician and compassionate public servant. He listened to their concerns, and, having seen their destroyed homes and the emptiness of their fields, I needed no understanding of the Kirundi language to know what they must be saying. When we stopped in Mabayi, where over 100 people had gathered to greet their governor and foreign minister, a peasant slipped a piece of paper into Jean-Marie's hand. Often people make requests or leave messages in that way, and Jean-Marie placed the paper in his pocket to read later. As he and I walked back to the car, he unfolded it and discovered the peasant had given him a 1,000-franc note—a huge amount for a subsistence farmer, representing two week's income for the average Burundian. Jean-Marie shook his head slowly in disbelief, commenting, "Even amid misery, the man is capable of generosity."

We had spent fifteen to twenty minutes in Mabayi, where people gathered in groups around both Jean-Marie and the governor to share their painful stories. But the commander was becoming increasingly agitated. He had not wanted to stop there, and was anxious now to proceed. Once he got the cars loaded, the convoy took off at breakneck speed. And although our American car had a large, powerful V8 engine, Eddie could scarcely keep up with the speed set by the Mercedes army truck leading the convoy. While I didn't want to embarrass the foreign minister about the protective convoy he had arranged, I was sufficiently puzzled to say, "Jean-Marie, the lead truck is going like a bat out of hell. Why do you think they're in such a hurry?" He agreed, but like me, had no explanation.

The road began climbing its twisting path into the mountains, the green foliage getting heavier as we neared Nyungwe Forest and Kibira National Park, a rare area of original, uncut, primeval forest remaining in Burundi and Rwanda. Racing along the treacherous mountain road, we flashed by giant trees, some with crowns eighty feet high and great arching branches from which hung multitudinous vines and occasional orchids. The floor of the forest was interlaced with ferns and mosses and, nearer the roadway, where sunlight could reach, longer grasses. Andrew Marvell's line, "a green thought in a green shade," flashed through my mind. But I could not concentrate on poetry, the majesty of the forest, or the demolished huts we were passing because my attention was riveted on whether we were keeping up with the cars ahead, sometimes visible, sometimes not, on the tightly twisting road.

THE ATTACK

Then, suddenly, I heard a plop-plop-plop, followed by a strange buzzing sound. "Flat tire," Chris and I said in unison. Probably a car up ahead, I supposed, as the Land Cruiser in front of us stopped and Eddie pulled up directly behind it. We could then see nothing ahead except its rear end, with its externally mounted spare tire, two feet in front of our hood. Immediately to our right, a vertical rock escarpment rose twelve or fifteen feet where the road had been cut through, and, above it, tall grasses led from the edge into the forest. Across the road, a steep incline dropped two hundred feet to a valley below.

Unable to move or to see ahead, we waited for what may have been only some seconds, but seemed a long time, since we were hearing nothing, knew nothing, and were wondering what was happening.

Then suddenly Chris jumped forward in his seat, shouting, "Jesus. It's gunfire." Bullets were kicking up puffs of dust all around us, on both sides of the road. I saw the right-side windows shatter in the car in front of us as the car body swayed, whether from bullet impacts or from the jostling bodies inside, where every passenger was hit by gunfire. The staccato sound of automatic weapons, even through the thick sealed windows of our car, punctuated our ears. As I turned to look over my shoulder, I saw the right-side windows of Larry Salmon's car blown apart.

Our car's shortwave radio crackled as Larry called, "Get 'em out of here, Chris—get them out of here."

Then Chris shouted, "Back up, Eddie, back up."

But Eddie froze.

Meanwhile, the MIOB Land Cruiser following Larry had pulled out and started forward. But just as it drew alongside the car ahead of us, it lurched to a halt as its driver passed out from bullet wounds. Then, its right front door opened and out fell the bloodied, dying body of Corporal Tharcisse, Ambassador Bassole's Burundian bodyguard. The ambassador stared, in shocked, open-mouthed, silent horror.

We heard Chris repeat again, "Back up, Eddie. Get us out of here."

Eddie, however, remained immobile.

In frustration, Chris reached across the front-seat divider, grabbed the steering wheel, put the gearshift into reverse, and set his foot on the accelerator pedal to start us backward. But now two cars, side by side, were before us. Chris would have to get us around both.

When Larry's voice next came over the radio, he cautioned, "Chris, you need to get 'em out of here, but I'm not sure you have room to get by both cars."

As I turned again to look out the rear, Ann Nosten was out of sight. I saw only Larry's long frame leaning across the front seat, his forearm and hand extending out the right front window and pointing upward while he emptied his .357 Magnum to give us covering fire.

Then, as Chris started forward to move around the second, stalled car, I could feel and hear the crunching sound of metal against metal as the right side of our Chevrolet sideswiped the length of the Land Cruiser's left side. Simultaneously, our left front fender scraped the trunk of a tree clinging to the cliff on the edge of the road. Had the second MIOB vehicle stalled even a few inches further left, we could not have gotten through the opening between the tree and the stalled car. Even so, if Chris had not guided the car carefully, our left tires might have slipped over the precipice, either stalling us helplessly in the line of fire or possibly sending us tumbling over the side into the valley below.

No more than twenty yards ahead, around a curve, Lieutenant Colonel Ndayisaba was standing in the center of the road, pistol in his holster, shouting to the soldiers ahead. One soldier was slowly exiting the first jeep. Ten yards farther along we saw half the truck's soldiers still sitting or standing on its open bed, the other six or seven slowly ambling along the road as if they were just stretching after a long sleep. Not a weapon was raised. Not a soldier took protective cover. Not a shot was fired. They might have been out for a Sunday-afternoon stroll, except that they were in full combat uniform.

What are they doing, I asked myself. I wondered if we might find a tree across the road, blocking our passage. After Ndadaye's assassination, felling trees had been a common practice of the bandes armées and Hutu villagers to halt army movements. There is no way this Chevrolet can jump a tree, I thought. Might there be a second ambush, I wondered. Only later did I realize that the soldiers had never been in danger, for they were not the target.

Right behind us was Larry Salmon. Over our radio, I heard him say that Jean-Marie's bodyguard had been seriously wounded. Ann Nosten was bleeding slightly from shattered glass. Larry himself noticed a slight nick above his left collarbone, but nothing more. In our car no one had been hit.

"There is an army camp with a health center just a few kilometers down the road," Jean-Marie said. "Go there, Eddie."

The camp was large enough to have permanent buildings, but there was no physician. Nonetheless, Jean-Marie's bodyguard, Corporal Bosco, was lifted from the embassy Land Rover and taken in for first aid. Although he had been shot twice in the back, he was conscious and, fortunately, not bleeding profusely. Ann Nosten's cuts were not so bad as to require treatment. Within a few minutes, the two MIOB Land Rovers arrived, one running on the rim of its front wheel, some shreds of the shattered tire still plop-plop-plopping as it pulled into the army camp. I watched the soldiers lift and carry inside two dead and seven wounded from the two bullet-ridden MIOB vehicles. Apparently not one person riding in them had escaped either death or injury. Our car had been far more fortunate, receiving only one bullet, which entered just below the main rear glass and exited through the left rear fender, missing Jean-Marie by two feet.

We did not wait for Lieutenant Colonel Ndayisaba and the feckless Burundi troops. After fifteen minutes, we decided it was time to get out of there.

The ambush, which occurred in the commune of Bukinanyana between the villages of Rusenda and Butara, had come at four thirty. By now it was after five, and in the tropical forested hillsides, darkness would soon approach. Not knowing at that moment whether the attack against us was an isolated incident or part of some larger, nationwide uprising, not having a radio or telephone capable of contacting the embassy, and not wishing to return to Bujumbura by night and after curfew, we decided to drive to the town of Kayanza. "We can stay at the nuns' convent," I said. "My family and I overnighted there just a few months ago."

As our two embassy cars moved out of the camp and along the highway, all eyes during the first few miles were searching the forests, uncertain what to expect. When we reached the convent on the edge of Kayanza, fluttering leaves were shimmering in the evening sun on the branches of the tall eucalyptus trees that cast their shadows across the parking lot. Then, as Jean-Marie sought the mother superior to ask about staying overnight, and Chris and Larry tried once more to reach the embassy by shortwave radio, I strolled slowly among the trees, determined to fix in my mind the events of the day and to try to comprehend their meaning.

Just then, a car arrived. Out stepped Mr. Barazingiza, the governor of Kayanza. After my February press conference on the killings in Butaganzwa, he was recorded on radio as saying in a public meeting, "If Ambassador Krueger returns to this area, he might very well have an accident on the road."

"*Comment allez-vous, M. Ambassadeur?*" he asked.

"*Bien, merci, M. Gouverneur. Dieu m'a protégé,*" I replied.

(How are you, Ambassador?)

(Well, thanks, Governor. God has protected me.)

And, that said, I smiled, turned away, and walked off to seek the mother superior and a telephone.

What the governor knew, I'm not sure. But what I said, I knew to be true.

The mother superior appeared—a tall, stately woman dressed in a full, traditional nun's black habit with a starched white collar and a headdress framing her face. Hands folded before her, she explained that the convent had no phone. Kayanza itself had few phones; the only one that might be available was at the local bar and restaurant.

We went there immediately. While we knew that we were well, we didn't know what our friends in Bujumbura might know or fear. But phoning Bujumbura from Kayanza proved no easy task. All long-distance calls had to be placed through one local operator using unreliable equipment. We first tried reaching the embassy, where all the lines were tied up in communication with Washington. After trying for an hour, Jean-Marie managed to reach his aunt at her residence and Ambassador Bassole contacted his office. After another hour we reached an embassy employee at home to say that we were fine. Fortunately, a shortwave-radio report had earlier reached the embassy that we were thought to have escaped without injury. But no one knew where we were.

REVIEWING THE AMBUSH TOGETHER

Once Bujumbura was informed of our true circumstances, we could relax, and relive the experience. And we did.

We were in a bar, and had been tying up its only telephone for over two hours; therefore, we felt it was time to buy something. So while we were gathered in his outer office, the owner brought us a round of room-temperature Cokes and local beer. And as we sank into deep, well-worn chairs, whose springs had given up long ago, we began to piece together a fuller picture of the ambush than any one of us could have remembered alone.

Saddest of our group was Ambassador Bassole. Both the known dead were his friends. During the attack, he had witnessed the body of his guard, Corporal Tharcisse, fall from the second MIOB Land Cruiser, face in the dust. And he had watched at the army camp as the lifeless body of Captain Sylvain Kabré Sana, from his home country of Burkina Faso, was carried from the bullet-ridden Land Cruiser that had been directly in front of us during the onslaught. A young transport engineer sent to serve as an observer in the MIOB group, Kabré had been scheduled to end his yearlong term of service at six that evening. He had already bought his airline ticket to return to his pregnant wife and two sons later in the week. By temperament a sensitive and quiet man, Bassole now had to search in himself for the right words with which to comfort two young wives and mothers who did not yet know that in the last four hours they had become widows.

Jean-Marie was quieter than usual. Perhaps he was already beginning to contemplate resigning his position as foreign minister and moving to South Africa, as he did eleven days later. If so, he gave no direct hint. But he spoke slowly and deliberately about how fearful his bodyguard, Corporal Bosco, had been about making the trip. And now Bosco had two bullets in his back. Larry Salmon, without malice but also without reservation, pointed out that when the shooting began, Bosco threw his AK-47 to the floor and lay on top of it, seeking to hide rather than to return fire.

Ann Nosten felt she owed her life to Larry Salmon. The instant the shooting began, Larry had reached his long arm around her shoulder and pushed her to the floor. There, a bullet smashed through the window and left a hole in the floorboard only three inches from her head.

Chris and Larry didn't know how many attackers there had been — perhaps several, perhaps only one. Larry said, "I looked out the right window and on top of the bluff above I saw two black arms through the tall grass, about fifteen to twenty feet away, strafing the cars with an AK-47. That's when I emptied my revolver."

"Do you know if you hit him?" I asked.

"No, I don't know. But I can tell you (he said with a slight smile) that one of the eleven bullet holes we found in our car afterwards was from an outgoing round that I fired as we drove away."

Chris had considered returning fire with his pistol, but the windows on our car were partially bulletproof—capable of deflecting a pistol shot, though not of stopping automatic-weapon fire—and could not be rolled down. Rather than having risked opening the door to shoot, his training was to get the passengers away as quickly as possible.

Ann Nosten asked me what I was feeling during the attack. I replied, "To my own surprise, I felt no fear—because I *knew,* in *absolute* terms—that nothing bad would happen to any of our immediate group. I saw the glass shatter; I saw the bullets hitting all around us; I heard the automatic-weapon fire. But it was as if all that was part of a movie, an action I was observing, but was not really participating in. Yes, I knew it was true: I knew that terrible things were happening. But I equally knew that no harm would come to our immediate group. I did not pray. I did not hope. I did not fear. I simply knew, as pure knowledge, *gnosis,* that we were safe. It wasn't intellectual knowledge of something separate from me, but absolute awareness of something that was part of me. It was as though an umbrella of divine light, impenetrable by any harm, was over us. I could not have predicted it. I've never before had such an experience. But this afternoon, I did.

"What makes all this more remarkable to me is a telephone conversation I had last night with a friend of mine, Ann Kunath, minister of a church in San Antonio. I almost always take notes on my telephone conversations, and I remember writing that she began the conversation by saying, 'You have nothing to fear; you are in no danger, and will not be; you are a warrior for peace.' I found that comment surprising, since we had never spoken of fear, and I felt none. She then talked about several other things, but she concluded with a comment that was unexpected then, and seems amazing now: 'I see three angels surrounding you. They are nodding, saying that all is well. They say they will be with you tomorrow.' Evidently they were."

Before returning to the convent, Ambassador Bassole, Ann Nosten, Jean-Marie, and I quietly toasted Larry and Chris. Their cool demeanor and careful teamwork entitled them to Diplomatic Security Awards for Heroism, which they received from the secretary of state several months later.

The next morning we were picked up by President Ntibantunganya's helicopter. Flying back, I thought I knew what would be in the minds of some people in Washington, and began mentally composing the message I wanted to cable back. Since Burundi was located in a time zone eight hours ahead of Washington, my cable could be on their desks when they arrived for work. My cable made the following argument:

> In Texas, when you fall off a horse, the first thing you do is get back on the horse. We do that for two reasons: (1) so we don't have time to get scared; (2) to show the horse who is boss. The worst thing the United States could do is to withdraw its ambassador simply because a bullet went through his car. That would convince the extremists that all they needed to do to get America to pull out of the country is to take a shot at the ambassador. That would not speak well for our professed firmness in support of democracy. We must stay here, and seek not to embarrass the fledgling democracy that is struggling so hard to take wing. If we pull out, we will pull out the props for democracy itself, and that would be a shameful legacy.

Perhaps my suspicion was baseless, and the cable unnecessary. No one ever suggested to me that the United States pull out, and to my knowledge the idea was never discussed.

Once we landed, Ambassador Ould-Abdallah and Colonel Bikomagu jointly met our helicopter. Ould-Abdallah handed me his cell phone; my wife, vacationing with her parents in Colorado, was already on the line. The sound of Kathleen's voice might have brought tears, so I turned my back and walked toward the helicopter to hold our conversation. Burundians seldom cry, and had I been seen with tears, it might have been misinterpreted as fear rather than affection.

POST-AMBUSH PRESS CONFERENCE

As in many less-developed countries, Burundi's failure to have a free, inde-pendent, and responsible press meant that rumor, however capricious, raced quickly through the capital and countryside. To shackle its start, Jean-Marie, Ambassador Bassole, and I had agreed as we were flying back to hold a press conference that afternoon at three. Gathered together in the Novotel's largest assembly room was a standing-room-only crowd of over 200 people. We three wanted to show that we had not been injured and would not be in-timidated from traveling to discover the truth. The majority of the press and audience had different interests. Overwhelmingly extremist Tutsi, they were hostile and often mocking. Those attending did not care, nor did they report that we had found overwhelming evidence of homes, vehicles, and property destroyed, and of populations that had fled. Their questions were, rather, why had we gone? Why had the foreign minister traveled in the American ambassador's car? Who did we think were the attackers? What was their purpose? Why had the foreign minister invited the American ambassador, a foreigner, to accompany him on such a trip?

One cannot expect clear vision or fairness from publications dedicated to furthering ethnic hatred; hence, I saw nothing different from what I should have expected from those who shouted taunting questions from the audience. My surprise was to see fourteen top-level Burundi Army officers, all in their gray-green dress uniforms with red epaulets and gold insignia, seated together in the front two rows directly before me. As I described the attack, the army officers, to a man, burst out in loud guffaws. That they might delight in hearing that the security car driven by Larry Salmon had been hit by eleven bullets did not surprise me. But that they should be so crass and coarse as to laugh about an ambush in which two members of their own military had been casualties—bodyguards Tharcisse and Bosco—was to me unconscionable. I spared telling the audience that the Burundian troops simply milled around in the road rather than offering protection. But in reply to a question about our convoy's response to the attack, I pointed to the back of the room and said, "The tall gentleman you see there is Larry Salmon, a U.S. Diplomatic Security guard. He is the *only* person to have returned fire against the attackers." That brought at least three seconds of silence before the next hostile question.

At that moment, my prime concern within Burundi was to keep the civilian government from being embarrassed that it had been unable to provide better protection to visiting diplomats. My main concerns in the United States were twofold: first, I did not want America to withdraw from Burundi; and second, I did not want the attack to be viewed as representing an anti-American, "Go home, Yankee" attitude from the Burundian people. When a country is as little known as Burundi, and is seldom covered by the international press, misconceptions can readily arise.

WHO DID IT?

During the first few days after the ambush, I was initially unwilling to think that an army that had never fought any foreign nation would have been willing to attack the representative of the world's most powerful country.

But I was wrong. Within a week or so I realized that the army, not one of the wilder bandes armées, had to have been responsible for planning and executing the operation. Myron Golden, head of USAID in Bujumbura, had suggested that on the day after the attack. But it was a conversation three days later with a European diplomat of long experience that convinced me. My memorandum of that conversation reads as follows:

> Asked who he thought was responsible for the attack on our convoy on June 14, the Ambassador said he was confident it was the Army for the following reasons:
>
> 1. The sequence in the convoy was wrong, according to his military adviser. The armed trucks should not have been leading the convoy, but should have followed the group intended to be protected, i.e. our vehicle.
>
> 2. The Army was angry with Jean-Marie Ngendahayo. "Don't show your shit in public" is a Tutsi maxim; that is, don't bring foreigners in to see domestic problems. Burundians do not like that.
>
> 3. The Army does not want me to travel in the countryside.
>
> 4. The Army dislikes the OAU: therefore, they could in this way intimidate the MIOB forces against seeking to observe carefully their actions in the countryside.
>
> 5. The Hutu armed bands appreciate the OAU since the OAU watches the Army. The Army "wants a free hand to murder," and therefore does not like OAU observers.
>
> 6. All the OAU and American Embassy cars were white. The Army vehicles were all drab brown colored. Therefore, there could be little doubt to the attackers whom they were attacking when they fired *only* at the white vehicles.
>
> 7. The Army did not fire back. This confirms that they were not anxious to kill the attackers, and that they themselves had nothing to fear.

The simple and clear logic of his thesis, plus the fact that he was closely tied to a large and well-informed expatriate community that had been in Burundi for several generations, gave particular resonance to his opinions. They were then confirmed by the intelligence service of the president's office, which was directed by Jean-Marie Ngendahayo's brother Déo. That office had learned that on the morning of June 14, Lieutenant Colonel Ndayisaba had met in Colonel Bikomagu's office to make final plans for the attack. But when Ndayisaba arrived in Cibitoke, he was surprised to learn that we wished to make a loop and would not be returning by the route on which we had departed. He then left us for an hour while he set up a new location for the ambush, and he returned with a different "protective convoy."

No "official," formal investigation of the incident was undertaken by the Burundian government. A civilian government too weak to provide reliable public inquiries into the assassination of its own president, vice president, cabinet members, and members of Parliament could not be expected to launch a formal inquiry into an attack that had resulted only in one bullet hitting the car carrying their foreign minister and two ambassadors. For that matter, the U.S. State Department's two-man Diplomatic Security investigation team discovered nothing. Neither member was familiar with Africa, and neither knew French. They were accustomed to getting most of their information from the police and military, who in this case were the culprits.

If the main intent of the attack was to discourage outsiders from trying to gain proof of the horrendous cruelty of the ratissage, nettoyage, persecution, and murder that was daily advancing in the countryside, it was partially successful. While the State Department did not absolutely prohibit me from going into the countryside, it sent out new instructions: no embassy official could travel more than fourteen miles outside Bujumbura without advance approval from Washington. This policy made even less sense than the policy followed during the Vietnam War of having all bombing targets selected in Washington rather than by commanders in the field. How would someone in a Washington office know which roads might be safe in Burundi? It was a policy intended to keep embassy travel on a tighter leash, and it would also ensure that Washington would remain ignorant of the extent of the daily genocidal activities in this small, distant, and easily forgotten country. I was determined to challenge this policy, but since it was announced in late June, only a few days before I was to join my family for a month in the United States, I decided to wait until my return to Burundi for that battle.

NINETEEN

INTERLUDE

Three Missionaries

Amid the corruption, cruelty, and confusion, there were, as in any society, always those whose altruism and perseverance shone through the darkest hours. Three missionary efforts come immediately to mind.

THE JOHNSON FAMILY: OVER FIFTY YEARS OF SERVICE

The Johnson family was legendary to many Burundians. As a young couple, Carl and Eleanor Johnson journeyed from America to the Belgian Congo in the early 1940s, and by 1949 had opened a mission in Bujumbura. Even during Bagaza's anticlerical persecutions, when most missions were closed, the Johnsons defiantly remained. When the head of immigration came to tell Carl Johnson that he and Eleanor had to leave the country within twenty-four hours, Carl simply replied, "No, I can't. I'm showing a movie at the mission tomorrow night." And he did.

Many years earlier, supported by their mother church, the Plymouth Brethren, the elder Johnsons had established Burundi's first school for the blind and its only school for the deaf. These provided lodging and instruction for a hundred or more so handicapped and helped the students discover within themselves the capacity for joy, merriment, and personal responsibility. All their mission buildings were situated upon large acreage at the base of the mountain range extending north from Bujumbura, and were directly across from the largest and poorest quartier in Bujumbura, Kamenge, where 50,000 or more Hutus normally lived. The mission boasted a primary school, pharmacy, and full-time physician. When the army and extremist Tutsi youth groups drove people from their homes, the Johnsons, assisted by various groups, sometimes fed as many as 5,000 people a day in their encampment. Mrs. Johnson, the matriarch, was a well-known, well-

*Harry and Ruth Johnson and their six children, the second and third generations
of the Johnson missionary family, 1995.*

loved figure who at age eighty could be seen driving her Volkswagen Beetle
through the streets of Bujumbura. Their son Harry and his family also lived
and worked at the mission. Harry's nine-year-old son, Luke, showed me
where bullets had taken out pieces of stucco from their second-floor balcony
a few weeks before my visit. And his mother, Ruth, privately told Kathleen
of his overwhelming grief upon seeing, during that attack, his best friend
and playmate, a Hutu child his age from Kamenge, get shot in the back and
killed while running away from a soldier outside their house.

The Johnson families lived not penuriously but simply. Like many missionaries, they ministered medically as well as spiritually to the wounded
seeking refuge in their compounds. There was no firearm in their houses.
They were armed only with their faith. Yet one would have to say that they
seemed likely to endure for many generations, like the rock of ages, a permanent part of the Burundian landscape.

SUSAN SEITZ: SOLITARY QUAKER

Solitary in her location and soft spoken in her faith, Susan Seitz, a Quaker
nurse-practitioner in her midthirties, lived by herself on a hillside near the

*Susan Seitz, a medical missionary living alone, welcoming
our family's visit, 1995.*

mountain town of Kibimba, a two-hour drive east from Bujumbura. There, she was responsible for a hospital established many years earlier by a Quaker physician who was the father of the U.S. ambassador in Rwanda, David Rawson. From Kibimba, the hospital was reached by passing through fragrant and stately eucalyptus trees along a rocky one-lane road that wound its steep way among terraced farm plots and ended at the hospital's one-story redbrick buildings. Most of the simple, bare rooms were vacant now, and the struggling mission treated or taught fewer people. I suspected that it was difficult today to find a physician prepared to bring a family to that remote outpost, especially after a mob of angry Hutus, on the day after Ndadaye's assassination in 1993, had cruelly incinerated over one hundred Tutsi schoolchildren and their teachers in a Kibimba gas station; the counter-vengeance had been severe ever since.[1]

But Susan Seitz, who had served as a physician's assistant in the U.S. Army, had come prepared to live alone, her brick house sheltered only by climbing roses, deeply colored purple flowers with bright yellow stamens, and her own commitment to her cause. Just a few hundred yards away was a small army outpost consisting of several canvas tents. On my first visit to Kibimba, I followed the trail from her house through the eucalyptus trees and found a half dozen troops stationed there. The only soldier who spoke French was partially drunk on banana beer, and I learned little from interviewing him except that, like most troops camping under canvas, he would rather have been assigned to the city. My visit, however, was intended less to gain intelligence than to let the troops know that Susan had friends in Bujumbura, the site of army headquarters. And fortunately, for the most part, the soldiers had left her alone, although their activities directly affected hers.

An excerpt from her handwritten letter to our embassy security officer on July 29, 1994, describes one week in this medical missionary's experience:

Dr. Mr. Reilly,

I would like to inform you about events that have taken place in the region surrounding Kibimba since approximately 20 July. I will be careful to indicate/differentiate between things I have *seen* and things I have *heard*. Beginning last week, 20 July, we began to see the hills of Mbuye burning at night. We *heard* rumors about soldiers stopping a public bus in this Mbuye area, ordering all the Tutsis off the bus, and then killing all the Hutus inside. We also *heard* that the Hutus had killed a Tutsi in retaliation. Tensions began to increase considerably. The number of fires visible to us at night also increased and came closer to Kibimba. We heard that soldiers had burned about 100 houses. This continued through the end of the week. Workers at the hospital from Mbuye and Muramvya province sought refuge in other locations in anticipation that the trouble would spread/spill over into their areas (toward Gitega province). The governor of Gitega came to the hospital on Friday.

On Saturday, we saw more soldiers moving around in our area. The hospital workers were very afraid. We heard rumors that the difficulties had come into Gitega province. We could see the dense smoke that hung over the hills toward Muramvya/Mbuye. Reports of many soldiers near the hospital reached us about noon. We began to hear gunfire from three directions starting around 15:30: 1) Musama, 2) Gitongo 3) Marumani (toward Mbuye). At one point, I heard guns very near the hospital. I ran from my home to the hospital to find everything/everyone safe: Then I heard guns being fired at my house, so I ran to my house to find that my cook was still alive.

At about 16:30 I took the car to Musama and someone stopped me to say that a hospital worker had been killed at Gitongo. I went to find him mortally wounded from a gunshot to the head. We took him back to the hospital and worked on him until he died a few hours later. The nun from Murayi brought us a child and man also mortally wounded as a result of gunfire. They died later that night. We continued to hear sporadic gunfire through the night. Also, while working at the hospital on this night, someone set a large bag of charcoal on fire that was leaning against my house. I returned in time to prevent the burning of my house. "Thieves" came at night to see if I was still there.

On Sunday, we heard the guns rarely. The road and houses were empty leading to Gitongo. We heard over 300 people had been killed in this area and 11 dead at Kabuguzo. The road to Bukinga was full of Hutu refugees. At Bukinga, I saw perhaps 4,000 people—perhaps more. Most of the hospital staff had left their homes to seek refuge in either Gitega or Bukinga. Soldiers set up a checkpoint at the road leading to the hospital. In the evening, the administrator for Giheta commune came with the military commander at the displaced camp in Kibimba, to investigate the death of our worker. I had seen the camp commander in the morning to tell him. I could smell alcohol on the breath of each one of the members in that party; therefore, I'm not sure how effective our meeting was, but he asked questions and took names.

On Monday, things had quieted down considerably. Some workers returned to the hospital, but many were still moving from place to place to seek refuge from soldiers. In particular, along the river between Muramvya and Gitega province, there were many soldiers and people fleeing in front of them: Sunday night then Monday morning early morning.

During one of my visits to her mission, Susan reported that a few nights earlier she had heard, coming from the nearby army camp where I had interviewed soldiers on my first visit to Kibimba, the screams of a young man being tortured slowly and persistently throughout the night. His beaten and lacerated body was discovered the next day. She further related that during the previous week the husband of a Hutu schoolteacher had been captured, tortured with knives, then burned alive till he expired. Yet in spite of the suffering that she saw and treated, she brought together small groups of Hutus and Tutsis so that they might talk openly and work out a way to live comfortably with one another. The quantity of strength, compassion, and courage that was required for her to persist in her medical work at the hospital, even after her pharmaceuticals had been stolen by army troops, was awesome. We at the embassy would have felt more secure about her safety if she had had either a telephone or a shortwave radio. Nonetheless, her sense of purpose so confidently overrode every challenge that she unfailingly conveyed a kind of buoyant good cheer wherever she went.

THE HANSENS RETURN TO DENMARK

Of the many missionaries in Burundi, I knew the Hansens best. And it was their experience on June 1, 1995, that most troubled me.

Knowing that they were coming to Bujumbura to get supplies, I had invited them to lunch. Upon their arrival in the driveway, they briskly stepped out of their well-worn but newly painted orange 1970-vintage Volkswagen minibus. I saw Knud's bright blue eyes sparkling behind his thick glasses and a familiar broad grin spread across his ruddy face. His handshake still had all the strength of a Danish farmer; his wife's embrace, the warmth and openness of one who had cared for countless suffering people. But as our conversation began, Knud led me over to his VW, which was riddled with bullet holes. The attack had come less than half an hour before, only a few miles away. As they came down the final hill, just before reaching the traffic circle on the more level plain where the edge of Bujumbura begins, they and the drivers of about thirty other vehicles were stopped at a military roadblock by a group of Burundian soldiers, still sweating after emerging from the heat of three enclosed steel blindés. The soldiers insisted that all the travelers crouch and lie down in the ditch and take refuge behind piled-up rocks. Then began a firefight with members of nearby Hutu bandes armées, which continued intermittently for over an hour. After a lull, the soldiers stated that it was safe to go on, but they would accompany the travelers, who should proceed in a convoy with one blindé in front, one in the middle, and the third in the rear.

A convoy of about thirty cars and trucks then headed down the mountain and started across the flat terrain where a mile-long stretch of Highway 1 separates the reddish mud-brick houses of Kamenge from the Johnsons' mission and church. It moved at perhaps twenty miles an hour, slow for a car or truck, but a good clip for a huge steel blindé. The Hansens were proceeding in file when the middle blindé, behind which they were driving, opened fire with both its mounted machine guns and its front cannon, shooting into the houses of Kamenge. "Get down, Jytte," he shouted, as he lowered himself, peering through rather than over the steering wheel to guide the car. Already sitting in back as a precaution, Jytte lay flat on the floorboards. A few seconds later, return fire from Kamenge tore through the thin sheet metal of the orange minibus, which had more than twenty bullet holes. Most bullets had undoubtedly been intentionally fired at their car, but Knud believed some may have ricocheted off the heavy, steel-plated armor of the blindé ahead of them. The holes were large; the rounds had been heavy. Knud showed me where one bullet had gone straight through the headrest of the seat where Jytte would normally have been sitting. Another bullet had torn through the left window frame, almost where it joins the windshield, missing Knud's head by two or three inches. Numerous other bullets also pierced the passenger compartment.

Somehow, I failed to notice a tear and a small bloodstain on the back of Knud's shirt. Only years later did Knud learn from an X-ray that a sudden (but not lasting) stinging sensation he had felt, from what he had thought was a piece of metal that grazed him, was actually half a bullet lodged in his back. He never even mentioned it at lunch. We talked at first about his car: seemingly, the motor and running gear were not damaged. But as then became clear, the Hansens' confidence about their usefulness in Burundi was. Knud explained: "We are no longer able to feed the refugees. The UN provisions are being cut back; the Burundi Army is driving most refugees back into Rwanda; and they are caught in between, while we are unable to help them."

And so, a mission that had provided sanctuary to Rwandan Tutsis during the genocide in 1994, and to Hutus during the massacres today, will be closed, I thought. In his accented but careful English, he continued: "And we cannot continue our instruction for ministers. They are too frightened, too intimidated to come. Then, too, the army comes now almost every day and questions refugees, and takes some away, and questions us. It all makes it very difficult to do our work. As you know, we were already planning to return to Copenhagen in about four months. We are just leaving a bit early. When the bullets came within a few inches of each of us, we decided that God was sending us a message that it was time to go back to Copenhagen."

I felt a rush of disappointment that I hoped would not well up into my eyes. Here was a man who had learned Hebrew, Greek, and Latin so that he would know the Bible of which he spoke; learned Kinyarwanda and Kirundi so he would know the people to whom he ministered; and had picked up five or six European languages along the way. This was a couple who lived alongside their church, dispensary, and school, in a simple rock house atop a mountain a few miles south of the Rwandan border; where Jytte cooked on the wood stove brought from Denmark and opened her Dutch-style half doors to watch my children playing with rabbits, looking as though she belonged in a Vermeer painting. This was a couple who lived without electricity except from seven to nine each night, when they could watch the television news from the capital, a three-hour drive away; the couple who had at times fed up to 1,000 refugees fleeing the Rwandan Patriotic Army. This was the former nurse who had given medical care to the wounded and suffering, and the pastor who had held up the multicolored rainbow to symbolize the message that God loved all his children equally.

Who now would tend the deep-throated flowers, those feeding stops each morning for the hungry, multicolored hummingbirds? What would happen to their simple but picturesque rock house? Would I ever again visit that hilltop, where on most days the only sounds were the songs of birds or the chatter of peasant women working their crops on the hillsides or, on Sundays, the hauntingly beautiful harmony created by Tutsi and Hutu singing together in their church?

The Hansens might say that in going to Copenhagen they were going home. But were they not at home when they had reared their daughter in Burundi, as they had their adopted Rwandan son, during years when they watched Rwanda and Burundi pass from colonialism to monarchy, independence, military dictatorship, nominal democracy, and now to new anarchy? Knud had written books about what they had seen and learned. They had ministered to needs—physical, educational, social, and spiritual—without ethnic favoritism or sectarian bias. When they had recounted their experiences, their tone was always tolerant, evenhanded, balanced and understanding. To me, Burundi seemed their home.

But now they were going home to Denmark. How could this missionary couple, with seemingly infinite patience, with vision and goals fixed from here to eternity, be leaving now? I knew that my rush of self-questioning was selfish: my family had left more than two months ago, and I still hoped that they might be able to come back. But if the Hansens, after a third of a century, were leaving Burundi, could I expect my wife and children to return? If home is where the heart is, they had given their heart and soul to the people of this area for thirty-four years. What did it say about this country at this time if people who loved it as much as they did were now leaving—if people as religious as they were said that they felt God was telling them to go?

My emotions subsided. I needed not conclude that their departure was triggered by despair. They still held hope for the country; they only felt that their time of service was complete.

After lunch I walked them to the car, embraced them both, and inescapably felt that I was more on my own than before.

TWENTY

EPIPHANY

Going Home

The weeks after the ambush were slightly different for me, but much the same for Burundians. The State Department directive cordoning off embassy members within the immediate confines of Bujumbura prevented my going into the countryside. Fortunately, I was visited by members of the White Fathers, Governor Mvutse of Cibitoke, the Hansens, Déo Ngendahayo (head of Presidential Intelligence), and others who kept us informed of events beyond our fourteen-mile limit, where 95 percent of the nation's people lived. And I was, of course, free to travel in the capital.

Nowhere was there good news. From Kamenge, smoke continued to rise. Not from charcoal fires to cook the rice, beans, manioc, or corn of Hutu villagers, but from the smoldering ruins of a neighborhood that had lost roughly half its homes and almost all its people. The capital had become virtually an entirely Tutsi city. No doubt the Hutu serfs would be admitted back in due course, because it is convenient to have servants near at hand, but the efforts to cow the majority into abject submission were continuing apace.

It was like watching lions at a water hole in an exceptionally parched dry season. The impala had to come in order to drink, and the lions had only to wait for their unresisting, nervous prey to arrive. Who was likeliest to die was unpredictable. The more highly a Hutu was educated, the more likely he was to be targeted, but as with the impala, the young and the females, generally being slower runners and easier capture, were taken in larger numbers. Burundi was, as a despondent Tennyson wrote in *In Memoriam,* "Nature, red in tooth and claw." The difference was that lions killed for food, and the Burundi Army for sport and dominance.

Knowing that the ravenous slaughter was continuing undiminished, I hesitated to take my scheduled vacation in the United States. However, it had been almost four months since I had seen my family, and my daughters did not understand the cause of the separation. Once again, my five-year-old Sarah was asking, "Mommy, are you and Daddy getting a divorce?" and never seemed to grasp the explanation. So I decided to go. After returning home, I realized that for Kathleen, the difficulty was not just that our family was divided by 8,000 miles, but that she was separated from Burundi. As we were vacationing in the West, staying in a cottage at the Grand Canyon, I awoke at three one morning to hear her crying. Because she was five months pregnant, I asked, "What is it, dear? Are you in pain?" Between her sobs, she replied, "No, I just want to be back in Burundi." Seeing the direction of events there, we both knew that was unlikely to happen soon, and we sensed it might not happen at all.

After four weeks at home, I returned to Bujumbura in mid-August and found things no better than before. I was witnessing not just lions waiting at the water hole for food, but the kind of pandemic fury found only in humans. The army had arranged for the purchase of additional heavy weaponry from China, but President Ntibantunganya had quietly persuaded the government of Tanzania, through whose country the arms needed to pass, to delay the shipment. The United Nations and its special representative, Ambassador Ould-Abdallah, however, concurred in the delivery, and when the president of Burundi could not hold out, Tanzania gave in. Thus, a military that already consumed one quarter of the national budget spent millions more dollars to buy armaments to use against the citizens of its own country. When the weapons arrived, portions of them were distributed to Tutsi youth groups, who were also receiving paramilitary training from the army in how to subjugate the local population. Meanwhile, at the suggestion of Tutsi extremists, the president had persuaded the Parliament to grant the army and gendarmerie additional emergency powers, thereby further restricting free movement and free speech for civilians while providing additional legal cover for military actions against the populace.

One morning soon after my return, I was breakfasting alone in the garden paillotte, enjoying the delicate color of pink and gold bougainvillea and the rich fragrance of a variety of African flowers, when Joseph, a gardener, and Emmanuel from the household staff approached me with this message: "Mr. Ambassador, last night the army attacked an area less than a kilometer away. They killed from thirty-five to forty people. The bodies are still there now, but the army will soon remove them. We believe Dr. Minani [the head of Frodebu] will come to see. But the army will come soon to take away the bodies, for sure."

"Let me call Mark Hunter, our new security officer, to bring a camera, and we will go right away," I said, reaching for a telephone.

Within twenty minutes I was joined by Mark; my new deputy chief of mission (DCM), Jim Yellin; and George Lambert, a security guard who replaced Larry Salmon; and we were on our way toward the site. But an army roadblock stopped us, forcing us to turn around, after which we went to the nearby office of Déo Ngendahayo, chief of Presidential Intelligence, to ask his intervention. He phoned Colonel Bikomagu, who told him, "If you allow Ambassador Krueger to go there, it will split the sheets between you and me. Absolutely not."

While we were still in his office, fuming at a diplomat's being denied free travel, word came that many of the peasants who had been driven out of their homes last night had gone to the Monument to National Unity, carrying bodies with them. "Let's go there before the army learns of it," I told Mark. And winding our way along the twisting, mountainous roads overlooking Bujumbura, we soon arrived.

High on a hill overlooking the city and the azure waters of Lake Tanganyika stands the Monument to National Unity, a modest stone-and-cement structure shaped partially like an amphitheater. In the surrounding hills one can see, amid the small farm plots, tiny tan mud huts, their thatched roofs scarcely differing from the vegetation surrounding them. At the monument itself were perhaps 250 people, some seated disconsolately, others walking slowly about. Some had been able to grab a few possessions and tie them up in large pieces of brightly colored cloth, from which protruded clothes and other personal items seized in the rush from their homes. Most, however, had brought nothing more than the clothes on their bodies. I saw a four-year-old girl wearing an elegant, full-skirted pink and white dress with small pleats tightly drawn about her chest and neck. Beside her was a boy with a thin bronze shoulder and collarbone projecting through a long and shapeless garment that may once have been a flour sack and seemed surely to have been passed on to him by someone who had worn it before. Among the entire group I saw one pair of feet in straw sandals; all others were barefoot, and all were poor.

In a country where half the population is age fifteen or younger, children are everywhere. At the monument I saw three boys kicking a ball that had been made from coconut shell fibers, enjoying their game, heedless of the bodies that had been laid out on the flat area beside the tribute to Prince Rwagasore. And in a country where the average family has six living children, and the average life span is only forty-four, there are always large numbers of mothers, each carrying her latest baby on her back.

As I approached the crowd, I found the irony striking. Here was one of Burundi's few monuments of any sort, enshrined to celebrate national unity, and honoring Prince Rwagasore, founder of the Uprona Party. Yet I was there not to celebrate national unity, but to witness national division; to view the bodies of women and children destroyed by an army collaborating with Uprona Party leaders dedicated to the proposition that all people are created unequal: some are entitled to rule, and others are destined to serve obsequiously or to die. At one edge of the semicircle, lying on a six-foot, woven straw mat of the type usually used to cover dirt floors, or else unrolled at night to sleep on, was a body wrapped from head to toe in brilliant yellow cotton cloth stamped with a design of purple, orange, and black leaves. A second cloth underneath, patterned in green and purple, had been darkened with a crimson-maroon stain of clotted blood. As a family member pulled back the two cloths for me, I first saw a young woman, perhaps in her twenties, her orange blouse and trousers soggy with blood where she had been shot in the chest. Nearby, on a similar straw mat, was another young woman with a large round stomach, and full breasts supported by a black brassiere. Just beneath her right breast were two bullet holes, still slowly seeping.

Two smaller bodies were lying nearby on straw stretchers curved and shaped almost like extended baby cribs that had been fastened to long poles. Someone identified for me the father of the two boys whose bodies lay on the stretchers. Accompanied by my new DCM, who spoke excellent French, we asked whether the father would mind our seeing and photographing his two sons. "I do not wish to do anything to add to your pain," I said, "but if we might photograph your sons, perhaps showing that picture to the world might help prevent some other father from losing his sons as well."

He had no objection. As I approached the longer body, wrapped in a white sheet, I saw pinkish red splashes of blood extending from top to bottom. Pulling back the covers, I found, beneath a second cloth of intense colors, the body of a twelve-year-old boy who had been bayoneted to death by soldiers, various stab marks extending from his neck to his shins. Lying next to him was a body about three feet long, wrapped in cotton cloth of brilliant gold with red and black leaf patterns throughout. When the father pulled back the white covering from the head of his five-year-old son, I saw that his skull had been split, perhaps by an axe, in a gigantic gash extending from the back of his skull across his right eye and nose. A second gash, exposing the white under-flesh beneath his dark skin, extended from his temple across his right eye. His face itself had been crushed, perhaps by a rifle butt. Then, at the father's direction, I pulled the gold cloth down even further,

Bob meeting with villagers driven from their homes, now gathered at the Monument to National Unity, Bujumbura, August 1995.

Amid the barefoot peasants, a father describing the deaths of his two sons, Bujumbura, August 1995.

and saw that the soldiers had not stopped with defacing his head. They had castrated the child and cut off his penis.

I stared at the mutilation before me. My first thought, of which I can never be proud, was "What chance had this poor child anyway?"

Then, with a flash of consummate embarrassment, I said to myself, "That's a terrible thought. You can't know what that child might have been: perhaps another Einstein, perhaps another Martin Luther King, Jr. In any case, you know that you cannot worship a God who does not love all His creation equally. If God loves this child as much as God loves you, then this child's life is as valuable as yours. And that means you must be prepared to give your life for his, or for that of some other child."

With that, my moment of epiphany was finished. Suddenly I noticed the loud, unmistakable roar of army trucks making their way up the mountainside. Within a minute they would arrive. I placed the gold cloth back over his body and head, and then watched the army trucks belching diesel smoke as they pulled to a stop in the parking area fifty feet away.

I had no further reason to stay. I thanked the father for his courtesy, expressed my regret for his loss, and started for my white Chevrolet, the right rear door held open and waiting for me as Mark and George walked with me on either side.

As the soldiers began climbing off the trucks, AK-47s in hand, I wondered who was more to be pitied: the child who had lost his life or the soldier who had taken it.

Within a week's time, I was gone from Bujumbura, a departure I neither expected nor wanted.

Periodically, roughly once a month, our embassy was visited by the CIA. A few of the visits were by a new agent, a pleasant woman in her late twenties who arrived, contacted one or two Burundians secretly on the CIA payroll, briefed me on the impressions that she had gained, and sent her report from the separate communications system left behind in the embassy from the days when a CIA agent had been permanently assigned to Bujumbura. Most visits, however, were from a more senior man in his late forties. Although his regular assignment was in another African country, Burundi's growing violence during the spring and summer of 1995 now brought him to Bujumbura more frequently than before. During his visit in the first week of September, he asked to see me to discuss a recent encounter.

As he was having a late afternoon drink by the swimming pool at the Source du Nil Hotel, he had met Dominique, a French woman responsible

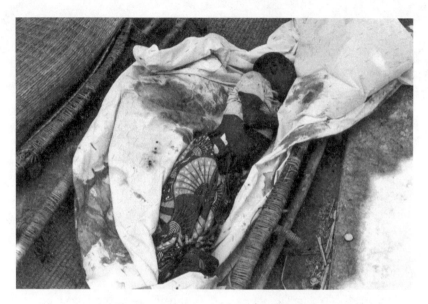

A twelve-year-old boy bayoneted to death by soldiers, Bujumbura, August 1995.

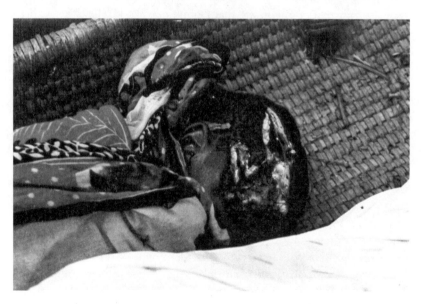

The split skull of a five-year-old boy, a gigantic gash across his right eye and nose,
Bujumbura, August 1995.

for the USAID condom-distribution program in Burundi. In conversation, Dominique mentioned that a number of influential local people (all Tutsi) were displeased with the outspokenness of the American ambassador, and believed, in consequence, that his life was in danger. If this visiting American cared to talk with some of these people, she could arrange a meeting.

The agent of course responded affirmatively, and on Sunday afternoon they had drinks together on the rooftop terrace of a bar overlooking Lake Tanganyika. While there, several Tutsis connected with the previous Buyoya government came by to convey their dissatisfaction with my public statements on Burundi's violence, which might, in their judgment, put me at risk of retribution. The agent, naturally, was concerned.

According to agreements between the State Department and the CIA, the CIA can maintain a separate communications system and send back messages unread by others in an embassy. Their agents are not, however, to make reports concerning embassy officers without giving those persons a chance to read and comment on the reports. This policy is more often honored in the breach than in the observance. In this instance, the obligation was breached. The agent cabled a report to Washington before informing me that he had done so. What he did not know, and what I was to learn from my secretary only that morning, was that Dominique had for the past year been living with a Tutsi lover. The head of the USAID mission had come to my secretary when Dominique was evicted from her previous quarters because of complaints by neighbors. He did not know whether the sounds coming from her house were those of excessive revelry or of her being beaten by her partner, but she had been moved to accommodations that by chance were located two houses away from my secretary. The USAID director confidentially asked my secretary to inform him if she heard either complaints from the neighbors or cries from the house.

The report by the CIA agent of my being in danger of renewed attack may well have been true. However, if Dominique's main concern was my safety, then as a U.S. government employee, she should have told her boss, the embassy security officer, or the ambassador of the danger—not a CIA agent whose "cover" story for being in Bujumbura was transparent. It therefore seems very possible that the meeting with Dominique may have been a setup by her lover as a way to get rid of an ambassador whose reports annoyed Tutsi extremists. In any case, whether Dominique's meeting with our James Bond was a setup or a valid concern, his cable back to Washington was sent before I was told. The arrival of the cable in Washington, and its distribution, was like the story of the bag of winds given by Aeolus to Odysseus. Once the bag was opened and the winds were released, there was no way of putting them back in the bag. Once the message was out that an ambassador who had been ambushed ten weeks earlier was the likely target of another assassination attempt, nothing that I might have said or written about the questionable motives and reports of Dominique's friends would have convinced Washington to let me stay.

Moreover, on the same day that the CIA cable was circulating in Washington, the following statement was being circulated on crudely typed, one-page photocopied leaflets in the streets of Bujumbura:

ATTENTION, LA JEUNESSE!

Le Moufrodebu Kruegger ne tolère en aucune façon qu'il y ait retour de la paix au Burundi. Il continue à soutenir surnoisement [sic] *les FDD, les Frolinat et autres Intagoheka en diabolisant l'armée qui vient de s'illustrer par sa bravoure dans la Kibira contre les FDD.*

Nous la Jeunesse pour le Progrès de la Nation Burundaise, ne pourrons plus longtemps tolérer le Palipehutu [Parti pour la libération du peuples hutu] *déguisé en Americain et promettons sans délai de le mettre hors d'état de nuire.*

La J.P.N.B.

(Attention, Youth!

The Frodebu member Kruegger [*sic*] does not in any way tolerate the return of peace to Burundi. He continues to insidiously support the FDD, Frolina, and other Hutu bandes armées by demonizing the army that has just won fame by its bravery in the Kibira forest against the FDD.

We, the Youth for the Progress of the Burundian Nation, shall no longer be able to tolerate this member of Palipehutu [the Party for the Liberation of the Hutu People] disguised as an American, and we promise to get rid of him without delay.)

The two messages, in combination, were too much. Within forty-eight hours of the cable's being sent, I received a phone call from George Moose, assistant secretary of state for African Affairs, asking me to return to Washington immediately for consultations. I responded that the next plane for the United States would depart thirty-six hours later, on Sunday morning, September 10. So, anticipating a stay of perhaps a week or two in the United

States, I packed a couple of summer suits and enough other clothes for a short visit, staying within the luggage weight limit of those traveling coach, and set out for Washington on Sunday morning.

I was never allowed to return.

Upon arriving in Washington, I gave an assessment of Burundi and my own position there to Strobe Talbott, the deputy secretary of state. I recall telling him: "Strobe, I may be the only person in this building who would say this, but if you gave me a choice between being U.S. ambassador to the Court of St. James in London or U.S. ambassador in Burundi, I would choose Burundi. I know what I'm doing there, and I think it's worthwhile work. On the other hand, I married late, I'm an older father, and my wife is pregnant now. If the departure order is not lifted in October for dependents of embassy staff, Bujumbura automatically becomes an 'unaccompanied post.' I would hate to be permanently separated from my family just as my son is being born and my oldest child is only seven, since I already have to anticipate having fewer years with my children than most fathers have."

Strobe replied that, since an election year was approaching, the administration preferred not to change the ambassadorial assignments of political appointees; partisanship might delay Senate approval of all such appointments. Nevertheless, he would see what could be done.

That meeting was followed by one with Tony Lake, the national security advisor at the White House, who asked, if Bujumbura became off-limits to families in October, whether I would like some other position with the administration, and if so, on what continent. I responded that the continent did not matter as long as it was "a real job," not a sinecure. He phoned three weeks later, by which time Burundi had been declared an "unaccompanied post," and offered several options. I accepted the nomination to be ambassador to Botswana, probably the best-run country in Africa, although it was not until July 1996 that I actually gave up the position as ambassador to Burundi and took on the new assignment.

During the intervening months, I sought without success to return to Burundi at least for a few days, to say proper good-byes to Burundi's leaders and my friends. I did not want to appear to have left in secrecy and fear. But after numerous discussions, months of delay, and, finally, a personal meeting with Secretary of State Warren Christopher, the decision remained the same: the State Department was unwilling to allow even a brief return.

During those ten months, I was in daily contact with the embassy and Burundian leaders by telephone, and watched, from a distance, as the fledgling democracy failed to take wing, dropped from the nest to the ground, and was devoured by the waiting predators.

Less than two weeks after I was replaced as ambassador, in July 1996, Pierre Buyoya launched one more military coup and again assumed the title of president of Burundi while Ntibantunganya sought refuge at the home of the newly assigned American ambassador, who had been in the country for little more than a week. With Buyoya's return, both the "creeping genocide" and the "creeping coup" could stand up, needing to creep no more. A full-blown military dictator was once more in the saddle and could ride across the parade grounds with all the trappings of legitimacy as country after country across the globe and at the United Nations accepted a genocidal killer into the family of nations, while the hopes of the majority of Burundians were once more buried in an unmarked grave.

TWENTY-ONE

CONCLUSION

In the preceding chapters, Kathleen and I sought to share our experiences in Burundi and, more importantly, to transmit a picture of the cruel and unnecessary punishment being imposed upon its population. Rather than relying on secondary sources, we drew upon our own direct observation, interviews, and documents that circulated on the streets of Bujumbura or were passed from hand to hand, often privately, in a fearful and shattered society.

Once we had both left the country, although we knew that the suffering and subjugation continued there unabated for many years, our own ability to observe it directly ended. I must now, therefore, end our narrative and address, in summary, three major questions: (1) Who is primarily responsible for the assassination of President Melchior Ndadaye on October 21, 1993, and the ensuing chaos in Burundi? (2) What has happened to Burundi since September 1995, the point at which the narrative ends? (3) What can Burundi's future hold?

COUPS AND CHAOS

The answer to the first question—who killed President Ndadaye—is, in my judgment, very simple: Pierre Buyoya, the president who, by his first coup, followed Bagaza and preceded Ndadaye, and who, by his second, succeeded Ntibantunganya.

Soon after my arrival in Burundi, in June 1994, a widely experienced European diplomat made the following observation in our telephone conversation: "When I came to Burundi I thought of Pierre Buyoya as a kind of George Washington figure: a father to his country who personally sought to bring Hutu and Tutsi together; one who gracefully accepted defeat in an election and a role as an elder statesman. The longer I stayed in Burundi, the less the picture fit. If you observe carefully, Bob, you'll notice that he will never criticize the army, no matter how horrendous the offense, and he will never support the actions of the civilian government. He claims to work for peace, but he never censures the real source of violence—not even the youth gangs that create villes mortes. So by now I'm highly suspicious of him." My own impressions followed the same curve from respect to contempt.

During my first few months in Burundi I so fully accepted what was then the standard Western interpretation of Buyoya that, at his request, I tried to help him obtain a position at an American university. He told me that he hoped to improve his command of English and broaden his education, which had been limited to secondary schooling in Burundi and military training in Belgium and Germany. I then telephoned the president of Duke University, where I had taught for twelve years, and the dean of the Lyndon B. Johnson School of Public Affairs at the University of Texas, suggesting to both that Buyoya be invited to teach or be given a temporary academic appointment in the United States. Fortunately, neither institution offered him a position.

When Buyoya approached me with a similar request a year later, I responded that I was unable to help. But this time he found assistance more influential or persuasive than mine. When visiting CIA headquarters, outside Washington, after my return to the United States late in 1995, I was invited to talk with a Yale University professor who was working temporarily with the CIA and whose expertise was African affairs. He mentioned that during his absence from Yale, Pierre Buyoya was using his office there while in residence as a visiting dignitary. I wondered then, and do now, who was responsible for Buyoya's receiving the invitation from Yale. Could it have been the same U.S. government agency now providing this professor a salary and office? Was it a coincidence, or, more likely, was there a causal connection? If it was the latter, it is certain that the CIA never contacted the embassy to get our view of Buyoya.

What I had learned by the end of 1994, after talking with priests, missionaries, and Burundians of various backgrounds, was that perhaps 20,000 Hutus had been slaughtered during one week in 1988 by the Burundi Army, which, under Buyoya's direction, had fired machine guns, cannons, and rockets from helicopters and blindés at defenseless citizens. And as I began to know and be trusted by some of those high Frodebu government officials who had survived the assassinations of October 21, 1993, I began to understand the simple arithmetic of who had put together the July and October 1993 coup attempts, and who would benefit from them.

The government that remained after Ndadaye's death had been too weak to put together a credible investigation of the October assassinations. Moreover, the law courts were filled with Buyoya appointees; the gendarmerie and its investigators were all Tutsis who owed their positions to Buyoya; and the entire legal apparatus was controlled by the old regime and used as a mechanism to maintain and justify its control. One might as well have expected a Nazi court in Germany to bring Hitler to trial as to expect the Burundi courts to call Buyoya to the dock.

Later, however, during Buyoya's second presidency, the tyrant held a show trial. In May 1999, thirty-eight people were charged with involvement in the October 21, 1993, assassinations of President Ndadaye, his cabinet members, and government leaders. All high-level officials and army officers charged with these crimes were acquitted. Many of them reportedly joked and laughed throughout the court proceedings. These trials identified a lowly lieutenant, Jean-Paul Kamana, as the mastermind who supposedly directed the October 21 coup, organized battalions from eleven different camps, and gathered the gendarmerie to join in a putsch against a president in whose defense not a single shot was fired. Kamana himself was absent from his trial. Once the October 21 coup had obviously failed, Kamana, on learning that he had been picked by superior officers to be the fall guy, fled Burundi on October 26, 1993, into exile in Uganda. When he was tried in absentia, convicted, and sentenced to death in the May 1999 proceedings, his French attorney was not even allowed into the courtroom.

In my interviews with Kamana, he did not deny having been present at the Presidential Palace on October 21 after five in the morning, and he stated that later that day he was sent as a driver to bring the Upronist leaders Alphonse Kadege, Libère Bararunyeretse, and Charles Mukasi to a meeting at the État-Major (Military Headquarters). But he denied any role in planning or preparing the putsch. Kamana's only role, he insisted, was to serve as driver and bodyguard to François Ngeze, who had been picked by the army leaders as the willing Hutu puppet to be named president after Ndadaye's assassination. Moreover, he claimed that during the four days after Ndadaye's assassination, when he was assigned to serve as François Ngeze's bodyguard, he accompanied Ngeze to the residence of Nicolas Mayugi, president of the Uprona Party, and also to Buyoya's home for a midnight meeting. There, Ngeze told Buyoya that the coup had failed and the international community would not accept Ngeze and his cohorts as leaders of the country. Buyoya then agreed that, for the present, power would have to be returned to Frodebu and the civilian government. Kamana stated in a BBC program, in an interview in the African journal *New Vision* (November 17, 1997), and in personal conversations with me that Buyoya was the master planner of the coup attempts against Ndadaye on July 3, 1993, and October 21, 1993. In each instance, Buyoya, behind a glove of secrecy, fingered others to take the blame. Kamana maintained that he himself was far too junior to have been invited to meetings attended by either Buyoya or the military leadership. In defending himself, he pointed to paragraph 213 of a UN report by an international commission appointed to look into the assassination: it states that the planning and execution of the coup were carried out by the high command of the Burundi Army.

One may suppose that Kamana has not necessarily told all that he knows or may have done. Even so, one may reasonably infer that he appears to have been selected to wear the bell in a small herd of scapegoats picked by Buyoya and senior officers in the Burundi Army to be blamed for the attack. Figures who were let off scot-free included the following: the would-be president, François Ngeze; former army chief of staff Colonel Jean Bikomagu; former defense minister Colonel Charles Ntakije; former head of presidential security Major Isaïe Nibizi; Uprona Party leader Charles Mukasi, who directed the preparation of the radio announcements used on October 21 to ask the public to support the military council; and Lieutenant Colonel Daradangwa and Libère Bararunyeretse, both present at planning and execution meetings for the October 21 coup. The fate of lesser fry was different: three soldiers who might have told embarrassing truths, while awaiting trial on charges similar to those against Kamana, were slain in their prison cells.

Another officer who escaped prison and, like Kamana, today survives in exile in Uganda is Commandant Hilaire Ntakiyica, once a close associate and adviser of Buyoya. Ntakiyica informed me that he was invited by Siningi (Buyoya's chief of staff for seven years) to attend a meeting at the home of Major Busokoza to prepare the final plans for a coup against Ndadaye to occur on July 3, one week before Ndadaye was to be sworn into office. Siningi left no doubt that the meeting was called upon then-president Buyoya's orders. That coup effort failed at the final moment on the night of July 3, however, because of the intervention of two diplomats, the papal nuncio and the French ambassador. Having learned of the plot, they called President Buyoya to warn him that grave consequences would follow from such an action. Ndadaye himself, seeing the movement of army trucks loaded with soldiers, called Buyoya on the same night to ask what was happening. Buyoya responded that the soldiers were simply new recruits engaged in a *baptême de feu* ("baptism of fire," a term used to describe army initiation ceremonies). Buyoya then called and reached Colonels Nzunogera and Girukwigomba, who halted their battalions. These troops came from the same military camp, housing blindé and elite commando units, that had been commanded by

Major Buyoya in 1987, when Buyoya used them in his first coup to force President Bagaza's resignation and install himself in power. Moreover, after the election of Ndadaye, in July 1993, Buyoya continued to use these units as his personal protective force. He would later call upon them again, on October 20–21, 1993, to lead the successful coup against President Ndadaye.

Other troops proceeded to Ndadaye's location on July 3, but were turned back by the Presidential Guard, which was under the direction of Captain Gratien Rukindikiza. After that failed coup attempt, Ndadaye insisted that Siningi and Ntakiyica both be placed in prison, where they remained until October 21.

Ntakiyica has told me that he was freed at four that afternoon, as was Siningi, upon Colonel Bikomagu's orders. He was then placed in a truck with Ndadaye's sister, a prisoner whom he claims to have saved from death at the hands of the soldiers transporting them, and was driven immediately to military headquarters in Bujumbura.

There, he says, he was taken to the office of Colonel Bikomagu, who was meeting with Ngeze, Simbanduku, and Daradangwa. Because Ntakiyica had worked with Buyoya since 1988, and held a graduate degree from a Canadian university, supposedly giving him some credibility with foreigners, Bikomagu directed him to speak on the radio in support of the proposed ruling military council. After refusing to do so, he was imprisoned four days later upon Bikomagu's order, but managed to escape in November 1995. Like Kamana, Ntakiyica states that Buyoya was behind both coup efforts, wanting, he believes, to sow confusion before Ndadaye could even take office, and then to assume control.

One need not, however, rely only on the statements of these two officers about the coup attempts. Common sense and experience in Burundi make Buyoya's responsibility obvious.

Let us suppose that an American president lost an election, and a hundred days after his successor's inauguration, most members of the former president's cabinet gathered with the military leadership that he had installed, and together they then planned and carried out the capture of the new president, took him from the White House to the Pentagon, there to be bayoneted to death. Meanwhile, the vice president and all the members of the new president's cabinet who could be found were on the same night assassinated by an army and police force put together by the previous president, the leadership of which was drawn largely from the village and county in which he was born and reared. Would we suppose that the entire action had been planned and directed by a lieutenant and performed without the former president's knowledge, encouragement, or blessing, and that the former president should neither be questioned nor taken to court? Suppose, additionally, that the former president had previously been a military dictator, and three years after the assassination of the legitimate president, he again took power in a coup supported by the army. Would that not add to our suspicions, especially if during the six years of his second rule he never once granted, encouraged, or prepared for a democratic election, but used all means in his power to prevent it?

And if, under his dictatorship, show trials declared all of his compatriots innocent of involvement in the coup, even though many of them were serving again in his cabinet and leading his army, which continued to assassinate leaders of the former president's political party, whereas a few junior officers and soldiers who stood to gain nothing from the assassinations were sentenced to death or killed while awaiting trial—would not all that cast additional doubt on the innocence of the two-time tyrant? If such events were to occur in the United States, no one would believe that the former American president was not behind the putsch. And no one should believe that in Burundi Pierre Buyoya was not responsible for the swift bayoneting of Ndadaye and the slower strangulation of democracy in his homeland.

BURUNDI SINCE SEPTEMBER 1995

Upon receiving a CIA report of new death threats against me in September 1995, the State Department instructed me to return to Washington for "consultations," but never allowed me to return to Burundi. I retained the title and authority of U.S. Ambassador to Burundi until June 1996, but had to conduct embassy business by telephone and cables from Washington, working through an excellent, newly arrived deputy chief of mission, Jim Yellin. My daily conversations with him made it clear that the violence continued unabated, and that the flaccid sinews of democracy were weakening further with each passing day. Within a month of the arrival of my replacement, Pierre Buyoya and the Burundi Army had completed a new coup, and the deposed President Ntibantunganya then took refuge for several months at the residence of the new American ambassador.

During much of the six years that followed with Buyoya as president, the reports that I received from Burundi, both from citizens and expatriate observers, indicated that human suffering continued undiminished, and that economic, social, and political turmoil intensified.

The subjugation of the majority by the minority grew after Buyoya's takeover on July 25, 1996. The Secretariat General of the Frodebu Party, in a document released in April 1997, stated that during "the eight months since the usurpation of power by Buyoya and the army, more than 50,000 people have died, killed by the military under a single justification: the pursuit of rebels." That number was twice my estimate in 1995 of 100 a day, but was probably correct, for Frodebu had representatives on almost every hill and in every village in Burundi and provided a highly accurate accounting of such matters. Agence France Presse quoted a Catholic Church official in Ngozi as saying that 3,000 civilians had been killed in two months in the province of Kayanza alone, and a community leader in the Giheta commune estimated that 10,000 of the 70,000 people living there had been killed between April 1996 and 1997.[1] Unfortunately, such statistics are not political propaganda, but simply information generally unknown to the outside world.

Fifty thousand deaths almost equals the total American deaths in the Vietnam War. Those, however, were military losses during a decade of fighting; these were noncombatant men, women, and children killed in less than a year. If we adjust for the difference in population between Burundi and the United States, it would be comparable to 2,350,000 civilians being murdered, a figure exceeding the combined American military losses in all wars from 1776 to the present. Exceeded in eight months. And all Hutus, except for any mistakes made by the soldiers. But not a single international newspaper reported this genocide.

Even in the face of such massacres, one of the most heinous examples of subjugation by the army was its policy of forcibly tearing families from their homes and interning them in "regroupment camps," which Nelson Mandela later accurately termed "concentration camps." In 1995 the army began a nationwide policy of "cleansing" areas believed to be shielding Hutu combatants: entire villages, communities, and hillsides, sometimes with only a few hours notice, were stripped of their inhabitants and placed in open-air encampments surrounded by soldiers. The abandoned homes and schools were then pillaged, and often destroyed by cannon fire and arson so that, in theory, the rebel forces would have no place to hide. The displaced families were marched off to waiting trucks or forced to walk at gunpoint to the campsites themselves. There they found neither buildings nor tents. Only open, exposed hillsides.

In 1997, some 700,000 people were forced to live in ramshackle hovels put together from tin, plastic sheeting, sticks, banana leaves, and grass. The government made no effort to provide food, clothing, shelter, or sanitation facilities. Massive deaths from malaria, malnutrition, cholera, exposure, and starvation resulted. Even Hitler's concentration camps provided buildings with roofs, doors, and nests of squalid bunks. On these mountainous, damp, and often chilly hillsides, men, women, and the children who composed the majority of the camp population spread leaves or tin over branches torn from trees to create hovels approximately nine by six feet. The size was seldom larger, since splicing together branches to sustain a larger roof was difficult. An average-sized Burundi family of eight persons was therefore crowded together in fifty-four square feet, insufficient space for all of them to lie down at once. Animals cannot survive well in such fetid, crowded conditions. Nor can Hutus. Depression, disease, and death stalked the camps, where within a few weeks almost 12 percent of the nation's population was crowded. Adjusted for the difference in population, it would be as if the entire population of California, 33,000,000 people, had been torn from their homes, dumped on bare land, and forced to snatch and grovel while fighting to live.

It goes without saying that the troops enforcing Buyoya's concentration-camp policy engaged in beatings, torture, cruelty, rape, and humiliation. A favorite punishment in many camps was for soldiers to tie their victims in a manner termed *invuto,* whereby they were suspended in the air before being beaten. Such torture could be used for any supposed offense, whether returning late to the camp from work outside, or resisting a soldier's request for sexual favors from one's daughter.

Those in camps for the displaced, normally Tutsi déplacés (but sometimes Hutus), could suffer as cruelly as those in the regroupment camps. A Human Rights Watch interview graphically describes one family's experience in such a camp:

> One family in a camp for the displaced has been victimized three times in the last six months, twice by armed men in uniform who forced their way into their home and robbed them. On the third occasion, on a Saturday night in mid-May, four men—three of them in uniform—forced their way into the home, where parents were sleeping with their eight children. They demanded money but, dissatisfied with the amount, two of them then raped two daughters of the family, one thirteen years of age, the other fourteen. Then they brutalized the girls, one by kicking her in the genitals, the other by sticking a wooden paddle in her vagina. The father of the family ran from the house seeking help. One of the men in uniform shot him in the back, killing him immediately. Relatives of the victims state that soldiers committed these crimes but have brought no formal complaint against them. Asked why not, one family member replied, "Complain? To whom?" In previous cases of crimes that they knew of, victims received no help from either local civilian or military officials, who always took the position that the crimes had been committed by

rebels. The attack took place in a zone where there are many military posts and aroused sufficient commotion that others resident in the area heard the sounds clearly. Yet no soldiers came to the rescue of the family during the attack nor did any civilian or military officials come later to inquire into the circumstances of the crime.[2]

Upon assuming the role of moderator at the Arusha peace talks, Nelson Mandela promptly and publicly castigated Buyoya for his "concentration camps," and closing them became a precondition for signatures from the CNDD-FDD and FLN to any peace agreement. Buyoya disbanded many of the camps that confined over 220,000 people in Bujumbura immediately before Mandela's July 2000 visit to the capital. Nonetheless, camps containing tens or perhaps hundreds of thousands operated for at least two years in some areas where permission to travel was denied to press, diplomats, and other expatriates, thereby making a reliable count impossible.

In the presence of such persecution, dislocation, and terror, the general economy scarcely functioned. As the army forcibly removed many people from their farms and homes, agricultural production plummeted. In a country in which 85 percent of the population lives by subsistence agriculture, the immediate and unavoidable consequences were malnutrition and starvation, conditions I never observed during my frequent travels in 1994–1995.

Consider this description of children fighting for kernels of corn at a food distribution center:

> With no school or other organized activities to distract them and with hunger ever present, young boys—especially orphans—hung around food distribution centers trying to pick up something to eat. They risked beatings by soldiers and others charged with food distribution as they struggled to gather any food spilled on the ground. Crouching under trucks in ankle deep mud, the desperate children picked up peas and kernels of corn that had fallen out of torn bags. Others dodged the long sticks that authorities whipped through the air in their direction as they darted in and out of the areas where the fifty kilogram bags of food had been divided, hoping to gather any extra fallen in the grass.[3]

Coffee production declined, shrinking sales of the only significant export product to generate hard currency. Average daily income fell from fifty cents a person to a figure so small as to defy accurate measurement. Meanwhile, the few remaining European expatriates continued their exodus, taking with them their expertise.

Amid this turmoil, almost all foreign economic development programs in Burundi expired. Germany ended its programs and closed its embassy; increased violence made Bujumbura into a "danger post" for diplomatic assignment; and at various times, numerous international relief agencies suspended their operations. The International Red Cross withdrew entirely from Burundi for several years after three of its workers were executed in a roadside ambush. Doctors Without Borders, winner of the Nobel Peace Prize, left when the Buyoya government refused to let it treat patients inside regroupment camps. Other organizations stopped their activities because of threats, theft, or intransigence and hostility from the ruling authorities.

Burundi's economic collapse was but one consequence of the dissolution of democracy after Ndadaye's assassination. Direct conflict between the army and Hutu rebels (or *combatants*, as they called themselves) became more frequent, and support rose for the only force willing to challenge the army—the Hutu *combatants*. During my residence in Burundi, the two main rebel groups, the FDD and FNL, together probably numbered only a few thousand members at most. They were nasty, generally incompetent pillagers, resented by the Hutu populace because their ineffectual military actions only aroused army anger, which was inevitably expressed against the civilian population. In all my time in Burundi, I personally talked with only two rebels and knew of only a handful of documented attacks by rebel groups. Outnumbered perhaps ten to one by the Burundi Army and gendarmerie, they held no territories, won no notable battles, and made no roads regularly incapable of passage.

But in the final years of the twentieth century, all that changed. Their numbers and results improved remarkably, as did support for them. They established bases not only in Tanzania and the Democratic Republic of the Congo, but even in the heartland of Burundi. In March 2001, combatants from the FNL occupied the quartier of Kinama, within the capital of Bujumbura, for two weeks. Most residents fled, but the army was afraid to enter. In this connection, a paragraph in *Proxy Targets: Civilians in the War in Burundi,* is telling and damning:

> Many people told Human Rights Watch that even when the possibility presented itself, the army rarely confronted the rebels directly. Armed forces took five hours to arrive at Buta, which is only ten minutes from Bururi, an important garrison town. When the FDD attacked the Catholic center at Kiryama, soldiers took forty minutes to respond, although their post is only a few hundred meters away. People told Human Rights Watch, "You never hear of direct battles. It is always the assailants coming

down to steal, which they have to do to survive, and then the army comes in and attacks the population. They never get the rebels. They always kill the civilians."[4]

The increased effectiveness of the Hutu *combatants* enlarged the world's interest in Burundi's political evolution. Late in 1995–1996, Hutu *combatants* engaged the army in a significant firefight and cut water supplies and major power lines to Bujumbura. Although the outside world had accepted uncomplainingly the killing of women and children by the Burundi Army, once the Hutu *combatants* began shooting back, and causing inconvenience for expatriates living in the capital, the possibility of significant armed conflict, instead of one-way genocidal killing, became real. Wars are harder for the world to ignore than quieter genocide. Thus, international pressure began for talks between the opposing factions. Under the leadership of Mwalimu Nyerere, the former president of neighboring Tanzania, discussions got underway between Upronists, Frodebists, and their allies, in Arusha, Tanzania. Western powers supported such talks, financially and verbally; the United States assigned Ambassador Richard Bogosian and former Congressman Howard Volpe to serve as special envoys to the region. Simultaneously, Sant' Egidio, an independent group with close ties to the Vatican, initiated secret meetings in Rome between Burundi's established political and military figures with representatives of Léonard Nyangoma's rebel group, the FDD.

Talks, already underway before Buyoya's 1996 coup, intensified after it. Buyoya had to attend: his coup had provoked an immediate economic embargo from neighboring African states and donor nations, thereby making his absence from negotiations impossible.

Joining Buyoya at the negotiating table was, inevitably, an extremely disparate group. Frodebu, which in 1993 had won over 80 percent of the seats in Burundi's only free election, had greater popular legitimacy than did any other group at Arusha. But between 1993 and 1996 Frodebu had split—twice. First, after Ndadaye's assassination Léonard Nyangoma went into exile to form the CNDD, which joined the Hutu military arm, the FDD, in Zaire. And as Ntibantunganya's leadership became lame and then helpless, Nyangoma's following grew.

By the time of Buyoya's coup, those Frodebu leaders remaining in Burundi were losing cohesion. Between October 21, 1993, and May 1996, hundreds of Frodebu local and national party leaders had been killed, including two presidents, thirteen governors or assistant governors, five cabinet ministers, scores upon scores of local officials ranging from communal administrators to village chiefs—and over one quarter of Frodebu's members of Parliament.

Under these circumstances, some survivors, like Frodebu party president Dr. Jean Minani, former foreign minister Jean-Marie Ngendahayo, Parliamentarian Norbert Ndihokubwayo—and others receiving either repeated threats or bullets—had sought safety in exile. Many of these exiles broke with the party leadership remaining in Bujumbura, finding the Parliament's accommodations to the returned dictator impossible to swallow.

After taking office, Buyoya soon disbanded Parliament, contradicting his statement to the *New York Times* upon taking power, "We have to bring back democracy."[5] Upon reconvening Parliament in 1998, he expanded its seats by 50 percent and packed them with members slavishly loyal to him. Buyoya understood that the outside world would often be satisfied with the appearance of democracy rather than the substance of it. With the blessing of the Western powers, Buyoya announced an "internal partnership" with the highest-ranking Frodebist remaining in Bujumbura, Léonce Ngendekumana, speaker of the National Assembly, in order to forestall negotiations with Burundians in exile, who were free to insist on real democratic reforms. Many of those in exile saw this unequal partnership as Frodebu's capitulation to fear, the sale of their democratic honor for a parliamentary salary. Others considered it a necessary accommodation to the Maoist assertion that political power grows out of the barrel of a gun. Frodebu's problem was that it had no gun to lay on the negotiating table, and it had lost, in Ndadaye, the one leader who had successfully united the majority and shaped public opinion into a powerful, nonviolent force. Thus the Frodebists in Arusha lacked strength both of arms and of coherence.

Buyoya and his Upronists obviously had the guns, and they knew both by the quiet success of their own creeping genocide against Hutus and by the flagrant success of the Hutu genocide against Tutsis in Rwanda that although the international community had many guns to brandish or sell, it was unwilling to commit troops bearing arms for use in defense of hundreds of thousands of poor black people in the heart of Africa. Seeing little likelihood of international military intervention, Buyoya could afford to stall. And he did.

Nevertheless, his participation in peace talks, both in Arusha and in Rome, helped trigger the break between Buyoya and the most extreme wing of the Uprona party. On April 18, 2001, while Buyoya was in Gabon negotiating with the CNDD-FDD, Burundi Army Lieutenant Pasteur Ntakarutimana led about thirty troops, perhaps pro-Bagaza, in a daylong capture of the national radio broadcast facilities, announcing an end of Buyoya's rule and of the Arusha negotiations. Their putsch fizzled by nightfall. Such events, however, contributed to Buyoya's policy of wishing to appear to Western diplomats as a "moderate," the lesser of two evils. Fear of a return to power by Bagaza (whom Buyoya had exiled in his first dictatorship and placed under house arrest in his second) was a useful Frankenstein-monster scenario with which to frighten the West. Meanwhile, throughout the negotiations, Buyoya followed the technique that had led to success for Uprona in the Convention of Government—i.e., have the army and youth groups violently attack the population, but simultaneously sit at the negotiating table and there engage in interminable delay.

Besides the two divided major parties, smaller satellite Hutu and Tutsi political parties added to the seventeen groups that participated in the Arusha talks. One temptation that attracted even some extremists to attend was a per diem payment for attendance, which, being based on Western standards of living, made each day's stipend equal to six months' income for the average Burundian. Unfortunately, by October 1999, about four years of intermittent talking had produced no accords that would improve materially the lives of Burundi's people, and then Mwalimu Nyerere, moderator of the discussions, died.

Into this swamp of distrust, where different malcontents crouched on every island of opinion, stepped one of the world's most respected statesmen. Africa's most revered leader, Nelson Mandela, former president of South Africa and Nobel Peace Prize winner, assumed leadership of the peace talks in January 2000. Having spent twenty-seven years as a political prisoner, he was freighted with moral authority, yet remarkably free of bitterness. His magnetism attracted African leaders from surrounding countries to give renewed attention to the negotiations, and his insistence that the FDD and FNL be invited to the talks brought recognition both that these combatants had become a genuine force in Burundi, and that the Hutus needed some weaponry at the negotiating table if Buyoya and the army were to yield any of their usurped authority. Mandela's effectiveness, as described by Human Rights Watch, "stemmed in part from his being held in such high esteem and in part from his willingness to challenge the prevailing wisdom that Buyoya and the precarious stability that he seemed to represent should not be questioned too vigorously."[6]

Nelson Mandela brought not only wisdom and towering stature to the talks, but a recognition that, to match the strength of Burundi's Tutsi army, the forces of democracy also needed some guns on the negotiation table. As a former member of a guerilla movement himself, Mandela recognized that no guerilla movement could exist without support from the population, and therefore he invited members of the Hutu guerilla forces to join the discussions. That movement, while growing during the previous five years, had undergone changes in leadership. Léonard Nyangoma had been over-thrown as leader of the CNDD-FDD early in 1998 by Jean-Bosco Ndayiken-gurukiye, an FDD officer who had been educated at ISCAM, the military academy in Bujumbura. A Hutu from Bururi, the home province of Buyoya and most Burundi Army leaders, he was a brother of Augustin Nzojibwami, a Frodebu leader of the "internal partnership" with Buyoya. Jean-Bosco was prepared to sit at the negotiating table, although he and the FNL leader were unwilling to agree to a cease-fire or sign the first accords reached on August 28, 2000.

Similarly, some signatories reserved points to which they would not agree. The document itself lacked enforceable provisions. Nonetheless, in a cere-mony attended by many African heads of state and by President Bill Clinton (by videoconference), an important step forward was taken. The strength of the agreement lay in this: many African leaders signed or witnessed the signing; all parties to the conflict were present; Africa's most respected states-man chaired the effort; and perhaps most importantly, the country of South Africa could not let its revered leader fail—that is, if South Africa had to provide troops to enforce peace, it would be willing to do so.

The August 28, 2000, Arusha accords gave Frodebu and its affiliated Hutu political parties (known as the G-7) a portion of the political pie with speci-fied governmental offices ranging from cabinet appointments, parliamen-tary seats, and governorships to local positions, while Uprona and its related parties (the G-10) also received their share. CNDD-FDD refused to sign, calling the agreement no more than a greedy division of power rather than a framework for democratic elections, and insisting that peace could come only if the existing Tutsi army were replaced with a truly national, multiethnic force. But Mandela was under pressure unknown to the CNDD-FDD.

A group of the ten top leaders of the Burundi Army had come to Mandela, asking for Buyoya to continue as president for the first eighteen months of a transitional government. If not, they threatened, they would create chaos. Mandela agreed, with the condition that Domitien Ndayizeye, the leader of Frodebu, would serve as Buyoya's vice president, and then succeed to the presidency after eighteen months, with a new vice president for the transi-tional government then to be chosen by the Upronist group. By this maneu-ver, Mandela accomplished three things: he avoided an otherwise promised renewal of violence; he set a limit on the time of Buyoya's presidency; and he placed himself in authority—Buyoya, who until then had been presi-dent under his own authority, had now given up his authority to Mandela. Meanwhile, Mandela sent through Jean-Marie Ngendahayo (the former for-eign minister and now political advisor to CNDD-FDD) a message that he would promise to remove Buyoya after eighteen months: if he could appoint Buyoya, he could remove him.

Having worked what Africans refer to as "Madiba magic," Mandela stepped off the stage in 2001 and passed the initiative on to the leaders of the nations in the region—Uganda, Tanzania, Rwanda, Kenya, Ethiopia, and South Africa. Monitoring progress daily was the assignment given to Jacob Zuma, deputy president of South Africa, who was to report to the African Union, the UN Security Council, President Mbeke of South Africa, and President Yoweri Kaguta Musevini of Uganda, chairman of the regional initiative. In sum, the effort was to give Zuma a mandate that would imply a political strength allowing him to pull the necessary strings to make a peace accord work, and to move toward democracy.

Next, a series of understandings moved Burundi closer to peace and democracy. Cease-fire agreements between the transitional government and the CNDD-FDD, led by Pierre Nkurunziza, were signed on December 2, 2002, January 27, 2003, and October 16, 2003. The last agreement not only reaffirmed the cease-fire, but granted CNDD-FDD four cabinet portfolios, including minister of state for good governance (the third-highest position in government), the third position in the national legislative branch, and a variety of governorships and communal administrative positions.

Most important of all was a merger between parts of the former Burundi Army and the armed forces of the CNDD-FDD: a new military force that, in effect, replaced the old monoethnic Burundi Army. The agreement required that 60 percent of the officers in the central headquarters (État-Major) be from the former Burundi Army and 40 percent be from the CNDD-FDD. At all lower command levels there would be interlocking, counterbalancing officers: if a member of the old Burundi Army was commander, the sub-commander would be from CNDD-FDD, and vice versa. The belief was that with a chain of command that throughout it had members from formerly opposing factions, instructions for a coup or unwarranted attack would be difficult to carry out.

One must remember that the existing Burundi Army, which had never once faced a foreign foe, had only been used against its own people. Therefore one cannot overemphasize the importance of replacing a monoethnic army with a multiethnic, integrated national defense force. For generations, Hutus had been at the mercy of a merciless, ravaging band of killers who engaged in slaughter as ethnic sport and a means of ethnic subjugation. No Hutu could feel secure about any new government, even one democratically elected, if the old Burundi Army continued. They needed not think back to the genocides led by Micombero and the army in 1972, or by Buyoya in 1988, for they could all remember the assassination of their only democratically elected president, Melchior Ndadaye, in 1993, when not a single soldier fired a shot in his defense. In a country in which the possession of guns has long been illegal for the general population (but not for Tutsis), and in which the cost of purchasing weapons and ammunition remains excessive for the peasant majority, confidence in the new multiethnic defense force now being developed offers a new experience for the majority of Burundi's citizens.

If the establishment of a multiethnic national defense force is one prerequisite for meaningful democracy in Burundi, equally important are fair and free elections ensuring multiethnic representation. And there too, Burundi has new hope. As part of a broader strategy for sharing governance with groups that had long been excluded from power, the five-year interim constitution agreed upon in the Arusha accords requires the membership of Burundi's political parties to be multiethnic and open to women as well as men. Further, parliamentary membership must be 60 percent Hutu and 40 percent Tutsi, with 30 percent of the total being female.

In July 2005, the national elections envisioned in the Arusha agreements took place. Judged by international observers to be free from intimidation and fairly counted, these elections resulted in an overwhelming victory by the political party led by a former teacher and college professor who had become military commander of the CNDD-FDD. Pierre Nkurunziza's FDD Party captured 59 of the 100 seats in Parliament, whereas Frodebu, once the party of Ndadaye and the Hutu majority, but weakened by more than a decade of assassinations, intimidation, subjugation, and internal conflict, garnered only 24 seats. Uprona, the Tutsi party that had ruled the country for four decades, now riven by inner divisions and forced to compete in an honest election, won only 7 places.

Following the national elections in July 2005, the Parliament in August unanimously elected Nkurunziza to be the new president; and in a nonpartisan unifying gesture, he then resigned his position as leader of the FDD. His magnetism draws the population to him and undoubtedly emanates less from successful battlefield stratagems than from inner qualities of character. Those who know him well define him as deeply religious, but not evangelical. One of the president's long-time friends told me, "He spends 30 percent of his time in prayer, and 70 percent on politics." His comfortable mixture of politics, social activism, and non-denominational Christian faith consistently appears in his public utterances, whether made in churches or in political forums.

In September 2006, I was invited to meet the president during his visit to New York to address the UN General Assembly. Throughout a private conversation that continued for more than an hour, my steady impression was that in this man, Burundi had found a leader who was at peace with himself, someone devoted to establishing peace and hope in his long beleaguered homeland. He expressed the self-assurance and assured faith that did not require him to proselytize, and this confidence allowed him to explain with candor and simplicity his background, his vision, and his plans for Burundi.

A Hutu born in 1963, he lost his father in the massive genocide against Hutus in 1972, and by the time he assumed the presidency in 2005, he had lost five of his six siblings to ethnic violence. Yet, in relating this, he showed no hint of bitterness, no hunger for revenge. He quickly left all talk of his personal history to express pride that in its first year in office, his government had built 220 of the 400 new schools that his nation requires. The need for these schools was illuminated by Nkurunziza's pledge in his inaugural address a year earlier to provide free primary education to all Burundian children. Like almost all African countries, Burundi until then had never offered free public education. Indeed, most Burundian families had previously been deterred from enrolling their children in school by the required yearly fee of two U.S. dollars per student, one of many impediments discouraging education in a country where half the population is illiterate, and roughly half completely unschooled. This project is only recently underway and faces formidable financial and administrative challenges in trying to provide instruction to almost twice as many students as in earlier years, but its popularity is immense and its ultimate success inevitable. After generations of genocide, fear, and subjugation, the ruling majority will finally insist on the project's continuance. Moreover, as Thomas Jefferson observed two hundred years ago, the most secure base for any democracy is an educated electorate. Few forces can more readily undermine longstanding ethnic hatreds than a multiethnic universal education.

While the president's vision for Burundi's future recognizes the need for more hospitals, greater foreign investment, tourism, and infrastructure, he knows that Burundi's success will above all depend on forming a unified society. In his inaugural address he pledged "to fight all ideology and acts of genocide and exclusion, and to promote and defend the individual and collective rights and freedoms of persons and of the citizen." His actions and statements thus far have demonstrated remarkable tolerance both toward his former enemies and toward those who historically have been excluded from respect or positions of power.

Sentenced to death by the Buyoya government in 1998 but granted amnesty during the peace negotiations in Arusha, Nkurunziza in his public statements avoids making any threats of trials or punishment toward past participants in Burundi's long tyranny. His focus has been inclusion, not exclusion.

In keeping with the new constitutional requirement that 30 percent of parliamentarians be women, the new government has taken affirmative measures to name seven women as cabinet ministers to some of the most important government departments: Foreign Affairs, Justice, Planning, Commerce and Industry, National Solidarity, HIV-AIDS Prevention and Treatment, and Tourism and Environment.

Burundi's early success in broadening the reach of democratic governance in its own country has brought it an unexpected and unprecedented role as an exemplar to other nations in the region. Since ethnic warfare had continued in Burundi for decades, its new government's success in conflict management has become a reference point for the region. People who had been fighting for control of the nation only a few months earlier are, after free and fair elections, now cooperating and achieving a society with free movement, a free press, and free discussion. Remarkably, Burundi is acting as mediator in a dispute between neighboring Rwanda and the Democratic Republic of the Congo. Further, at this time Burundi expects to release over six hundred prisoners, after the establishment of a Truth and Reconciliation Commission, to help heal long-standing divisions.

For the first time since Ndadaye's inauguration in 1993, optimism seems justified. With each passing day the multiethnic army, cabinet, and Parliament, working peacefully together, seem to reflect a society more eager for peace than retaliation.

BURUNDI'S FUTURE

In light of both Burundi's hellish past, to which Kathleen and I were witness, and some promising signs of peace, represented by recent accords, the question becomes: what, then, is its future? Surely the world cannot say to the people of Burundi, "Abandon all hope, ye who enter here," and undoubtedly Burundians are saying to the world, "Do not abandon us." And we need not.

Nor need we despair. The same German soil that produced Hitler and Himmler also gave birth to Handel and Haydn. The same America that bore both John Wilkes Booth and James Earl Ray bore Abraham Lincoln and Martin Luther King. And the same mountainous land that grew Micombero and Buyoya also brought forth Melchior Ndadaye. Germany made democracy work after being governed by warlords. Once Hitler and his fascist co-horts were gone, leaders like Konrad Adenauer and Willy Brandt stepped forward. The power of democracy to change a society should not be under-rated by those who, having been born to it, may take it for granted.

Establishing democracy was a major purpose of the Arusha talks. It is true that not all participants wanted to see it, and true that, given Burundi's long spell under tyrannical rule, many outsiders doubt its capacity to sustain it. But I do not share that view. Burundi was well underway to providing demo-cratic government in an ethnically impartial, unified nation when the army snuffed out that hope on October 21, 1993. Yet if Burundi could produce an Ndadaye under despotism, under democracy it could be expected again to produce democratic leaders committed to sharing power and opportunity among all citizens.

Unfortunately, at this moment perhaps the thing most shared among all citizens, and by all those at the negotiating table, is the recurrent memory of terror. Haunting, daily, nightly, inescapable terror. The Hutu remembers lying sleepless, listening for the sound of the diesel army trucks, fearing that his door may be kicked down and his family forced to flee or be slaughtered, or that his children may be victims of a grenade tossed from a passing Sans Échec car as they walk to school. His family's defense has been that of the impala or the wildebeest: to travel in numbers, hoping that when the lion attacks, it will bring down a smaller, slower, or weaker member of the group and that they may escape to safety.

If the Hutu's safety has lain in numbers, the Tutsi's remembered terror lies there also. He knows he is outnumbered six to one. He knows that the Hutu wants the same opportunity as he for education, a government job, or a chance to advance financially and socially. And he fears that the same genocide carried out by Hutus against Tutsis in Rwanda could happen in Burundi. And if, to the Hutu, the army has been the agent of death and sub-jugation, to the Tutsi the army has been the dike of protection and salvation against the Hutu deluge.

There has been between Hutu and Tutsi, however, no balance of terror, as existed between nuclear powers for the last half century; no balance regard-ing weapons too terrible to use. The terror of those who engage in genocide and of those who fear genocide is unlike lesser fears. Genocide says to you: not only you, but your parents, children, spouse, relatives—all your pos-terity, including not only every person most cherished by you, but the values themselves that you most respect and expect to continue after you, may be obliterated and forgotten. Genocide can make a Rwandan Hutu slice off the four fingers of a Tutsi woman and force her to hold her baby with the palm of her hand and a single distended thumb. It can make a Tutsi soldier cut off the penis and testicles of a five-year-old boy after splitting open his head with an axe. The fear of genocide overwhelms the simple fear of one's own death. Those in its grip strike out wildly, in actions so heinous and irrational as to be incomprehensible to those of us who have only known normal fears. Their frantic reaching for "security" justifies any action, however abominable or cruel.

The question for those seeking peace in Burundi is can the terror be slaked? Or at least controlled? Somehow reduced to milder fear or apprehension? If so, that is the first step to be taken in a pilgrimage from terror to the trust necessary for civil society.

An absolute requirement for the Hutu has been the complete transformation of the Burundi Army and gendarmerie. No group that has known decades of subjugation could be expected to trust a genocidal army simply because a peace treaty was signed. No European from a state conquered by Germany in the Second World War would afterward have trusted a German soldier just because the Nazi insignia was removed from his uniform; hence, the German Army was disbanded. No Hutu today could have trusted the troops of Buyoya's military forces. Their replacement by a new multiethnic military was inescapable.

Just as an army responsible for genocide needed to be disbanded for a new society to develop, so too the members who served in Buyoya's dictatorial government in upper-level official positions should, in my opinion, be removed and proscribed from holding governmental positions in future, as was done in Germany after the Second World War. That is the extent of the formal, governmental punishment that I would wish to see imposed on them. However, the real challenge for Burundian society, as for every nation emerging from civil warfare, is to decide how to deal with past misdeeds in a way that will lay a strong foundation for the future.

Across its northern border, Burundi sees the example of Rwanda, which, twelve years after the end of a major genocide, is still struggling with ethnic hatreds, dishonest elections, widespread dissatisfaction, and an essentially divided nation. Thousands have died awaiting unfair trials in Rwanda's fetid, overcrowded prisons. Justice is no more available to the Rwandan population under Kagame's Tutsi tyranny than it was under Habyarimana's Hutu despotism. And although the European Union is now trying to lessen the court backlog by funding *gacaca* courts, in which local villagers try cases instead of waiting upon actions in the existing court system, it is unlikely that fair trials, free of ethnic intimidation and bias, can be achieved.

Even though the International Criminal Tribunals in Rwanda and the former Yugoslavia have been underway for roughly a decade, and have cost in excess of one billion dollars (a sum greater than the annual GDP of Burundi), no satisfactory closure on past genocide or healing of past wounds has resulted in either location. Their populations remain weary, fractious, and disappointed. There is no sense that justice has been done, that a hunger for revenge has been sated, or that the nations have been unified in common purpose. In short, tribunals and traditional court systems seem to offer no strong hope of forging national renewal and common purpose.

Fortunately, as this book goes to press, Burundi seems to be looking south, at South Africa's remarkably successful Truth and Reconciliation Commission (TRC). The current plan is to have a seven-member commission made up of four Burundians and three international members. Decisions have not yet been made regarding the extent of the proposed commission's authority, the manner in which testimony may be taken and accountability determined, and the possibility of instituting amnesty or prosecution. But the decision to have a commission has been made.

Obviously, Burundi's legacy of genocide differs in a number of ways from South Africa's legacy of apartheid. But the overarching similarities are there: a minority ethnic group that long subjugated the majority militarily, politically, economically, and educationally; horrendous violence as the military and law-enforcement officers utilized terror tactics; the impossibility of any legal recourse for the majority population; the long-standing practice of tyranny, denying voice or vote to the majority. The reborn, postapartheid South Africa, in its plan for renewal, put the need for truth first. Truth that revealed the policies, actions, murders, beatings, and all the many practices under apartheid government that led to death, degradation, humiliation, persecution, and misery for the majority of the population. This truth telling was used, first, to bring accountability to the world: who was responsible for specific murders, rapes, torture, and the panoply of cruelty that had persisted for generations? The intent was to have truth and public accountability so that past injustices could never be repeated.

As Archbishop Desmond Tutu, chairman of the TRC, observed, the sentence inscribed over the entry to the Holocaust Museum at Dachau is philosopher George Santayana's famous caution: "Those who forget the past are doomed to repeat it."[7] The South African TRC found that victims were comforted and relieved simply by telling their stories to the TRC or some of its committees. The opportunity to do so served to validate the grief they had experienced, but also to diminish their pain, since the horror they often had held internally, in isolation, could now be shared with others, thereby allowing them to overcome some of the humiliation and weakness they had felt.

And as thousands of victims and thousands of perpetrators (many seeking amnesty) spoke of the history they shared, a nation that much of the world expected to implode after holding elections emerged as one of the strongest of the fifty-three nations on the African continent.

As Archbishop Tutu points out throughout his book *No Future without Forgiveness,* a perpetrator's telling the factual truth is the step that leads toward accountability and accepting responsibility for one's actions. Doing so then allows the victim to extend forgiveness, as an act not of weakness, but of strength: the victim is now in the magnanimous position of extending comfort to one who has inflicted hurt, and in the process has risen above an earlier vulnerability. And in the process of personal reconciliation, fuller national reconciliation is achieved.

I believe that the adoption of a Burundian version of a reconciliation committee—perhaps, like South Africa's, not excluding all possibility of prosecution—focused on truth, accountability, and the possibility of amnesty and forgiveness is a worthwhile goal, possible of attainment. Given the misery and injustice imposed on the population in Burundi, many people might consider the possibility of amnesty to be excessively lenient. However, having witnessed Burundi's capacity for revenge, I am convinced that the possibility to gain amnesty for all crimes will be far more salutary and efficient than an attempt to mete out punishment for past misdeeds, however heinous and extensive. There are practical reasons for this approach.

First, as one of the poorest and least-educated countries in the world, Burundi has no administrative capacity to bring to justice even a small portion of those guilty of murder, cruelty, torture, rape, and countless other criminal acts of violence. Burundi has suffered several hundred thousand killings, by tens of thousands of perpetrators, since October 21, 1993. But only 30 percent of its population is literate. During my time as ambassador, there were only approximately forty lawyers (about thirty-five Tutsi and five Hutu) to prosecute or defend a population of 6 million (or, one lawyer for 150,000 people). The judiciary is over 90 percent Tutsi in a country that is 85 percent Hutu— and was characterized by a visiting group of Belgian magistrates and legal experts in 1995 as woefully untrained, uninformed, and ethnically biased. It could not possibly provide a court system that could fairly process even a few cases. If the international community provided hundreds of judges, prosecutors, and defense attorneys for the trials of all those who could reasonably be charged with killing innocent citizens, there would not be courtrooms, hotels, copying machines, or even typewriters enough to enable justice to proceed satisfactorily. Moreover, the majority of the population speaks only Kirundi, a language so little known that it is not even among the hundred or so languages taught at the language-instruction center for U.S. State Department officers going overseas. How could an attorney effectively represent a client with whom he could not speak? Trying to establish in Burundi a legal process such as is followed in the developed world might give us a partial accounting of irremediable acts, but would result only in a mockery of justice that would stain the prospects of a country requiring a revitalized future.

Second, any attempt to bring to trial all those guilty even of murder (ignoring an array of other ignominious crimes) would but perpetuate conflict, not resolve it. Burundi's atmosphere will remain ethnically charged for many years to come. Fair trials at this time would be impossible. Yet for civil society to function effectively, justice must not only be done and be seen to be done, but must be *believed to be done.* Burundi could not, overnight, establish the trust in its Hutu society that if a Hutu were convicted, it did not result from Tutsi machinations; and if a Tutsi were convicted, Tutsis would believe the action represented international revenge.

For over half a century Burundi has been captive to its past, unwilling to "let the dead bury the dead." It has embraced the maxim "an eye for an eye, and a tooth for a tooth," a teaching that, when fully practiced, leaves both parties toothless and blind. Revenge has so stalked the countryside that its people have lived in perpetual fear. No legalistic accounting and attempt to bring to a courtroom those seemingly most responsible for this parlous state can either rectify the past or project the country into a better future.

The question is not whether certain persons deserve punishment. Most people would think they do. The real question is whether a desire for their punishment should be allowed to delay the establishment of a society that might offer justice and opportunity to millions of suffering people. Perhaps the desire to see certain people punished is only a way of giving easy satisfaction to our collective consciences for having allowed the suffering to go on so long. We should not, however, allow our desire for revenge against the genocidists to overcome the far more important need of the people for a just and humane society. To make even so-called "just revenge" more important is but to repeat Burundi's past mistake. Every day that the amnesty that is a necessary precondition for establishing democracy and justice is delayed withdraws energy that could be devoted to concord, not conflict—to reconciliation, not revenge. Surely the thirst for vengeance is not worth that price. Ultimately, is it not more important to try to save the life of a child, or of thousands of men, women, and children, than to try to force guilty leaders to trial? Which action really shows greater respect for human life and dignity?

Let me be clear, I loathe the actions sponsored by men such as Pierre Buyoya and Jean Bikomagu: the death of Melchior Ndadaye; the slaughter of 20,000 Hutus in 1998; the concentration camps with their torture and humiliation; the overturning of democracy; the abolishment of Parliament; the daily slaughter of innocents; the mock trials regarding Ndadaye's assassination; the closing of schools; the rape of young girls and old women; the disemboweling of pregnant mothers; the cruelty and callousness in which children are reared and in which the entire society lives. But I would rather see Buyoya and Bikomagu walk as free men along the streets of Bujumbura than to perpetuate suffering and hatred.

If Buyoya and Bikomagu and others must be punished, let their punishment be to see men and women whom they had held in abject servility walk past them and smile with the liberty of free citizens advancing together. If they be spat upon while moving among their former subjects, let their punishment be the spittle on their clothing and the fact that in a new society, people need not fear torture for expressing their disdain. Let that be their daily and hourly punishment. Not the swift death of the hangman's noose or the firing squad, but the knowledge that the country Buyoya twice headed has been freed of fear, and the population has moved into the broad uplands of hope and opportunity—perhaps not opportunity for riches, but an opportunity for decency, self-respect, and justice from their neighbors. Such punishment would not trivialize the suffering and the agonizing cruelty the population has experienced. But it would put it past, and allow a society to move forward with lighted candles rather than to curse the darkness.

After declaring in a public meeting in 1988 that he believed Burundi should, in the next decade, move toward establishing full democratic government, Melchior Ndadaye was three days later locked in solitary confinement by President Buyoya, his prison cell periodically partially flooded so that he would be chilled and unable to rest. His response? The experience was so terrible, he told his friend Jean-Marie Ngendahayo, that he would never wish anyone else to experience it. Therefore, among his first actions as president, he abolished all torture cells, converted a new prison facility into a school, and declared a broad, inclusive amnesty for almost all the nation's prisoners. My hope is that Burundi will be guided not by the policies of Pierre Buyoya, whose presidencies have looked to the example of Adolf Hitler, but by the example of Melchior Ndadaye, an admirer of Martin Luther King. My hope is that Burundi, like South Africa, will find a way to combine accountability with amnesty—for Buyoya, Bikomagu, and all Burundians.

It is with the hope that the world will take note of the small, isolated, and long-suffering country of Burundi that this book has been written. Kathleen and I have sought to serve as guides across an infernal landscape, largely unknown to the world lying beyond its borders. Upon completing that journey, we believe that the pain that Burundi has experienced can be that of *Purgatorio,* not *Inferno,* of purgation rather than despair.

Burundi has leaders who have shown their commitment, oftentimes at great personal peril and cost, to the values of individual dignity and mutual respect, which are nurtured by democracy. And Burundi has a citizenry that urgently seeks to exchange suffering for civility, tyranny for democracy, discouragement for hope. It has, as well, the capacity to rise from the ashes of Kamenge and Cibitoke to enter the bright prospect of forming a new nation in a new millennium. Its ability to achieve that vision depends on helpful encouragement from other nations with longer experience in self-government. If other countries respond to its need, Burundi can take its place as a full participant in the community of nations that by painful experience have learned to respect the value of every human life.

On March 4, 1865, as America neared the end of a civil war that had already taken almost as many lives as were to be lost during all of its other wars across two centuries, its most loved and most compassionate president, Abraham Lincoln, foretold how his nation could bury its destructive hatreds and conceive a new birth of freedom. Those in Burundi seeking escape from the fiery wheel of genocide and civil strife might listen to his words:

> With malice toward none; with charity for all; with firmness in the right, as God gives us to see the right, let us strive on to finish the work we are in: to bind up the nation's wounds; to care for him who shall have borne the battle, and for his widow and his orphan, to do all which may achieve and cherish a just and lasting peace among ourselves, and with all nations.

— SECOND INAUGURAL ADDRESS

NOTES

CHAPTER 1

1. *Blindé* is the term used in African francophone countries to describe an armored personnel carrier, similar to a small tank, which runs on tires instead of tracks.

CHAPTER 2

1. René Lemarchand, "Burundi: The Killing Fields Revisited," *Issue: A Journal of Opinion* 18, no. 1 (Winter 1989): 22.

2. Catherine Watson, "After the Massacre," *Africa Report* 34, no. 1 (Jan.–Feb. 1989): 51.

3. Reginald Kay, *Burundi since the Genocide* (London: Minority Rights Group, Report No. 20, 1987), 5–6.

4. Gérard Prunier, "Burundi: Descent into Chaos or a Manageable Crisis?" (March 1995), a WRITENET report available on the Web site of the United Nations High Commissioner for Refugees: http://www.unhcr.org/cgi-bin/texis/vtx/home/opendoc.htm?tbl=RSDCOI&page=home&id=3ae6a6c00.

CHAPTER 3

1. Zaire in 1997 was renamed the Democratic Republic of the Congo, or DRC.

CHAPTER 4

1. In Rwanda, the Tutsi guerilla movement that for three years fought against the established Hutu government called itself and its fighting forces the Rwandan Patriotic Front, or RPF. When their victory in July 1994 made them the official government, they

thereafter referred to their political party as the RPF and renamed their armed forces the Rwandan Patriotic Army, or RPA.

2. By September 9, 1994, Hugh Johnstone, director of the European Economic Community program in Burundi, reported that the number of known dead from the attack had reached 126. How many more wounded died later, and how many dead were never reported, remains unknown.

CHAPTER 5

1. Ahmedou Ould-Abdallah, *Burundi on the Brink, 1993–95: A UN Special Envoy Reflects on Preventive Diplomacy* (Washington, D.C.: United States Institute of Peace Press, 2000), 71.

2. Ibid., 70.

CHAPTER 8

1. Amnesty International, *Rwanda: Reports of Killings and Abductions by the Rwandese Patriotic Army, April–August 1994* (London, October 20, 1994, AI Index AFR 47/016/1994), 4:

Many . . . killings by the RPA . . . appear to have gone largely unreported. . . .

In mid-September [1994] the United Nations High Commissioner for Refugees (UNHCR) said that it had received dozens of testimonies from refugees . . . alleging that the RPA had carried out numerous killings, forcing many people who had returned to the[ir home] area to flee. The UNHCR suspended repatriation of refugees from neighbouring countries [to Rwanda]. A controversy soon arose when some other UN agencies expressed or implied doubt over UNHCR findings. . . . The United Nations Assistance Mission for Rwanda (UNAMIR) sent several dozen soldiers to monitor the situation. The Rwandese Government denied that its soldiers had been involved in any massacres.

The report is available online at http://web.amnesty.org/library/Index/ENGAFR 470161994?open&of=ENG-RWA.

2. Ibid., 9:

There have been numerous reports of abductions and "disappearances" carried out by the RPF since April 1994. There are fears that those who were abducted or "disappeared" may have been killed and their bodies secretly disposed of. . . .

There were . . . reports of "disappearances" in July 1994 of about 600 people from a camp for the displaced at Rango, several kilometres south of Butare. Amnesty International representatives were told that the RPA was thought to have killed and buried those who had "disappeared" in mass graves in a valley next to the *Groupe scolaire* in Butare. However, Amnesty International's representatives were prevented from going to the valley by RPA soldiers.

3. Alison Des Forges, *Leave None to Tell the Story: Genocide in Rwanda* (New York: Human Rights Watch, 1999), 553–556.

CHAPTER 10

1. Within the next year, all three features were gone. In a coup, the military dictator Buyoya overthrew the legitimate president of the majority party, who failed to finish his term, and Parliament became a powerless sham.

CHAPTER 19

1. The story of Gilbert Tuhabonye, the only survivor of the attack on the school, is poignantly narrated in Michael Hall, "Running for His Life," *Texas Monthly,* Aug. 2003. Tuhabonye has written (with Gary Brozek) a memoir that includes an account of the massacre: *This Voice in My Heart: A Genocide Survivor's Story of Escape, Faith, and Forgiveness* (New York: HarperCollins, 2006).

CHAPTER 21

1. Timothy Paul Longman, *Proxy Targets: Civilians in the War in Burundi* (New York: Human Rights Watch, 1998), 36, 59.

2. Human Rights Watch, *Emptying the Hills: Regroupment in Burundi* (New York: Human Rights Watch, 2000), 72.

3. Ibid., 104.

4. Longman, *Proxy Targets,* 97–98.

5. D. G. McNeil, "Leader of Coup in Burundi Hints at Tribal Reconciliation," *New York Times,* July 27, 1996.

6. Human Rights Watch, *Emptying the Hills,* 147.

7. Desmond Tutu, *No Future without Forgiveness* (New York: Doubleday, 1999), 179.

INDEX

Page numbers in *italics* refer to photographs. BK in index refers to Bob Krueger.

displaced-person camps for Tutsis, 170–174; and Ndadaye, 36, 269; and Ould-Abdallah in Burundi, 41–42, 71–74, 136, 144; and refugee camps, 58–61, 65, 161–165, *162, 164,* 173, 184, 187; and refugees, 29, 54, 58, 61, 62, 65, 81, 94, 97–101, *98, 99,* 103, 105, 161–165, *162, 164,* 292n.1; and Rwanda genocide, 104, 106–112; Security Council of, 73, 108, 211, 280; and weapons for Burundi Army, 256

United Nations Assistance Mission for Rwanda (UNAMIR), 100–101, 106–112, 292n.1

United Nations Commission on Human Rights, 142–143

United Nations High Commissioner for Refugees (UNHCR), 61, 62, 81, 107, 111–112, 161, 167, 292n.1

University of Burundi, 115, 117, 220–221, 225, 228

University of Rwanda, 32, 117

Uprona Party: and Arusha accords, 279; and assassinations, 141; and Bimazubute, 11; and Buyoya, 33, 35; in colonial period, 27–28; and Convention of Government, 74, 140, 143, 278; after coup against Ndadaye, 37–39; demonstration by, in Bujumbura, 155; and elections of 2005, 281; founding of, 258; and genocides, 258; and Kanyenkiko as Prime Minister, 143–144; leaders of, before Ndadaye presidency, 1–2; in Ndadaye's cabinet, 1, 5; and Nduwayo as Prime Minister, 144; and Ntibantunganya government, 74, 140, 143; and Odeon Palace meeting (June 1995), 218, 220; and Ould-Abdallah, 72–73, 144

USAID, 50, 52, 62, 84, 159, 244, 262

U.S. Defense Department, 106–107, 213

U.S. embassy in Burundi: BK's appointment to, 43–44, 185; BK's arrival at,

49–50; and coup against Ndadaye, 9, 11, 13–15; and evacuation of Americans from Burundi, 44, 52–54, 179–183; foreign-service nationals (FSNs) employed by, 50; Kennedy's establishment of, 36; and Ould-Abdallah, 73; photograph of, *50;* protection for, 155; and return of American families to Burundi, 75, 77–78; and town-hall meetings for all American citizens, 156, 181; and violence in Bujumbura, 83, 153–154. *See also* Krueger, Bob

USIS, 13, 87

U.S. State Department: and ambush of BK's convoy in Cibitoke, 242, 245; BK's appointment as ambassador to Burundi, 43–44, 185; BK's departure from Burundi, 260, 262–265, 271; BK's visit to Washington offices of, 212–214; Bureau of Diplomatic Security, 230; and CIA, 262; and death threats against BK, 136; and embassy travel policy, 245, 255; and genocide, 83, 105–106, 111, 133, 135, 211, 212; and ordered departure of Americans from Burundi, 44, 52–54, 179–183, 195, 211; proper procedure on ambassadors' comments, 104, 133; and return of American families to Burundi, 75, 77–78; tour of Burundi refugee camps by, 158–166

Van Craen, Ambassador and Mrs., 176–177

Vasser, Charles, 175

vehicles and driving conditions: automobiles in Burundi, 6; bicycles, 224; BK's and U.S. embassy's vehicles, 44–46, 54, 79, 114, 147, 166, 185, 230, 260; Bujumbura streets, 44, 46, 147, 155; in Butaganzwa, 121, *122,* 126, *126,* 197–198; and Cibitoke tour, 230–231, 234–236; converted minivan, 17; Han-